YALE HISTORICAL PUBLICATIONS

Leonard Woods Labaree · Editor

MISCELLANY

XLI

THE TWENTY-EIGHTH VOLUME
PUBLISHED UNDER THE DIRECTION OF
THE DEPARTMENT OF HISTORY ON THE
KINGSLEY TRUST ASSOCIATION PUBLICATION FUND
ESTABLISHED BY
THE SCROLL AND KEY SOCIETY
OF YALE COLLEGE

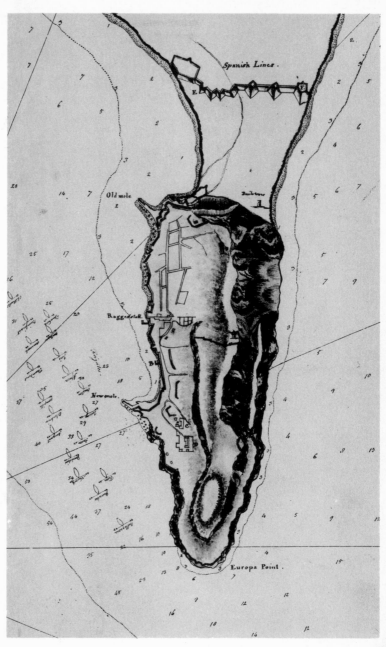

GIBRALTAR

GIBRALTAR
IN BRITISH DIPLOMACY IN
THE EIGHTEENTH CENTURY

BY

STETSON CONN

INSTRUCTOR IN AMERICAN HISTORY
AMHERST COLLEGE

NEW HAVEN · YALE UNIVERSITY PRESS
LONDON · HUMPHREY MILFORD · OXFORD UNIVERSITY PRESS
1942

TO MY FATHER
WALLACE THOMPSON CONN

PREFACE

GIBRALTAR served as the principal European focus of Anglo-Spanish enmity in the eighteenth century. Spain was forced to cede it to Great Britain in the Treaty of Utrecht, but from the beginning the Spanish entertained hopes for the recovery of the Rock. The English soon discovered that Gibraltar had little real value as a military or commercial outpost and that no solid reconciliation with Spain would be possible as long as England held it. For these reasons, James Stanhope promised to restore Gibraltar to Spain; and after his untimely death his successors in the ministry, in order to secure a resumption of trading privileges in the Spanish dominions, were compelled to pledge a fulfillment of Stanhope's promise. The failure of England to carry out the obligation incurred by the famous royal letter of George I of June 1721 gave rise to the Gibraltar question —a problem which rankled in England's relations with Spain until the French Revolution and involved her in dangerous diplomatic complications with the other powers of continental Europe. Most notably, the Spanish quest for Gibraltar lured Spain into a Bourbon Family Compact with France that became the chief threat to England's constant effort to maintain a balance of power on the Continent. The Bourbon allies, with Spain seeking the restitution or capture of Gibraltar with a single-mindedness that was frustrated only by French artifice, finally seized the opportunity of intervening in Britain's domestic struggle with her American Colonists; not only did they register the sole defeat suffered by England in the "Second Hundred Years' War," but also they helped to disrupt the first British Empire. Gibraltar, then, became one of the principal pivots in European diplomacy; the "Gibraltar question" posed one of the most difficult and insoluble problems that English statesmen had to face in the eighteenth century.

In this study I have tried to trace the origin and development of this problem down to the French Revolution. For my information, I have relied principally upon the manuscript and printed diplomatic correspondence of Great Britain, and to a lesser extent on similar material from the French and Spanish archives. This work is in no sense a complete history of Gibraltar in the eighteenth century; I have touched upon other aspects of its history—military, naval, and commercial—only as they seemed to affect the rôle of Gibraltar in British diplomacy. Nor does the story end in 1789; indeed, the modern significance of Gibraltar as a vital British outpost on the "life-line" to the East makes the recent history of the Rock seem far more momentous than any account of its fortunes as a British possession in the eighteenth century. This study only provides an historical background for one of the most persistent problems in Britain's international relations. The events of today illuminate the prophetic forecast of George III, made in December 1782, that "this *proud fortress*" would be the "source of another war, or at least of a constant lurking enmity."

A few words of explanation are necessary regarding the chronology and form employed in footnotes and quotations. Unless otherwise indicated, the dates given are New Style, except for those of correspondence originating in England or Gibraltar before 1752, for which double dates have been inserted. The year dates are New Style throughout. In English quotations, I have retained the original spelling, capitalization, and punctuation. Translated excerpts have been modernized.

To all who have contributed to the completion of this work I express my appreciation. In particular, I am deeply indebted to Samuel Flagg Bemis, Farnam Professor of Diplomatic History at Yale University, for his constant criticism and encouragement. My research in the public archives of Great Britain and France, and in the manuscript collections of the British Museum, the Library of Congress, the William L. Clements Library, and the New York Public Library, has been facilitated by a friendly courtesy on the part of custodians and staffs that I gratefully acknowledge. A Yale University Fellowship made it possible for me to spend several months in London and Paris transcribing material for this study, first undertaken as a doctoral dissertation at Yale. I wish to thank my colleague Professor Alfred F. Havighurst of Amherst, and Professor Stanley M. Pargellis of Yale, for careful reading of the manuscript and helpful suggestions. The inspiration and assistance of my wife have been invaluable. I assume the entire responsibility, however, both for the contents and the imperfections of this study.

S. C.

Amherst, Massachusetts,
   August 8, 1941.

CONTENTS

MAPS

GIBRALTAR IN BRITISH DIPLOMACY
IN THE EIGHTEENTH CENTURY

I

THE ENGLISH ACQUISITION OF GIBRALTAR

AS strong as the Rock of Gibraltar" is a household
phrase. The Rock, acquired by England in the
War of the Spanish Succession, has stood as a
symbol of the power and prestige of the British Empire.
Yet this proud fortress, long known as the Key to the
Straits, became a possession largely by accident, not by
design. It fell into the hands of England as an incidental
in her long struggle with France for supremacy. The full
measure of its future worth was not, and could not have
been, realized by British statesmen in the eighteenth century. They could not foresee that one day it would be the
strongest link in the life-line between Britain and her dominion in the Far East, or that modern armaments would
make possible the control of shipping through the Straits
from land fortifications. Such changes have given to the
Rock a worth far greater than any it possessed in the century after its acquisition.

Informed Englishmen in the eighteenth century regarded Gibraltar rather as an incubus than as a pillar of
strength. "Two or three such Acquisitions as Gibraltar
would be the splendid but certain Ruin of us," wrote Horatio Walpole in 1739.[1] In 1782, Sir John Jervis (subsequently Earl of St. Vincent and Admiral of the Fleet)
commented: "In a Spanish War the Anchorage is bad,
and except the single advantage of watering a Fleet, I
cannot see the real importance and utility of it, tho' I have
always considered it one of the brightest ornaments of the

1. *The Grand Question, Whether War, or no War, with Spain* (London, 1739).

Crown."[2] That it remained in England's possession must be attributed not to the stout defense maintained by British generals against Spanish attacks on the fortress, but to the failure of repeated attempts to negotiate a restitution of the Rock to Spain in return for advantages elsewhere. The story of those negotiations and their relation to the larger aspects of England's continental diplomacy in the eighteenth century provides the central theme for this study. This story is not without significance, for at times the question of Gibraltar became almost a focal point in British relations with Spain, France, and the Empire. Furthermore, the problem of Gibraltar entered as a vital factor into the formation and maintenance of the Family Compact between France and Spain. Despite the earnest efforts of England's ministers and diplomats, Gibraltar proved invulnerable to the assaults of diplomacy, and remained in Britain's possession to become not only a link in the life-line to the East, but also a link between the old British Empire and the new.

Gibraltar passed into the hands of Christian Spain in 1462, after being held by the Moslems for seven and a half centuries. Famous in ancient times as one of the Pillars of Hercules, and as the Mons Calpe of the Romans, it had remained uninhabited and unfortified prior to the Moslem occupation. The Moorish conquest was made by Tarik ben Zaide, who gave his name to the Rock, *Jebel Tarik*, since corrupted into *Gibraltar*. The erection of strong fortifications and a castle enabled the Moors to withstand a number of Spanish sieges. After being held for some years as the private property of the Dukes of Medina-Sidonia, Gibraltar was surrendered to the Spanish crown in 1501.[3]

During the sixteenth and seventeenth centuries, Spain improved the fortifications on the Rock and constructed moles in the open and treacherous harbor for the protec-

2. Jervis to Lord Shelburne, Sept. (?) 1782, William L. Clements Library, Shelburne Manuscripts, vol. 83.

3. Ignacio López de Ayala, *Historia de Gibraltar* (Madrid, 1782), p. 208. This is the best work on the early history of Gibraltar.

tion of vessels. Since the possession of both Gibraltar and the opposite promontory of Ceuta gave Spain a means of controlling the Straits, the Rock was highly prized by the Spanish. But the rapid decline of Spain in the seventeenth century, especially in naval power, removed any threat of the closure of the Straits to foreign nations. Although the Spanish people cherished Gibraltar in much the same fashion as the English did later, the garrison languished under the last of the Hapsburgs.

As soon as Louis XIV decided to accept his grandson, Philip of Anjou, as King of Spain after the death of Charles II, he urged the Spanish to strengthen their ports, especially Cádiz, Port Mahón, and Gibraltar; and he sent technical advisors into Spain to oversee the work. Renaud, a leading French engineer, went to superintend the remodeling of the defenses of the Straits. The reports of these projects greatly alarmed the Protestant powers. "What will become of the commerce of the English and Dutch," wrote a correspondent of the Elector of Hanover, "if he [Louis XIV] has Gibraltar fortified and keeps a strong garrison there with a squadron of galleys and ships of war?"[4] Count Schonenberg, the envoy of King William at Madrid, reported the plans for strengthening Gibraltar; but he was more amused than alarmed, for he felt sure that Spanish initiative would run true to form, and that practically nothing would be done.[5] The ease with which the English and Dutch captured the fortress in 1704 confirmed this forecast and exploded the myth of Gibraltar's impregnability.

The primary objectives of English naval strategy in the Mediterranean area during the War of the Spanish Succession were to seize control of the Straits in order to bottle up the French fleet at Toulon, and, secondarily, to support land operations in Spain and Italy with an Eng-

4. J. S. Corbett, *England in the Mediterranean . . ., 1603–1713* (London, 1904), II, 194.

5. Corbett, *England in the Mediterranean*, II, 194–198. George Macauley Trevelyan, *England under Queen Anne* (London, 1930–1934), I, 262.

lish fleet. Admiral Sir George Rooke sailed in 1702 with orders to seize Cádiz; if that were not possible, he was instructed to capture Gibraltar or any other convenient Spanish port. For the first time, a Spanish-Mediterranean naval expedition had as its primary objective a check to French naval power by dividing it and cutting off the French Mediterranean fleet from egress to the Atlantic. This maneuver had been accomplished accidentally by Blake under Cromwell; now the step was fully premeditated. It should be noted that the seizure of Gibraltar was only a secondary alternative in Rooke's instructions; he returned without having captured any Spanish port.[6]

The Methuen Treaty with Portugal in 1703 marked a vital step toward the acquisition of Gibraltar. By this treaty England secured the use of Lisbon as a base of operations. Without Lisbon as a supply base, Gibraltar probably could not have been held, for it could not itself be readily adapted for use as a strong naval base. The Portuguese alliance, followed by the conquests of Gibraltar and Port Mahón, paved the way for English sea power in the Mediterranean.[7]

6. Corbett, *England in the Mediterranean*, II, 203–205; I, 318–320. The following interesting commentary on the merit of acquiring Gibraltar is to be found in the Godolphin Papers: "Gibraltar and Ceuta make the very mouth of the Mediterranean, the first, vizt Gibraltar may be taken and afterwards kept much easier than Cadiz, for tis but badly fortifyed, and may quickly be made an Island: And Ceuta must soone fall for want of Provisions from Spaine: The Bay of Gibraltar is capable of holding as many, and as bigg shipps, as that of Cadiz; and being in the very passadge may much better hinder shipps and gallies passing into and out of the Streights, than at so great a distance as Cadiz is. Besides the Bombing or pretending to take Cadiz will fright the commerce to Sevilla, to the prejudice of all other natives, especially the English and Dutch, because of the freedom of the Port, and the great conveniency there in shipping off silver and gold in time of Peace: For if the commerce is once removed, it wont easily be returned. And the People of Spaine in General will be more affected with the loss of Gibraltar, than Cadiz, this [Cádiz] being envyed for the many Strangers residing in it; And the other esteemed the Key of the Kingdome." British Museum, Additional Manuscripts 28,058, fol. 31. (Hereafter cited as Add. MSS.) The authorship and date of this memorandum are not indicated, but it must have been written shortly before 1704.

7. Trevelyan, *England under Queen Anne*, I, 300–302.

Admiral Rooke again sailed to the Mediterranean in 1704 with instructions to prevent the junction of the Toulon and "West France" fleets, and to coöperate with Eugene of Savoy in a secret and sudden attack on Toulon. If the latter project failed, he was ordered to assist the archduke's cause in Spain as best he could. Reaching the Mediterranean, Rooke abandoned the attack on Toulon as impracticable and fell back to the Spanish coast, where he made an abortive attack on Barcelona. He then sailed back through the Straits, but returned into the Mediterranean after being reinforced by Sir Cloudesley Shovell's squadron. The commanders then held a council at which they decided, with the approval of the Archduke Charles, to attack the enemy in Andalusia by capturing a port on the Straits. Probably with a knowledge of its weakness, they chose to launch their assault against Gibraltar.[8]

The attack opened on July 23/August 3 and the Spanish governor capitulated the following day, the capture being made with ridiculous ease because of the wretched state of the defenses, which were manned by only a few hundred troops.[9] It is important to note that Gibraltar succumbed to a fleet consisting of both English and Dutch vessels and operating—at least nominally—under the auspices of the Austrian archduke as King of Spain. From 1704 until the Peace of Utrecht, Gibraltar was garrisoned jointly by English and Dutch soldiers, and its legal position was identical with that of the other portions of Spain captured and held for the archduke by the allied forces. It must also be emphasized that the capture

8. Corbett, *England in the Mediterranean,* II, 242–245. *A Narrative of Sir George Rooke's Late Voyage to the Mediterranean* (London, 1704), pp. 2–3.

9. There are numerous printed descriptions of the capture, the story of which is hardly relevant to this study. Rooke secured his niche in the Hall of Fame by this exploit. As to his ability, Corbett has written: "There can be no doubt that Rooke was one of those men whose popular reputation will sometimes remain proof against the most glaring exhibition of incapacity and lack of understanding." *England in the Mediterranean,* II, 232. A eulogistic account of Rooke's expedition and the capture is to be found in the previously cited *A Narrative of Sir George Rooke's Late Voyage to the Mediterranean.*

of Gibraltar was only an after-thought and secondary to the main objectives of Rooke's expedition.

The report of Gibraltar's capture aroused no great enthusiasm in England. The news of Marlborough's great victory at Blenheim overshadowed it. Secretary Hedges thought that Gibraltar would be a great advantage to the allies, "it being a Footing for the King of Spain [Charles] in the Strongest Fort belonging to that Country," and that it would also be useful in securing English trade, and interrupting that of her enemies.[10] Robert Harley wrote: "The taking of Gibraltar may turn to great account, it being [on] the greatest thorofare of trade in the world."[11] A member of Parliament commented, shortly after Gibraltar's capture: "It will not protect a fleet against a superior one, but 'twill be of use and safety for single ships, or four or five men-of-war, and in that respect of great advantage to our trade."[12] The limitations of the exposed harbor at Gibraltar were well known in England, but the impression rapidly grew that it could be utilized as a valuable point of support for the Levant trade and that it would also serve to overawe the Moors, thus protecting trade to the Barbary states. There was no hesitation in sending out troops for a permanent garrison in response to Rooke's plea for reinforcements to replace the men taken off his ships. Yet there is no contemporary evidence to indicate that Queen Anne's ministers contemplated retaining Gibraltar as a permanent English possession; they did their best to get the Dutch to share the cost of its upkeep; and as long as they recognized the archduke as King of Spain, they could not very well consider Gibraltar as English territory.[13]

10. Sir Charles Hedges to George Stepney, Aug. 22/Sept. 2, 1704, Add. MSS. 7,058, fol. 360.
11. Harley to the Duke of Newcastle, Sept. 5/16, 1704, *Historical Manuscripts Commission, The Manuscripts of . . . the Duke of Portland*, II, 186. (Hereafter cited as *H.M.C., Portland MSS.*)
12. Trevelyan, *England under Queen Anne*, I, 415.
13. Trevelyan, *England under Queen Anne*, I, 414–415. Lord Godolphin to Robert Harley, Feb. 1706, *H.M.C., Bath MSS.*, I, 80.

The capture of Gibraltar roused the Bourbon courts to action. A combined Franco-Spanish force laid siege to the fortress and prosecuted the attack with great vigor during the winter of 1704–1705. Naval control of the Straits enabled the English to protect and relieve the beleaguered garrison, and the exhaustion of French and Spanish resources compelled the Bourbon monarchs to raise the siege in April 1705. Thereafter, they were never in a position to threaten Gibraltar during the remainder of the war.

The English and Dutch had as their primary goal in the Spanish phase of the war the acquisition of "securities" for the protection and expansion of their commerce with Spain and the Spanish Indies. They stood united in their determination to prevent the realization of the French monopoly of the Indies trade proposed by Louis XIV. During the war, the maritime allies extracted secret assurances from the Archduke Charles that they themselves should control Spanish trade. Thus it became obvious that the English and Dutch would agree to the retention of the Spanish throne by Louis' grandson only if they were given adequate securities for their commerce with Spain and the Indies.

In a secret exchange of correspondence during the fall of 1707 between the Marquis de Torcy, the French foreign minister, and Petkum,[14] a secret French agent at The Hague, the latter proposed that the English and Dutch keep Cádiz and Gibraltar as securities for their Spanish commerce. He asserted that the Dutch longed for peace, if the freedom of their commerce were assured; but that a mere treaty promise would be insufficient. Torcy refused to consider the cession of either of these Spanish ports, since Spain would never agree to surrender Cádiz, and Gibraltar in English hands would give them control of the Levant trade. Then too, such a cession would be construed as a sign of weakness, and the French minister

14. Petkum was the minister of Holstein at The Hague; he also used the noms de plume of *Riviac* and *Riviere*.

would not consent even to submit such a proposition to King Philip.[15]

The secret Anglo-French negotiations leading to the Treaty of Utrecht had their origin in the rise to power of the Tories in the summer of 1710. Until then, English policies had been controlled by the Whigs under the leadership of the Duke of Marlborough, and under their direction England had shown no disposition to accept any terms short of the project of the Grand Alliance.[16] When Marlborough's opponents, headed by Robert Harley, came to power, they were anxious to secure a peace if one could be made on favorable terms.

The initial contact with the French began under the auspices of Edward Villiers, Earl of Jersey. Jersey held no public office, but he acted with the knowledge and approval of Harley and his associates. The Abbé Gaultier, secret agent of the French minister Torcy in London during the war years, served as the intermediary through whom Jersey conducted his exchange with the French. Though a mere prelude to the official negotiation of the following year, the main outline of the English peace objectives took shape in the preliminary exchange of correspondence between Torcy and Gaultier in the latter half of 1710. The essentials of these objectives were: modification of the Barrier Treaty of 1709; Philip of Anjou to be recognized as King of Spain and the Indies; and England to secure substantial commercial concessions in the Spanish dominions.[17]

15. H.M.C., MSS. of the Earl of Buckinghamshire, etc. (Round MSS.), pp. 321–323.

16. The Grand Alliance between England, Holland, and the emperor, signed on September 7, 1701, provided that the signatory powers should concert their efforts to rescue the Spanish Netherlands, the Spanish possessions in Italy, and the Spanish Indies from the control of France. In case of war, they agreed "that no peace shall be made unless jointly," and that peace would never be made until measures had been taken to insure that the Spanish and French thrones should never be united under the same government or ruler. J. W. Gerard, The Peace of Utrecht (New York, 1885), pp. 131–133.

17. G. M. Trevelyan, "The 'Jersey' Period of the Negotiations Lead-

The Earl of Jersey commissioned Gaultier, in January 1711, to go to Versailles with the message that the new Tory ministry was anxious for peace. The English ministers did not feel their position strong enough to permit them to initiate negotiations with France, but they would be glad to receive French terms. Furthermore, the English promised not to let Dutch objections stand in the way of favorable proposals. The French accepted this as a sincere overture and sent Gaultier back to London with general assurances that they too wanted peace. The English then informed the French through Gaultier that if France would submit proposals no less advantageous than those presented to the Dutch at Gertruydemberg,[18] England, in concert with Holland and the other allies, would give them active consideration. France responded with a proposal for a general peace conference; England rejected this overture as too vague, and sent Gaultier back to Paris to secure more specific terms which might be submitted to Holland.[19]

With these preliminary maneuvers as a background, the French minister Torcy, on April 22, 1711, drew up a set of propositions as preliminaries for a general peace, and included among them the promise: "Que les Anglois auront des Securetez reeles pour exercer desormais leur Commerce en Espagne, aux Indes, et dans les Ports de la Mediterranée."[20] Gaultier carried these terms back to England; the English communicated them to the Dutch, but nevertheless informed the French that the terms were still

ing to the Peace of Utrecht," in *English Historical Review*, XLIX (Jan. 1934), 100–105; Trevelyan, *England under Queen Anne*, III, 176–179.

18. In the spring of 1710, the French king offered peace on very favorable terms, even agreeing to acknowledge the Archduke Charles as King of Spain. The inexorable demands of the Dutch and Marlborough that Louis himself at once remove his grandson from Spain led to a rupture in the negotiation, for the French king felt that he could not submit to such a humiliating proposal. Gerard, *Peace of Utrecht,* pp. 187–191.

19. France, Ministère des Affaires Etrangères, Correspondance Politique, Angleterre, vol. 233, fols. 79–116. (Hereafter cited as Cor. Pol.)

20. Great Britain, Public Record Office, State Papers Foreign 105: 258. (Hereafter cited as S.P.)

too vague. In particular, England demanded an explanation of the term "Securetez reeles" in the clause cited above.[21]

Three days after the French had drafted these proposals, news of the death of the emperor reached Paris. King Louis realized that England would probably prefer the retention of the Spanish throne by his grandson, with proper restrictions and securities, to the prospective union of Spain and the Empire under the Archduke Charles, whose election as emperor was virtually certain. Therefore, he at once wrote his emissary at Madrid, the Duc de Vendôme, to secure as favorable a project as possible from the Spanish court.[22] The French king did not suggest specifically that Spain give up Gibraltar; but soon after the receipt of this letter, Vendôme wrote his master that the Spanish king would grant Gibraltar and Port Mahón to England if the rest of Spain were left to him. On May 31 Torcy informed the English through Gaultier that Spain would cede Gibraltar as a security for English commerce in Spain and in the Mediterranean; he said nothing about Port Mahón, for France wanted to keep that concession as a point for further bargaining.[23]

Internal difficulties of the Harley ministry delayed the negotiation with France for several weeks. In the meantime, the English discovered that the Dutch would not willingly consent to the exclusive acquisition of Gibraltar by England.[24] This discovery, a forecast of future trouble with Holland over Spanish spoils, undoubtedly helped to

21. Gaultier to Torcy, May 8, 1711, in *Letters and Correspondence . . . of the Right Honourable Henry St. John, Lord Viscount Bolingbroke* . . . (Gilbert Parke, ed., London, 1798), I, 178.

22. Louis XIV to Vendôme, April 26, 1711, Cor. Pol., Espagne, vol. 206, fol. 209.

23. *Bolingbroke Correspondence*, I, 178–179. Louis XIV to Vendôme, May 31, 1711, Cor. Pol., Espagne, vol. 207, fols. 113–114. A copy of the Spanish king's authorization to France to cede Gibraltar and Port Mahón to England was sent to the French king on June 11; the original, in Philip's own hand, was retained by Vendôme. Cor. Pol., Espagne, vol. 207, fol. 219.

24. See below, p. 13.

persuade Harley and his associates to attempt to conclude secret terms with France. Louis XIV was perfectly willing to proceed on this basis. Indeed, he believed that he could sow dissension between the two maritime allies by offering to England exclusive advantages in the Spanish dominions; and he counted on future internal disturbances in England to retrieve any concessions granted to the English themselves.[25]

The ministry finally sent Matthew Prior, a confidential agent of Harley, and Gaultier to Paris in July with the secret territorial demands of England: in Spain, Gibraltar and Port Mahón; in the Indies, four ports, as sureties for her commerce. Prior carried no powers to negotiate, but only to receive *ad referendum* the French response to these demands. The French minister Torcy made no objection to the cession of Gibraltar; but he did object to giving up Port Mahón, and was adamant on the question of surrendering ports in the Spanish Indies.[26]

Since nothing could be settled through Prior, the French decided to send a responsible emissary to England; they chose for this purpose Nicolas Mesnager, who had already acted as French representative in previous peace negotiations in Holland. Mesnager reached England in the latter part of August. He held many conferences with the English ministers, the principal point of contention being the English demand for four ports in Spanish America.[27]

25. Louis XIV to Vendôme, May 31, 1711, Cor. Pol., Espagne, vol. 207, fols. 113–114.

26. Cor. Pol., Angleterre, vol. 233, fols. 11, 59–62. For Prior's own account see *H.M.C., Portland MSS.*, V, 34–42. Prior's part in the negotiation of the preliminary terms of 1711 has been related in L. G. W. Legg, *Matthew Prior* . . . (Cambridge, 1921), pp. 144–167. For Torcy's account of his interviews with Prior, see the mémoire from the French archives edited by L. G. W. Legg, in the *English Historical Review*, XXIX (July 1914), 525–532.

27. Louis XIV was willing to press his grandson to give up either Puerto Rico or Trinidad in addition to Gibraltar and Port Mahón. At the same time that Mesnager left for England, instructions were sent the French minister at Madrid, the Marquis de Bonnac, to prevail upon Philip to consent to the cession of one of those islands, if necessary. *Recueil des instructions données aux ambassadeurs et ministres de*

There was no discussion of the cession of Gibraltar, which was regarded as a *fait accompli*. The surrender of both Gibraltar and Port Mahón was made a *sine qua non* in the preliminary demands presented by the English to Mesnager on September 9, 1711.[28] Mesnager transmitted these demands to Versailles; and, in response, the French king gave his formal promise of the cession of Gibraltar and Port Mahón.[29] On October 8, Mesnager and the English signed two sets of preliminary articles: the first, a declaration by the French king of the general bases upon which he was willing to treat with the allies in the forthcoming peace negotiation; and the second, a secret agreement specifying the particular advantages that France promised to secure for Great Britain. Points four and five of the secret Anglo-French agreement stipulated that Britain should obtain Gibraltar, Port Mahón, and exclusive trading concessions with the Spanish Indies.[30]

From the viewpoint of this study, the important thing to note is that the cession of Gibraltar presented no difficulty whatsoever in this secret negotiation, having been accepted without question by English, French, and Spanish alike after the preliminary overtures in May. Provided

France, vol. XII (*Espagne,* II, Paris, 1898), pp. 212–214. In a long memorandum of instructions for Mesnager, the French had indicated their willingness to attempt to persuade Philip V to relinquish Puerto Rico and Trinidad. Aug. 3, 1711, Cor. Pol., Angleterre, vol. 233, fols. 79–116.

28. Cor. Pol., Angleterre, vol. 233, fol. 239. Article four of the English demands read: "Gibraltar et le Port Mahon resterons entre les mains de ceux qui les possedent presentement. Gibraltar et le Port Mahon sont à present entre nos mains, nous ne les regardons tous deux que comme une seule sureté pour notre commerce dans l'Espagne et dans la Mer Mediterranée. Ainsi on ne se departira point de cette demande."

29. Cor. Pol., Angleterre, vol. 234, fols. 39–40. The French response read: "Le Roy [Louis XIV] promet au Nom du Roy d'Espagne son petit fils, et Suivant le pouvoir qui Sa Majesté en a receu de ce Prince, qui Gibraltar et le Port Mahon demeurement entre les mains des Anglais qui possedent presentement l'une et l'autre." Full powers for the French to negotiate peace on behalf of Spain on the basis of the cession of Gibraltar and Port Mahón were transmitted to Paris by the Spanish king through the Marquis de Bonnac on September 5.

30. For texts, see *Bolingbroke Correspondence,* I, 374–381, 402–404.

no rupture occurred to nullify the preliminary articles of October 8, there remained only the problems of securing Dutch acquiescence to the exclusive English possession of Gibraltar, and the settlement of the specific terms regulating the cession of the Rock to England by Spain.

The Dutch had a sound claim to participation in the possession of Gibraltar. Under the terms of the Grand Alliance and the Barrier Treaty of 1709, England had agreed to share with Holland any advantages obtained by the allies in the Spanish dominions. Furthermore, Gibraltar had been captured by a joint Anglo-Dutch force; and in May 1711 the Rock was garrisoned by one Dutch and two British regiments. But the English had no intention of sharing Gibraltar with the Dutch. Even before the receipt of the French proposal of May 31, the English secretary of state, St. John, wrote to the English minister at The Hague, Lord Raby, urging him to get the Dutch to withdraw their regiment from the garrison, at the same time admonishing him not to arouse Dutch suspicions by this request. If the Dutch refused to withdraw, Raby should insist that they pay their portion of the expense of Gibraltar and recruit their regiment to its full strength. Preferably, however, England wanted to ease the Dutch troops out of the garrison; St. John told Raby: "Your Excellency will endeavour on this occasion to make them desire us to give way to Their doing of that which we shall be heartily glad to see done." Raby responded that he would do his best to persuade the Dutch to withdraw their troops, but he observed that under the terms of the abovementioned treaties Holland expected to participate in any advantages obtained from Spain.[31]

At first Raby was hopeful that the Dutch would agree to withdraw, but when he discussed the matter with Buys, the Pensionary of Amsterdam, he met with what amounted to a refusal. Concerning this conversation, Raby wrote:

31. St. John to Raby, May 11/22, 1711, S.P. 84:241. Raby to St. John, May 26, 1711, Add. MSS. 22,205, fol. 107.

I insinuated I believed if the Queen was solicited she might
give them leave to remove that Batallion, but he answered,
no, then they must send another in its place. I told them perhaps I might obtain they might be dispensed with, but he
looking upon me said then we should have no troops there,
and would you have that place alone? No, My Lord, says he,
'tis better we guard it between us and [he] gave me a look
which shewd me plainly they would be very sorry to have us
alone masters of that place. . . . 'Twill be a very hard thing,
I believe, to persuade these People to quit any things they
have got hold on.[32]

This attitude vexed the English, but in order not to arouse
Dutch suspicions St. John told Raby merely to urge the
Dutch to recruit their Gibraltar regiment and "to persuade them you had no other view by your first proposition."[33]

Shortly before returning to England in June, ostensibly
to attend to private affairs, Raby wrote that Buys was
very uneasy about the rumored interchange of correspondence between France and England. Buys did not feel that
the retention of a few "seaport towns" would be a sufficient surety for Spanish commerce; if such towns were
kept, he insisted that their garrisons must be equal, half
Dutch and half English, an arrangement which he feared
would inevitably cause future dissension with England.
What made the Dutch most uneasy, Raby reported, was
the thought that "whilst the thing is carrying on through
our hands we may make our Terms better than they would
trouble themselves to do for Us."[34]

Having discovered that the Dutch were unwilling to
give up their claim to a share in Spanish acquisitions, the
English carefully abstained from telling their ally that
France had offered the cession of Gibraltar to England
alone. Nor were the Dutch informed about the particulars

32. Raby to St. John, June 2, 1711, S.P. 105:279.
33. St. John to Raby, May 29/June 9, 1711, S.P. 84:241.
34. Raby to St. John, Add. MSS. 22,205, fol. 151.

of the secret Anglo-French negotiation that culminated in the preliminaries of October 8. Lord Raby's return to England brought a convenient hiatus in official communication with Holland until after those preliminaries had been signed. During his absence Harley (now Earl of Oxford) and St. John carried on an unofficial exchange with Holland through John Drummond, a Scottish merchant of Amsterdam. Early in July, Drummond reported that the Dutch were reconciled to the retention of the Spanish throne by Philip, but felt that the Spanish Indies trade must be placed on an equal footing for all nations and that England should give up Gibraltar and Port Mahón. Shortly thereafter, Drummond informed Oxford that the Dutch entertained but slight hope of persuading England to give up those strongholds, but they still insisted that Holland must have a share in their garrisons.[35] After Mesnager's arrival in London in August, St. John informed the Dutch through Drummond of the progress of the negotiation; but the English secretary gave no hint of the particular terms being discussed, merely stating that England would not enter into a separate treaty with France, and that Raby (now Lord Strafford) would take with him the terms of the French proposal on his return to Holland.[36]

Immediately after the signature of the preliminaries of October 8, the English proceeded to tell their allies about the general bases for a peace negotiation upon which they and the French had agreed, but they maintained a discreet silence on the particular advantages France had promised England herself. In accordance with this policy, the Earl of Strafford was sent back to Holland in October with a copy of the general terms of the Anglo-French peace project. The queen's instructions directed him to inform the Dutch of these terms, and to arrange for the opening

35. Drummond to Oxford, June 27/July 7 and July 13/24, 1711, *H.M.C., Portland MSS.*, V, 22–24, 47–49.

36. St. John to Drummond, Aug. 17/28, 1711, *Bolingbroke Correspondence*, I, 316–317.

of a formal peace conference in the Netherlands at the earliest possible date.[37] At least officially, Strafford had no knowledge of the particular terms that had been agreed upon by France and England, and he certainly did not tell them to the Dutch. But the Dutch suspected the worst, and, despite British efforts to dissuade him from so doing, Buys hastened to London to ferret out the truth of the private Anglo-French agreement.

Buys, in a series of conferences with the queen and her ministers, did his best to force the British to disclose the particulars of their secret negotiation. In this effort he failed, but he seems to have guessed their true import from the beginning. Realizing that the British had appropriated for themselves alone Gibraltar, Port Mahón, and special advantages in trade to the Indies, Buys joined with the Whigs in their attempt to overthrow the Tory ministry and block its efforts to negotiate a peace based on the terms of October 8. Oxford and St. John triumphed after a sharp struggle, and the Utrecht negotiation opened on schedule in January 1712.

The real reason for this Dutch effort to upset the secret Anglo-French negotiation of 1711 was the action of the English ministry in excluding Holland from the particular advantages to be obtained from Spain, an action contrary to the letter and spirit of the Grand Alliance and Barrier Treaty. As St. John later recorded, Buys frankly "declared himself ready and authorized to stop the opposition made to the Queen's measures . . ., provided the queen would consent that they should garrison Gibraltar and Port Mahon jointly with us, and share equally the Assiento, the South Sea ship, and whatever should be granted by the Spaniards to the queen and her subjects."[38] When Buys proposed that peace negotiations be dropped and the war prosecuted with renewed vigor until the Bour-

37. Instructions for Strafford, Oct. 2/13, 1711, and St. John to Strafford, Oct. 12/23, 1711, *Bolingbroke Correspondence*, I, 397–408.

38. *The Works of the Late Right Honorable Henry St. John, Lord Viscount Bolingbroke* (Dublin, 1793), II, 464.

bons should be ousted from Spain, the English queen and
ministry responded that they would do so only if Holland
and the other allies would promise to supply their full
quotas of men, money, and material (as specified in previous treaties), for further operations in Spain and on the
high seas as well as in the Netherlands and Germany.
They asked Buys if the Dutch were in a position to make
good their quotas, and he had to confess that they were
not.[39] Finally Buys openly demanded that the English secretary of state disclose the particular advantages that had
been offered to England; but St. John refused, and threatened to withdraw from the war and negotiate a separate
peace with France unless the Dutch stopped their machinations to upset the Anglo-French preliminaries.[40] Faced
with such intransigence on the part of the English ministry, and with the defeat of the Whig effort to block the
negotiation, the Dutch had to permit the peace negotiation to proceed and tacitly to consent to England's acquisition of the Mediterranean strongholds and the Asiento.

After the opening of the Utrecht conference the Dutch
attempted to revive their claim to a share in the Spanish
spoils, but with no success. The instructions for Thomas
Harley, special emissary to Holland and Utrecht, noted
that the principal reason for Dutch resistance to the negotiation stemmed from their displeasure at the exclusive
advantages to be granted by Spain to England. Nevertheless, these instructions stated categorically:

. . . that she [Queen Anne] will insist to have the assiento
granted to her subjects, and to keep Port Mahon and Gibraltar. That from these three points, no extremity shall
ever oblige her to depart; and that, providing the States-
General will agree with her upon these heads, her Majesty
does then promise that she will join with them in reducing

39. *Mémoires de Torcy pour servir à l'histoire des négociations* . . .
(London, 1757), III, 109. Memorandum of a conference between Gaultier and Torcy, Nov. 17, 1711, Cor. Pol., Angleterre, vol. 234, fol. 103.

40. St. John to Strafford, Dec. 18/29, 1711, *Bolingbroke Correspondence,* II, 80–81.

the trade to Spain, and to all the Spanish dominions both in
Europe and elsewhere, in every other respect, to the condi-
tions under which it was carried on before the death of King
Charles the Second.[41]

The Dutch had to be satisfied with this crumb of comfort,
and thus to agree to the exclusive possession of Gibraltar
by England.

The reluctance of the Dutch to give up their claim to
Gibraltar is illustrated by their delay in withdrawing their
troops from the garrison. In October 1711, Governor
Stanwix was instructed to exclude soldiers of all other nations from the Rock; and further orders in June 1712
emphatically stated that the Dutch were included in the
previous instructions. But Dutch troops did not finally
withdraw until March 1713.[42]

During the negotiation of the Anglo-Spanish Treaty of
Utrecht, the cession of Gibraltar was never seriously in
question.[43] Queen Anne's instructions to her plenipotentiaries at Utrecht were adamant on this point. In June
1712 she announced to the English Parliament and people
the particular advantages, among them the cession of Gibraltar, that England was to secure in the forthcoming
peace.[44] An armistice with France in August 1712 provided for the cessation of Anglo-Spanish hostilities and
the blockade of Gibraltar, and complete freedom of action
for the English in the possession of the Rock.[45] The ces-

41. Instructions of Feb. 23/March 6, 1712, *Bolingbroke Correspondence,* II, 185–190.
42. Reports of Stanwix, Feb. 18/29, 1712 and March 31/April 10, 1713,
Public Record Office, Colonial Office Papers, 91:1. (Hereafter cited as
C.O.) Lord Dartmouth to Stanwix, June 10/21, 1712, S.P. 105:269.
43. In April 1712, Philip V, loath to relinquish his claim to the French
throne, insisted that he would not renounce that pretension unless further
compensations, including the restoration of Gibraltar, were granted him.
Louis XIV managed to dissuade his grandson from presenting any such
demand to England, and succeeded in obtaining the necessary renunciation of the French throne without any reservation on Gibraltar. A. Baudrillart, *Philippe V et la cour de France* (Paris, 1890–1901), I, 476–517.
44. *The Parliamentary History of England* . . . (London, 1806–1820),
VI, 1141–1144.
45. Armistice of August 19, 1712, Articles 5 and 7, S.P. 104:25.

sion was formally consummated with the signature of the
Anglo-Spanish treaty of peace in July 1713. The final
stages of the negotiation produced one point of significance: the official British position, subsequently maintained, as to the true foundation of England's claim to
Gibraltar. The British then and thereafter claimed that
Gibraltar became a property of the Crown through conquest and not through diplomacy. While arranging the
terms of cession with the Spanish envoy, the English insisted that Gibraltar was "conquered by her [Queen
Anne's] Arms and it was urg'd that the Treaty did not
give her a title, but only acknowledged what She had already; that She would hold it by that Right and accept
of no Cession from the King of Spain under the Conditions he proposed. With much difficulty, the Marq. de
Monteleon yielded it."[46] Even though they may have
"yielded it" on this occasion, the Spanish never accepted
this point of view in subsequent negotiations relating to
Gibraltar; they always insisted that England derived her
title from the Anglo-Spanish Treaty of Utrecht and not
from conquest; and that it might be revoked if England
did not abide by the terms of cession as stipulated in the
treaty. Though the cession itself was never in dispute
during the course of the peace negotiations, the settlement
of these terms started a number of controversies that forecast trouble for the future.

England naturally wished to protect her tenure of Gibraltar by securing an extent of land adjacent to the Rock
that would prevent the Spanish from erecting land fortifications within range of the fortress. After the English
plenipotentiaries failed to settle this point with the French
at Utrecht, the matter was referred to a future adjustment by direct negotiation between England and Spain.[47]
First, however, the English attempted to secure the inter-

46. Earl of Dartmouth to Lord Lexington, May 8/19, 1713, S.P. 105:
269.
47. Lord Bristol to St. John, April 26, 1712, Add. MSS. 22,206, fol.
402.

vention of the French court in this effort to obtain additional territory. In secret negotiations carried on by St. John and Torcy during the spring of 1712, the English minister included among his demands: "That an extent of country round Gibraltar, equal to two cannon shot, and the whole island of Minorca be ceded to England." In response the French minister declared that it would be impossible to persuade the Spanish king to yield any territory in the vicinity of Gibraltar. On the other hand, the French king offered to support England's demand for the entire island of Minorca, "as a sort of equivalent for territory round Gibraltar; and on this consideration, and from this time, his Majesty promises that the whole island of Minorca shall be ceded."[48] The English accepted this compromise, securing in the peace the entire island of Minorca instead of Port Mahón only, and in turn dropping their demand that the French intercede and prevail upon King Philip to surrender territory in the vicinity of Gibraltar. Henceforth, the English sought (though unsuccessfully) to secure this objective in their direct negotiations with Spain.

Following the armistice of August 1712, the English sent Lord Lexington to Madrid with instructions to secure the cession of Gibraltar on as favorable a basis as could be obtained. Since the expressed purpose of England in acquiring Gibraltar was to obtain a security for Spanish and Mediterranean trade, the English naturally sought to free the Rock from restrictions that might hamper its utility as a trade entrepôt. The Spanish, on the other hand, strove to circumscribe England's possession of the Rock in every possible way, and succeeded in inserting restrictions in the treaty of peace that effectively prevented England from developing Gibraltar as a trading center. The Spanish absolutely refused to cede anything but the fortress and bay; jurisdiction over the narrow neck of level land connecting the Rock with the mainland remained in dispute, the British occupying it, but the Spanish

48. *Bolingbroke Correspondence*, II, 288–289.

claiming that all land to the very walls of the fortress continued to belong to Spain. Professedly for religious reasons, the Spanish insisted that the Jews and Moors be
evicted from Gibraltar, to which the English agreed. England also promised not to give shelter to armed Moorish
ships. Spain refused to open up trade between Gibraltar
and the adjacent mainland except by water, and stipulated that no supplies were to be furnished by land to the
garrison save in emergency. At Spanish insistence, England guaranteed that the Spanish inhabitants should be
free to exercise their Catholic faith. Lastly, England
agreed that if she should ever give up Gibraltar, Spain
should have a prior claim to it over any other power.[49]

The failure of Lexington's efforts at Madrid to win
more liberal terms of cession led the English ministry to
transfer the negotiation back to London. But the Spanish
envoy, the Marquis de Monteleon, succeeded in maintaining the Spanish position on most of the points in dispute.
He even attempted to secure Britain's approval of the retention by the Spanish king of religious suzerainty over
the inhabitants of Gibraltar and Minorca; but that the
English refused to grant, since the exercise of religious
control might have qualified the queen's "absolute and independent Sovereignty over those Places."[50]

During the course of the negotiation, it was rumored
that Spain was ceding Gibraltar and Port Mahón to England with the understanding that they might be redeemed
for money at some future date.[51] There was some foundation for this rumor. In an interview on July 21, 1711,

49. Correspondence with Lexington in S.P. 105:269. For the text of
Article Ten of the Anglo-Spanish Treaty of Utrecht, regulating the
terms of the cession of Gibraltar, see George Chalmers (ed.), *A Collection of Treaties Between Great Britain and Other Powers* (London,
1790), II, 83–84.

50. Dartmouth to Lexington, May 8/19, 1713, S.P. 105:269. Lord Bolingbroke (St. John) to the English plenipotentiaries at Utrecht, April
25/May 6, 1713, Add. MSS. 22,206, fols. 301–302. See below, p. 176 n.

51. *H.M.C., MSS. of Buckinghamshire, etc.*, pp. 360–361. *H.M.C., MSS.
in Various Collections*, II, 180. See p. 100 below, quoting a remark of the
French minister Brancas in 1728.

Gaultier told Torcy that, while Spain would have to cede Gibraltar and Port Mahón in the peace, England might be willing to sell them back in a subsequent negotiation. Gaultier knew that this was the intention of the Earl of Jersey, who still was playing an important rôle in the conduct of the secret negotiations with France. Reflecting this report of Jersey's disposition, the instructions of the French emissary Mesnager, carried to London in August 1711, stated that "the view of the English ministers in demanding the retention of Gibraltar and Port Mahón, is less to obtain securities for their commerce in Spain and the Mediterranean, than some day to extract considerable sums of money from the King of Spain in selling him those two places."[52] But Jersey died suddenly in August 1711. St. John, his successor in the conduct of the secret negotiations with France, valued the acquisition of Gibraltar and Minorca more highly than any of his colleagues in the Tory ministry, and certainly never repeated the suggestion that they might be retroceded at some future date for a money equivalent.

To Spain, the surrender of Gibraltar to England in the Treaty of Utrecht was an unpleasant necessity. Through stipulations severely restricting the utility of the Rock to England, Spain made certain that it would be virtually worthless as a trade entrepôt. Furthermore, the discord in Anglo-Spanish relations engendered by England's possession of Gibraltar that began during the peace negotiations was destined to continue throughout the eighteenth century. In the light of this discord, Gibraltar's usefulness as a security for Britain's Spanish and Mediterranean trade was indeed dubious.

Before proceeding with the narrative of Gibraltar's rôle in Britain's diplomatic relations, we may note the condition of the surrendered fortress. Until 1720, Gibraltar suffered from neglect and maladministration of the worst

---

52. Cor. Pol., Angleterre, vol. 233, fol. 106. See also Torcy's mémoire of conversations with Prior and Gaultier in *English Hist. Rev.*, XXIX (July 1914), 525–526.

sort; there was a continual shortage of provisions, and the arbitrary exactions of the governors kept the garrison almost in a state of mutiny. In 1718 the defenses of Gibraltar were in no better condition than they had been in 1705, at the close of the siege; and it is unlikely that Gibraltar could have withstood any determined assault by the Spanish during this period. The garrison was greatly undermanned, having less than half the number subsequently considered the minimum strength necessary to defend the fortifications.[53]

Until the capture of Port Mahón in 1708, Gibraltar was of real value as a base for British operations in Catalonia. Subsequently it was practically deserted by naval vessels, with the consequence that many English merchant ships were taken by the Spanish within view of the fortress, which caused "great loss to Her Majesty in her Customes, and damage to Her Subjects, and the place looked upon as if it were in nobody's hands."[54]

The town of Gibraltar was in no better condition than the fortifications. The lower town was wrecked by the siege of 1704–1705, and the upper town largely destroyed by the soldiers, who tore down the houses to get firewood. Most of the trees and brush on the mountain were also destroyed, and there was practically no wood left available. Both soldiers and officers were very badly housed. The governor seized the few livable houses that were left and rented them to traders, principally Jews, for exorbitant sums.

At the peace, Queen Anne declared Gibraltar to be a

53. This and subsequent paragraphs on the state of Gibraltar are based principally upon material in C.O. 91:1, 5 and 6; and on a report, dated at Gibraltar, Nov. 22/Dec. 3, 1712, entitled "Some Remarks Concerning Gibraltar Humbly Offered by Col. Joseph Bennett to the Honourable the Commissioners Appointed to Examine the Publicke Accompte of Spaine and Portugal, etc.," to be found in the Liverpool Papers, Add. MSS. 38,329, fols. 157–159. See also *The Report of the Commissioners sent into Spain, Pursuant to an Address of the House of Commons to her late Majesty Queen Anne, Relating to Gibraltar, and some other Places, never Printed before* . . . (London, 1728).

54. Add. MSS. 38,329, fol. 157.

free port and the English hoped it would become an important trading center. The earnest efforts of Spain to prevent all trade between the town and the mainland, coupled with the numerous taxes and excises imposed by the governors, frustrated that hope. In fact, most traders avoided the place. All trade that remained was licensed by the governor, and neither soldiers nor inhabitants could buy provisions from any but those so licensed. The merchants who sold provisions to the garrison charged exorbitant prices, "knowing very well that such commodities must be had at any rate."[55] The arbitrary rule and peculation of the governors brought many complaints, and led to the removal of one of the worst offenders (Colonel Congreve) ; yet for many years the governorship of Gibraltar continued to be regarded as an opportunity for the aggrandizement of the personal wealth of the incumbent.[56]

The civil population of Gibraltar largely melted away after the English occupation, and numbered less than a thousand, of whom 150 or more were Jews. About three hundred, who claimed to be original Spanish inhabitants, were supported by the British government with provisions and other necessaries, at a cost of some £5,000 a year— more than was expended on the fortifications of the place. The business of the town was almost entirely in the hands of Jews, Moors, and Genoese.

Immediately after the signature of the Treaty of

55. Add. MSS. 38,329, fol. 158.

56. The neglect and maladministration of the Gibraltar garrison in the first half of the eighteenth century were by no means unique. Similar conditions prevailed at other British army posts, both at home and abroad. See J. W. Fortescue, *History of the British Army* (London, 1910), vol. I (chap. XI) and II (chaps. I and II). Conditions improved after 1720, but there is much evidence that the management of Gibraltar continued to be one of the blackest spots in British colonial administration. A pamphlet appearing in 1748 (*Reasons for Giving Up Gibraltar*) argued, sarcastically, that the administration of Gibraltar was so rotten that it ought to be returned to Spain before its example corrupted the whole colonial system. A French observer, as late as 1760, wrote: "The governors of this place have conducted themselves up to the present in a manner for which there is no parallel in the other domains of England." M. Durand, "Sur Gibraltar," March 10, 1760, M.A.E., Mémoires et Documents, Angleterre, vol. 58, fols. 103–106.

Utrecht, the Spaniards cut off all provisioning of Gibraltar from the mainland. The Earl of Portmore, who was sent to investigate conditions at the garrison, stated that it was evident that the Spaniards would "put us to all the inconveniency they can in the possession of this place, and watch all opportunitys for recovering it, in the same manner, as if wee were still in a State of War." Under the circumstances, it was obvious that the garrison would have to depend on England for both provisions and fuel. Such supply was most undependable. For some years no more than two months' supply of provisions was available at any one time. "This garrison must be victualled by the queen," wrote Portmore, "and the least diminution of the present allowance . . . would occasion a mutiny; as it is, the soldiers are so harassed since the late reduction, by being upon continual duty, and under a necessity of eating the salt provisions almost raw for lack of coals, that they desert dayly." He concluded his report by warning the ministry at London that "if a speedy supply is not sent and solid settlement made for this garrison, it is a great question if the town of Gibraltar will be long in Her Majesty's possession."[57] For several years this warning went unheeded. In 1717 Spain reopened communication with Gibraltar,[58] but war again closed it in the following year.

Under the terms of cession in the Treaty of Utrecht, England had agreed to evict the Jews and Moors from Gibraltar; and orders were sent to the governor to carry out this provision. Since the trade of the town was principally in their hands, such an action would have seriously injured the garrison. And since much of the governor's private revenue came from these people, naturally he was not enthusiastic about evicting them. Most of the Jews came from Barbary, and were under the protection of the Emperor of Morocco. Spain's refusal to permit communication with the garrison forced England to look across the

57. Earl of Portmore to Lord Bolingbroke, March 21/April 1, 1714, C.O. 91:5.
58. *H.M.C., Polwarth MSS.*, I, 166.

Straits for supply. When the emperor agreed to permit the export of lime, timber, bricks, and other materials to rebuild the fortifications, he did so only with the proviso that Gibraltar should be open to his subjects, both Jews and Moors. As time passed, the garrison also came to depend on Morocco for provisions. England was thus placed in a dilemma, for by carrying out her treaty promise with regard to the Jews and Moors she would cut off her only local source of supply. The situation was solved by repeated promises to Spain that these people would be evicted, and constant non-performance of orders to that effect sent to the governors of Gibraltar.

During the invasion of England by the Pretender in 1715, Spain massed troops about Gibraltar, and the governor and the commander of the Mediterranean fleet feared that the place might be attacked. The failure of the Pretender's effort forestalled such an attempt; but it was believed that if Louis XIV had not died and if the Pretender had appeared to have some chance of success, Spain would have fallen upon both Minorca and Gibraltar.[59] It is interesting to note that these alarms seem to have aroused no precautions on the part of England; no attempt was made to strengthen or relieve the garrison.

59. C.O. 91:5, especially the report of Admiral Baker to Secretary Stanhope, Sept. 27/Oct. 8, 1715. Subsequent to the uprising of 1715, the Jacobites contemplated offering the restoration of Gibraltar and Minorca as a consideration for Spanish aid to the Pretender's plans. During the summer of 1716 a plot was on foot whereby (with the aid of their British army garrisons) Gibraltar and Minorca were to be seized for the Pretender and used as points of support for a projected descent upon England; afterward, they were to be turned over to Spain. *H.M.C., Calendar of the Stuart Papers . . .,* II, 348 ff. Again in December 1717 it was proposed to make a definite offer of Gibraltar and Minorca to Spain in return for a promise of armed support. But the Pretender was not anxious to make any open offer to Spain of Gibraltar; on Jan. 26, 1718, he wrote to Cardinal Gualterio as follows: ". . . it is by no means agreeable to me to name Gibraltar etc. [in a memorial to the Spanish court], it is not in my power positively to make such an offer, and, if it should come to be known, that would antagonize the English, but, if Spain wishes to enter into a treaty, the end of the mémoire speaks sufficiently clearly in general of my disposition in favor of his Catholic Majesty." *H.M.C., Stuart Papers,* V, 332, 408.

This is in striking contrast to similar situations in 1720 and later years, and would seem to be another indication of the slight esteem which Gibraltar commanded in England before 1720.

The expense of maintaining Gibraltar was said to be about £90,000 annually in 1716, exclusive of the cost of the shipping by which it was supplied. The Prussian minister reported that he had been reliably informed in London that if the fear of the union of France and Spain were removed, England would voluntarily cede both Gibraltar and Minorca to Spain for commercial advantages; and that this measure would be highly popular in England, and very advantageous to the Crown.[60] The neglect and bad administration which the garrison suffered in its early years as an English possession certainly corroborate this statement.

The English acquisition of Gibraltar in the War of the Spanish Succession introduced a complicated and perplexing problem into the arena of European diplomacy, especially into the sphere of Anglo-Spanish relations. The continued possession of the Rock by England prevented the reëstablishment of the close friendship that had characterized relations with Spain in the preceding century. England had acquired Gibraltar almost accidentally, and had retained it as a check upon the Bourbon monarch of Spain. Instead of serving as a lever with which to enforce respect for English rights and interests in the Spanish dominions, Gibraltar created an irritation that was never healed throughout the century. Contention over its possession was stimulated by a conditional promise to restore the Rock, presently to be considered. The Rock of Gibraltar, so significant to the modern imperialism of Great Britain, became a constant threat to the peace of Europe for many decades, without the justification of an adequate return to the power of the first British Empire.

60. W. Michael, *Englische Geschichte im Achtzehnten Jahrhundert* (Leipzig and Berlin, 1896–1937), II, 632.

II

THE RISE OF THE GIBRALTAR QUESTION

TO understand the meaning of Gibraltar in British diplomacy in the decade after Utrecht, we must review the new and complicated international setting which appeared after that epoch-making peace.

In England the accession of the Hanoverian dynasty, together with the overthrow of the Tory party, wrought profound changes in foreign policy. The Tories were in disgrace because of their alleged desertion of England's allies in the recent peace negotiation and their suspected support of the Pretender. The Whigs naturally sought to return to the old connection with Holland and Austria, with enmity toward France as the natural order of things. Equally significant was the entanglement of England's external policy with that of Hanover. Hanover was in the process of absorbing a portion of Sweden's German possessions; and her relationships with the other German states and with the emperor were naturally very different from those of Britain. The Act of Settlement forbade the king, without the consent of Parliament, to draw England into a war in defense of Hanoverian interests; most of the Whigs strongly opposed the subordination of English interests to those of Hanover. But George I was far more attached to Hanover than to England. His wide control over the conduct of foreign affairs enabled him indirectly to utilize England's strength against the enemies of Hanover and to subvert English policy in favor of Hanover's continental interest in the German war against Sweden. After the return of Charles XII, England sent several fleets into the Baltic, avowedly to protect English trade; but they behaved in a most unneutral manner, creating enmity between Sweden and England. In retaliation, Sweden planned an invasion of Great Britain in favor of the Pretender, a plan which was prematurely discovered. The difficulties with Sweden, and later with Russia, that arose chiefly out of the interests of Hanover created a northern problem which for many years influenced English relations with the powers of southern Europe. The new king's predilections for his native state left him with slight concern for affairs in the south, and unimpressed by the significance of England's newly won possessions in the Mediterranean.[1]

The Treaties of Utrecht did not bring about a settlement between the original protagonists of the late war, the Empire and Spain. The emperor refused to recognize Philip V as King of Spain, and Philip refused to recognize the acquisition by Austria and Savoy of Spain's Italian possessions. The nub of this problem was the settlement in Italy, and its solution occupied western Europe for twenty-five years.

Immediately after their assumption of power, the English Whigs signed a new alliance with Holland and Austria, designed to straighten out this Austro-Spanish tangle and other matters left unsettled by the Treaties of Utrecht. The death of Louis XIV created a new situation. The Duke of Orleans, as regent, had a deadly fear of the pro-Spanish faction in France, which favored the candidacy of Philip V to the French throne in the event of the death of Louis XV, then a sickly infant. The regent naturally turned to England for support and negotiated an alliance which lasted for almost two decades, in name if not in spirit.[2] England presently took the initiative (1717) in formulating a Quadruple Alliance between herself and France, Austria, and Holland, which would mutually guarantee their own interests and force a settlement between the emperor and Spain. The moving figures be-

1. J. F. Chance, *George I and the Northern War* (London, 1909). Michael, *Englische Geschichte im Achtzehnten Jahrhundert,* vol. I.

2. See Sir Richard Lodge, "The Anglo-French Alliance, 1716–1731," in *Studies in Anglo-French History during the Eighteenth, Nineteenth, and Twentieth Centuries,* edited by A. Coville and H. Temperley (Cambridge, 1935), pp. 3–18.

hind this plan were James Stanhope, whose talents in diplomacy had won him the position of chief minister under George I,[3] and the Abbé DuBois, a satellite of the regent, who secured during this negotiation the control of French foreign policy.

In Spain Giulio Alberoni, an Italian priest who had been minister of Parma at Madrid, gained the chief power in the government. The marriage between Philip V and the fiery Elizabeth Farnese, niece of the Duke of Parma, was followed by the domination of the queen over her weak and vacillating husband. This domination continued for many years and served to orient Spanish policy in favor of the queen's ambitions in Italy. The queen secured positions of power for her Italian advisors; and Alberoni was only the first, albeit the greatest, of the Parmesan ministers who were destined to influence Spanish policy.

Alberoni formulated a grandiose scheme of using Spanish power to overwhelm practically all Europe. His first step was to enhance his personal prestige by securing a cardinal's hat. This done, he proceeded to attack the emperor in Italy. Alberoni probably was forced, by pressure from the Spanish king and queen, to act before he felt that Spanish power was sufficiently strong. But Sardinia, the first objective, was conquered without any great difficulty in the fall of 1717; and it was rather obvious (despite Alberoni's protestations) that this expedition was to be followed by an attack against Naples or Sicily in the following year. Secretly, Alberoni's eventual project included a grand coalition with the northern enemies of England and Austria, and an invasion of England in favor of the Pretender. The English did not realize the extent of the ambitions and inimical schemes of Alberoni, and his blandishments made them believe that he favored a moderate settlement with Austria.

3. For the larger aspects of Stanhope's diplomacy, see Basil Williams, *Stanhope: A Study in Eighteenth-Century War and Diplomacy* (Oxford, 1932).

Acting on their impression that Spain was prepared to accept a reasonable accommodation, Stanhope and DuBois drafted the Quadruple Alliance, and finally secured the adherence of the emperor to its terms (August 2, 1718). Under this new pact the Spanish king was to be granted recognition by the emperor, in return for an acknowledgment of the emperor's possession of the former Spanish portions of Italy; an investiture of the succession to the Italian duchies of Parma and Tuscany was promised to the sons of Elizabeth Farnese; Spain was offered an alliance guaranteeing her remaining territories; and, secretly, England offered to restore Gibraltar as an incentive to Spanish acceptance.[4] The chief obstacle was to secure the acceptance of these conditions by Spain, and the

4. According to the memoirs of Saint-Simon (Paris, 1919 ed., XXX, 224–226, 245–246), England had previously offered to restore Gibraltar to Spain in 1716. In order to combat Italian influence at the Spanish court, France had sent several secret emissaries to Madrid after the Peace of Utrecht. One of them, the Marquis de Louville, sent in July 1716, is said to have had secret instructions to offer Gibraltar to Spain in return for Spanish coöperation with the rapprochement then under way between France and England. As related by Saint-Simon, the matter was to be arranged as follows: the governor of Gibraltar was to be given secret instructions suddenly to withdraw his garrison to Tangier; the Spanish would occupy the fortress; and England, France, and Spain would then enter into a general agreement or alliance. Alberoni, however, was so distrustful of Louville that he would not let him see the Spanish monarchs, but compelled him to leave Spain. Consequently the offer of Gibraltar was never made.

There is no doubt about the general purpose of Louville's mission (an intrigue to combat Italian influence), but there is no documentary evidence to support Saint-Simon's story of his secret instructions to offer Gibraltar to Spain. Most historians of the period have ignored the story or treated it as a fabrication of Saint-Simon. But Wolfgang Michael (*Englische Geschichte im Achtzehnten Jahrhundert*, II, 261–265) believes that Saint-Simon's account may be true. Michael bases this belief not on documentary but on circumstantial evidence: Saint-Simon, though not always trustworthy, seldom fabricated such an elaborate account; the report of the Prussian minister Bonet (*ibid.*, II, 632) testifies that Gibraltar was considered a burden to England; and the subsequent readiness of James Stanhope to give up Gibraltar for a similar purpose in 1718 would support the idea that England was equally willing to do so in 1716. Without more substantial evidence, I cannot credit this story. See also P. Lémontey, *Histoire de la Régence* . . . (Paris, 1832), II, 394–398.

offer of Gibraltar in this negotiation thus connected the Rock with general European diplomacy.[5]

Under this new European setting, the Abbé DuBois journeyed to London at the end of December 1717 and entered into confidential negotiations with Stanhope. During January they worked out the terms of the new treaty designed to settle the differences between the emperor and Philip of Spain. Separately, through DuBois, Stanhope secretly authorized the regent to offer Gibraltar to Spain as a *douceur* for the immediate and unqualified acceptance of the treaty.[6] Precisely how this offer was communicated, and upon what terms, is not clear from the records. But DuBois' instructions to Nancré, the French emissary sent to Madrid, leave no doubt that the offer was made; other letters of DuBois indicate that Stanhope approved the offer of Gibraltar as early as January 15, 1718. As to the terms, DuBois wrote on February 21 that Gibraltar would be procured for his Catholic Majesty "sans qu'il lui en couste aucune somme d'argent ni aucun autre dédommagement."[7] Yet subsequent references, including the offer which Nancré was instructed to make to Cardinal Alberoni, specified that Gibraltar was to be given up only for a proper equivalent in money or other exchange. Two years later, the English insisted that the offer had been made on the latter basis.[8]

The draft of the treaty completed, it was carried to

5. This brief review of the diplomatic situation, 1715–1718, is based on the following: Michael, *Englische Geschichte im Achtzehnten Jahrhundert,* vols. I and II; Baudrillart, *Philippe V et la cour de France,* vol. II; E. Armstrong, *Elisabeth Farnese* (London, 1892); and A. Ballestros, *Historia de España* (Barcelona, 1919–1936), vol. V.

6. Abbé DuBois to the regent, Jan. 15, 1718, Cor. Pol., Angleterre, vol. 314, fol. 130. While DuBois was in London in November 1717, he had proposed to Stanhope that Gibraltar should be offered to Spain in order to secure Spanish adherence to the projected alliance, and Stanhope had agreed to attempt to secure the restitution. See Lémontey, *Histoire de la Régence . . . ,* II, 395, quoting a portion of DuBois' letter to the regent, dated London, Nov. 11, 1717.

7. DuBois to M. de St. Brice, Feb. 21, 1718, Cor. Pol., Angleterre, vol. 315, fol. 194.

8. Secretary Craggs to Earl of Stair, Feb. 18/29, 1720, S.P. 104:31.

Paris by Luke Schaub, Stanhope's trusted subordinate; Schaub was instructed to submit it to the regent for his final approval, and then proceed to Vienna to secure the emperor's adhesion.[9] After Schaub's departure, DuBois drew up the instructions for Nancré, dated February 5, promising that "His Royal Highness [the regent] will propose to the King of Great Britain the sale or exchange of Gibraltar, in order that he [the regent] can return it to His Catholic Majesty."[10] Three months later, King George officially authorized DuBois to make such a proposal as a means of securing Spanish adhesion to the projected treaty.[11]

In this attempt to force an Austro-Spanish settlement, it should be noted that England, more eager than France to effect an Italian settlement, took the leading part. It was England's interest to keep a victorious *status quo* after her great exertions of 1701–1713. Stanhope and his colleagues were anxious above all to avoid a general war, although they felt confident that English support would be forthcoming against Spain alone, if necessary. But the Tories and opposition Whigs, led by Robert Walpole, had been dangerously threatening the ministry's majority in Parliament, and attempting to force the government to reduce the size of the army. Undoubtedly the Anglo-French Alliance, the keynote of Stanhope's diplomacy, aroused opposition in many quarters. But Stanhope and DuBois had strong hopes that Spain would accept their plan for peace; for, if the emperor accepted and Spain refused, the latter would be faced by the united armed op-

9. Cor. Pol., Angleterre, vol. 314.

10. "Mémoire pour M. le Marquis de Nancré allant a Madrid, au mois de Février, 1718," *Recueil des instructions . . .*, XII, *Espagne,* II, 311–319. London copy, dated Feb. 5, 1718, in Cor. Pol., Angleterre, vol. 315.

11. A memorandum of DuBois, dated Paris, March 13, 1720, stated: "Pour persuadir le Roi Catholique de consentir à la paix . . . le Roi de la Grande Bretagne se porta genereusement a declarer le 10ᵉ de May 1718 à l'Abbé Dubois, Ambassadeur de France en Angleterre, que S. A. R. [the regent] pouvoit offrir Gibraltar au Roi d'Espagne si il vouloit accepter la paix." Cor. Pol., Angleterre, vol. 6 (Supplement), fol. 266.

position of Europe.[12] This prospective isolation of Spain, coupled with the offer of Gibraltar, apparently convinced the English and French ministers that Spain would come to terms.

The Marquis de Nancré left for Madrid early in March, with instructions to collaborate with the English minister, William Stanhope (a cousin of James), in an effort to secure Alberoni's assent to the terms of the Quadruple Alliance. For several weeks Nancré did not mention the offer of Gibraltar to Alberoni, merely hinting that if Spain would agree to accept at once and unconditionally the terms offered, the regent would procure for Spain some further advantage. Strangely enough, although the two envoys supposedly were collaborating in their representations to the cardinal, William Stanhope seems never to have been informed of the offer of Gibraltar. Nancré himself did not know whether his colleague had been instructed on the subject, and therefore refrained from mentioning it to him or in his presence to Alberoni.[13]

Alberoni showed no enthusiasm for Spanish adhesion to the Quadruple Alliance. Finally, on April 26, 1718, Nancré hinted that the regent would endeavor to secure Gibraltar from England for Spain. This suggestion failed to impress the cardinal; in a confidential memorandum, Alberoni noted: "A l'Egard de Gibraltar, il est onereux aux Anglois, et cela a esté avoüé en Plein Parlement."[14] Obviously, Alberoni felt that Gibraltar's restoration would

12. Lord Stanhope to Earl of Stair, Feb. 17/28, 1718, in Mahon, *History of England* . . . (London, 1836–1854), I, appendix, lix–lxi.

13. Nancré's negotiation at Madrid can be followed in Cor. Pol., Espagne, vols. 268–271. On May 23, Nancré wrote the regent: "Col. Stanhope has taken no step forward. . . . I have not spoken to him of Gibraltar as yet, nor he to me about it; I have recommended to Cardinal Alberoni that it be kept secret . . . for it is not possible to judge from the letters of Abbé DuBois if they still desire in England that the secret should be kept or not." Cor. Pol., Espagne, vol. 270, fol. 211. A letter of Wm. Stanhope to the Earl of Stair, Aug. 8, 1718, seems to indicate that he had no knowledge of the offer of Gibraltar which had been made through Nancré. S.P. 78:162.

14. Alberoni to Nancré, April 26, 1718, Cor. Pol., Espagne, vol. 269, fol. 195.

be no great sacrifice for England, and certainly not an adequate compensation for giving up practically all of King Philip's Italian pretensions. During the following month, Nancré repeated the suggestion on several occasions, with no greater success. Alberoni was perhaps somewhat suspicious of the offer, for he asked Nancré whether he might discuss the subject with William Stanhope, and also communicate the proposition to the Spanish ministers at London and Paris, Monteleon and Chelamare. Nancré objected, but finally consented to its communication to Chelamare, for, as he remarked, he understood the matter was by then an open secret in Paris.[15]

During May, Nancré drew up a project for a supplementary treaty to govern the various arrangements to be made with Spain by France and England. He included the promise that England would cede Gibraltar to Spain, but did not mention any equivalent for it. In response, Alberoni wrote: "This cession is the only real advantage which is offered at present to Spain; but it is too insignificant to be bought at such a price."[16] After the end of May, the Spanish preparations for hostilities against Italy were so manifest that Nancré felt it was useless to press the point further, and the subject of Gibraltar does not seem to have been mentioned again until August.[17]

The Spanish fleet sailed for Italy in the summer of 1718, and attacked and captured Palermo in Sicily on July 3. Originally the expedition had been destined against Naples, but had been diverted to Sicily in order to stave off British resistance. Great Britain was bound to protect the emperor's Italian possessions; but Sicily was still under Savoy, although destined for Austria in the projected settlement. Nevertheless England determined to

15. Nancré to [the regent?], June 3, 1718, Cor. Pol., Espagne, vol. 271, fols. 37–39.

16. Cor. Pol., Espagne, vol. 270, fol. 165. The draft and this response of Alberoni are undated, but probably were composed about May 19.

17. On June 12, Nancré referred to the Gibraltar proposal as one "dont il n'est plus question parce que je cesse d'en parler." Cor. Pol., Espagne, vol. 271, fol. 67.

take active measures to check the Spaniards in any event. Admiral Byng, commanding the squadron which had been sent into the Mediterranean, was ordered to prevent by force the Spanish conquest of Sicily.

Meanwhile, Secretary Stanhope did not lose hope that peace could still be made. In July he rushed to Paris and then on to Madrid, hoping by a personal visit to succeed where Nancré and William Stanhope had failed. He reached Madrid early in August, and repeated to the Spanish the offer of Gibraltar. Stanhope thought that Alberoni showed some disposition to come to terms, but news suddenly arrived of the Spanish capture of Messina and this disposition vanished. Secretary Stanhope forthwith left Madrid, but not without assuring Spain that the Allies would grant her three months' grace in which the Quadruple Alliance might be accepted, and the offer of Gibraltar hold good.[18]

Fortunately for Stanhope, he reached the French border before news of the destruction of the Spanish fleet by Admiral Byng off Cape Passero arrived at Madrid. This defeat, which at once enraged Spain and frustrated any further Spanish attack in Italy, made war between the allied powers and Spain virtually certain. Although Nancré was still sanguine in September that Spain would accept the treaty within the period of grace offered, William Stanhope believed that there was no longer any hope of Spanish adherence. Nevertheless, the British offer to re-

18. For Nancré's report of Stanhope's visit, see Cor. Pol., Espagne, vol. 272, fol. 212. Lord Stanhope's own correspondence on his mission is scanty; some information is to be found in his letter to Craggs, Aug. 22, 1718, S.P. 94:88, and his optimism in believing that war might yet be prevented and that Spain would accept the Quadruple Alliance and Gibraltar is indicated in his letter to Stair, dated at Bayonne, Sept. 2, 1718, S.P. 78:162. A Jacobite report of Stanhope's visit and of the offer of Gibraltar is that of Lieutenant-General Dillon to the Duke of Mar, Aug. 23, 1718, printed in H.M.C., Calendar of the Stuart Papers, VII, 196. That the English had but slight hope of a peaceful settlement with Spain even before Stanhope reached Spain is indicated by the instructions dispatched by Lord Stair to Admiral Byng (Aug. 10, 1718, S.P. 78:162), directing him to prevent, by force if necessary, the occupation of Sicily by the Spaniards.

store Gibraltar remained available to Spain until November 2, 1718, though there is no evidence to indicate that England ever offered to surrender Gibraltar as a *quid pro quo* for Spanish adhesion to the Quadruple Alliance subsequent to that date.[19]

In reviewing this negotiation, it is obvious that the king and ministry in England attached but little significance to Gibraltar, and were entirely willing to sacrifice it to preserve the peace. Although the suggestion of the cession came from the French, the English seem to have made no objection to it. England took the initiative in the negotiation, and France saw to it that Spanish bitterness over the blocking of her ambitions in Italy fell principally on the British.[20] The French would not have been averse to leaving Sardinia with Spain. Stanhope seems to have given this some consideration,[21] but eventually refused to negotiate with Spain on that basis. Alberoni refused to negotiate on any other. So eager was England for a pacific settlement that it was rumored that she was willing to surrender Minorca in addition to Gibraltar, although at the time Minorca was regarded as by far the more valuable of the two to England.[22] All England's efforts were unavailing, and this offer of Gibraltar engendered a long diplomatic struggle with Spain.

In the war that followed this unsuccessful negotiation, France invaded Spain from the north, and the English

19. Wm. Stanhope to Lord Stanhope, Oct. 5, 1718, S.P. 94:88. Stair to Wm. Stanhope, Oct. 18, 1718, S.P. 78:162. The original three-month period given Spain to sign the treaty was technically extended several times, and Spain's actual agreement to sign occurred just before the last of these extensions expired. But the English did not renew the offer of Gibraltar after November 2.

20. An example of this is the following extract from the regent's letter to Nancré of April 19, 1718: "It is very likely that Col. Stanhope will not have put off until the present opening himself to the cardinal on the matter of Sicily, and that he will spare you the odium resulting from that proposition. I am counting on the restitution of Gibraltar to be a good palliative. . . ." Cor. Pol., Espagne, vol. 269, fol. 47.

21. Dillon to Mar, Aug. 23, 1718, *H.M.C., Stuart Papers,* VII, 196.

22. Reported in a letter by an unknown writer to Nancré, Aug. 30, 1718, Cor. Pol., Espagne, vol. 272, fol. 217.

fleet blockaded the Spanish army in Sicily, so that its capitulation was only a matter of time. Alberoni tried desperately to foment an attack on England by the northern powers, and he fitted out an expedition on behalf of the Pretender under the Duke of Ormond, which came to grief in a violent storm off Cape Finisterre. All the cardinal's schemes miscarried. Spain was in a desperate military situation by August 1719. Alberoni was loath to make a direct capitulation, for that would bring his certain downfall. His one hope lay in the possibility of separating the Allies by opening up secret negotiations with one or two of them, and thus creating suspicions and recriminations which might lead to Spain's obtaining at least some of her desired objectives.

With this idea in view, Alberoni dispatched the Parmesan minister at Madrid, the Marquis Scotti, to Holland, via France, with the terms of peace; these were to be given to Beretti Landi, the Spanish ambassador at The Hague, for presentation to the Allies. There was no real occasion for Scotti's traveling by way of Paris, save that Spain may have hoped to open up secret negotiations with France herself. When Scotti requested a French passport (after reaching Paris), and yet declined to divulge the peace terms entrusted to him, the regent refused to grant the request without the consent of England and Austria (who both refused), in order not to create the suspicion that Spain rather obviously hoped would be aroused. Both England and France feared that if Scotti proceeded to The Hague, he might stir up friction between them and Holland. Bad feeling already existed. Holland, true to form, had been supplying the materials and munitions without which Spain could not have sustained the war. His passport refused, Scotti remained at Paris; and it became increasingly apparent that a direct capitulation must be made by Spain. England and France were determined that its terms should include the expulsion of Alberoni, the "firebrand" of Europe. The Duke of Parma played the decisive rôle in forcing the issue. His duchy was surrounded by the emperor's forces, and to save himself he ordered Scotti to press their Catholic Majesties in the strongest terms for peace. Secretly, the duke instructed Scotti to arrange Alberoni's downfall. Scotti returned to Madrid late in October. After some difficulties he reached the queen's ear. Alberoni was dismissed in disgrace on December 4.[23]

Scotti probably carried with him assurances from the regent that if Alberoni were dismissed and the Quadruple Alliance accepted by Spain, France would use her good offices to secure the restitution of Gibraltar. The regent, upon entering the war, had published a manifesto setting forth the reasons for his conduct, in which he referred to "la promesse que Sa Majesté lui procurerait la restitution de Gibraltar."[24] He apparently assumed that England was still willing to approve the restoration whenever Spain agreed to accept the Quadruple Alliance. At any rate, shortly after Alberoni's fall, he renewed his promise to King Philip that Gibraltar would be given up.[25] When DuBois on December 19 informed the British ambassador at Paris, the Earl of Stair, that Alberoni had been dismissed and Spain had agreed to the terms of the Alliance, he failed to mention any details of the proposed adhesion; and the British knew nothing about the renewed promise of Gibraltar until Lord Stanhope's visit to Paris early in January. When the English secretary of state for the Southern Department, James Craggs, heard of Alberoni's fall and Spain's capitulation, he lost no time in informing Stair that England no longer felt bound to give up Gibraltar on any terms. He insisted that the offer had been made only as a *quid pro quo* for immediate acceptance of the

23. The above is based principally upon material in S.P. 78:165, especially the Earl of Stair's letters to Secretary Craggs of Aug. 16 and Oct. 21, 1719.

24. Manifesto of Jan. 8, 1719. In a letter to DuBois of Dec. 20, 1718, Stanhope had authorized this reference to Gibraltar in the manifesto. See L. Wiesener, *Le Régent, l'Abbé Dubois et les Anglais* (Paris, 1891–1893), II, 320–329.

25. Earl of Stair to Secretary Craggs, Feb. 22, 1720, in J. M. Graham (ed.), *Annals of the Earls of Stair* (Edinburgh, 1875), II, 146.

treaty by Spain; that the ensuing war, entailing considerable expense and loss to England, had nullified the offer;
and that Britain now had no disposition to make peace
with Spain save on the basis of unconditional acceptance
of the Quadruple Alliance.[26]

Lord Stanhope took advantage of the Christmas recess
of the English Parliament to make a hurried trip to Paris,
both to discuss the terms of the Spanish settlement and to
investigate the quarrel which had developed between Stair
and the French minister of finance, John Law.[27] Reaching
Paris on January 9 (New Style), he conferred with the
regent and DuBois, and reported that the Spanish negotiation had been satisfactorily adjusted. They discussed
the subject of Gibraltar; Stanhope made no commitment,
but DuBois and the regent understood from their conversations with him that England would raise no objection
to an exchange of the Rock for a suitable equivalent. Both
the French and English agreed that Spain must accept
the Quadruple Alliance unconditionally, with the understanding that Gibraltar and other matters in dispute
would be arranged subsequently. Before Stanhope left
Paris, a letter arrived from Madrid containing extravagant demands which Spain insisted must be met before the
treaty could be signed. Among other requirements, Spain
asked for the cession of both Gibraltar and Minorca. Stanhope and DuBois answered that Spain must accept the
treaty without any reservations whatsoever. To convince
the Spanish that it was impossible to divide France and
England, Stanhope's assistant, Luke Schaub, was chosen
to go to Madrid to arrange the details of the settlement.[28]

26. Stair to Craggs, Dec. 20, 1719, S.P. 78:165. Craggs to Stair, Dec.
24/Jan. 4, 1719/1720, S.P. 104:31. A similar response had already been
made to the advances of Claudio Ré, an Italian emissary of the King of
Spain at London.

27. Law was pursuing a strongly anti-English policy at this time, and
trying to undo the Anglo-French Alliance of Stanhope and DuBois. As
one means of stirring up trouble, he did all he could to persuade the
regent to press the Spanish claim to Gibraltar. See E. Bourgeois, *La
diplomatie secrète au XVIIIe siècle* (Paris, 1909), III, 192–195.

28. Craggs to Stair, Dec. 22/Jan. 2, 1719/1720, S.P. 104:31. Lord Stan-

The Spanish envoy at The Hague, Beretti Landi, signed the Quadruple Alliance on behalf of his country in February 1720. Before signing, Landi attempted to persuade the English representative, the Earl of Cadogan, that Spain must be granted certain advantages, including the cession of Gibraltar, before she would sign the treaty. In response, Cadogan informed Landi that the English "were not under any sort of obligation to restore it [Gibraltar] to Spain, and furthermore, we were so far from any intention of doing so, that if Spain continued to insist on the Restitution, we would continue the war." When Landi signed the treaty on February 17, Cadogan insisted that Spain's adhesion should include the words *without reserve or limitation;* in answer to Landi's protest that these words were superfluous, Cadogan asserted that they were necessary in order to forestall any pretension to Gibraltar. To make assurance doubly sure, Cadogan stated to Landi, as the treaty was about to be signed, and in the presence of other signatories, "that if they [the Spanish] understood at his Court that their Accession would place us under any obligation towards them, in relation to Gibraltar, we would never sign ourselves; to which he replied to me that the terms of the Treaty explained so precisely that the Accession was pure and simple, and without reserve, that neither he, nor any one in the world could think, that placed us under the least engagement to cede Gibraltar to them."[29]

That Spain acceded to the Quadruple Alliance without extracting any promise whatsoever from England in relation to Gibraltar cannot be doubted. But Stanhope's later attitude, and that of Schaub in his letters from Madrid, give the impression that the French were not unjustified in assuming that England would make no difficulty about surrendering Gibraltar in a subsequent negotiation and

hope to Craggs, Paris, Jan. 12 and Jan. 19, 1720, S.P. 78:167. Stair to Craggs, Feb. 22, 1720, *Annals of Stair,* II, 146.

29. Earl of Cadogan to Secretary Craggs, London, Dec. 24/Jan. 4, 1720/1721, S.P. 100:56.

for a suitable equivalent. Plans were already afoot for convening a congress, at which matters in dispute between the powers could be thrashed out. Apparently it was assumed on all sides that Gibraltar would then come up for negotiation. What Stanhope desired was to prevent Spain from claiming any *right* to Gibraltar as a result of her signature of the treaty. He favored its cession for a desirable equivalent and hoped to secure in exchange further trade concessions in the Spanish Indies. At the time he returned from Paris in January 1720 it probably did not occur to him that serious obstacles to the cession would arise in the English Parliament and in public opinion.

Upon Stanhope's return to London, he found feelings already aroused by the rumor that England had agreed to surrender Gibraltar.[30] He therefore decided to sound Parliament and anticipate any effort which might be made to block the cession. This the opposition Whigs hoped to do by proposing a bill forbidding the king and ministry to give up Gibraltar without the consent of Parliament. Indeed, such an attempt was forestalled only by "assurances given by the ministry from man to man, that nothing of that kind should be done."[31] Through Secretary Craggs, Stanhope informed the Commons that the king had never intended to cede Gibraltar except for a satisfactory equivalent. Craggs even suggested that if it would suit the Commons better, he would propose that Gibraltar be formally annexed to the Kingdom, so that it could not be

30. On the first day of the new year, the young Scottish pamphleteer, Thomas Gordon, published his *Considerations Offered upon the Approaching Peace and upon the Importance of Gibraltar to the British Empire, being the Second Part of the Independent Whig* (London, 1720). This was the opening gun in the pamphlet war on the subject that continued intermittently throughout the eighteenth century. Gordon eulogized Gibraltar as "the most important Place in the World to the Trade and Naval Empire of *England,* the Key of the *Mediterranean,* the Terror of our Enemies, and the best pledge of our new friendships." (p. 28.)

31. Thomas Broderick to Lord Chancellor Middleton, Jan. 24/Feb. 4, 1720, in Wm. Coxe, *Memoirs of Sir Robert Walpole* (London, 1798), II, 183-184.

given up save with the assent of Parliament itself.[32] Thus
assured, the Commons took no further action.

Early in February Stanhope had to tell the French
chargé Destouches that the restitution of Gibraltar was
not going to be as easy a matter as the regent had anticipated. The English secretary declared that, when originally proposed, the cession could probably have been carried through without opposition; but the expense of the
war, together with its successful outcome, had created an
alarming opposition to any such concession on England's
part. He assured Destouches that the English king and
ministry were willing to give satisfaction to his Catholic
Majesty by restoring Gibraltar, but that he could do
nothing at the moment because of the violent hostility
which had been encountered in Parliament. To proceed in
the face of this opposition would threaten the overthrow of
the ministry. The matter, having been raised in Parliament, would have to be settled there; and all that the king
and ministry could do now was to support the restitution

32. Chammorel (a French agent) to the regent, Feb. 8, 1720, Cor. Pol.,
Angleterre, vol. 330, fol. 79. The sentiment of the opposition is well expressed in the following extract: "Our great men seem to be under no
small difficulties, they can have no peace abroad, it seems, without giving
up Gibraltar, and I see not how they can hope for peace at home, if they
part with it. Are we, who had nothing to do with this war, and who have
borne the chief part of the charge, and to whom the success of it is entirely owing, to be the only losers by it, and to purchase for everyone else
what he wants at our expense? If the Utrecht peace deserved impeach-
ments, what will this do?" Dr. Wm. Stratford to Edward Harley, March
10/21, 1720, *H.M.C., Portland MSS.,* VII, 271.

There seems to have been a close connection between the Commons'
opposition to the cession of Gibraltar and the affairs of the South Sea
Company. Stanhope, Craggs, et al., were the principal backers of the
South Sea Company, which triumphed over the opposition leaders who
had supported the Bank of England in the great refunding project.
Therefore the opponents of the South Sea Company opposed the cession
of Gibraltar, principally as a partisan measure. The subsequent South
Sea scandal and the fall of Stanhope's party (after his death) had much
to do with discrediting, regardless of merit, all the policies of the old
ministry, including the cession of Gibraltar as planned by Stanhope. See
the letter of Destouches to the regent, Feb. 15, 1720, Cor. Pol., Angleterre, vol. 6 (Supplement), fols. 262–263.

as best they could before that body. Stanhope informed Destouches that personally he considered Gibraltar useless to England and believed that the possession of it exposed the nation to the jealousies and enmities of her neighbors and created a heavy and unwarranted expense. He also assured the French chargé that, while he could not foresee the outcome of the question, he would give his word of honor to do everything possible to secure its restitution. At this point in the conversation, Craggs and Lord Sunderland (first lord of the Treasury and nominal leader of the ministry) entered and strongly seconded Stanhope's sentiments about the impossibility of carrying through the cession at that time. Destouches concluded his report by observing: "These gentlemen are so intimidated by the clamor which has been raised against them in relation to this restitution, that they do not imagine that they can hope to succeed in it. Only Lord Stanhope retains some hope in that connection, and he is resolved to do all possible to overcome the obstacles which have presented themselves."[33]

Lord Stair transmitted to London on February 4 a copy of King Philip's unconditional acceptance of the Quadruple Alliance. The Spanish minister Grimaldo appended to this document a statement of the terms the King of Spain felt himself entitled to expect in the forthcoming peace. This statement included the right to demand "the restitution of Gibraltar, which was offered to his Majesty by England and can not be denied him." In response Secretary Craggs again stated in unequivocal terms that the war and its burden to the subjects of Great Britain had absolved England from any obligation to renew the offer of Gibraltar made in 1718 as a device for preventing war.[34]

When the attitude of the British ministry, as revealed in Craggs' reply, became known in Paris, reproaches were

33. Destouches to the regent, Feb. 12, 1720, Cor. Pol., Angleterre, vol. 330, fols. 86–87.
34. Stair to Craggs, Feb. 4, 1720, S.P. 78:167. Craggs to Stair, Feb. 1/12, 1720, S.P. 104:31.

immediately forthcoming from the regent and DuBois to Stair. DuBois said that the Duke of Orleans had secretly assured King Philip on repeated occasions since the mission of Scotti to Paris that if Spain would adhere to the Alliance he would give his word that Gibraltar would be restored. To tell the Spanish king now that Britain was no longer willing to make the restitution would force the regent to break his word and compromise his honor. The duke had chastised DuBois for communicating the unconditional acceptance of the treaty to the English before extracting a promise to give up Gibraltar; the French felt certain that the English would have agreed to the cession if they had not been informed that it was no longer necessary. DuBois was doing everything in his power at this time to effect a solid reconciliation with Spain. The refusal of Gibraltar, after the regent had pledged his word to secure it, conceivably might prevent the consummation of this understanding. As Stair had no authority to answer DuBois, he merely reported the matter to London. Secretary Craggs responded in a letter (purposely written in French so that it could be shown to the regent) explaining in detail the dangers of the European situation that had originally prompted the offer of Gibraltar, but insisting that England was now under no sort of obligation to surrender the Rock. He complained bitterly of the unauthorized assurance which the regent had made to Spain that Gibraltar would now be given up.[35]

Craggs' answer did not appease the Duke of Orleans. The duke assured Stair that personally he preferred Gibraltar in English rather than in Spanish possession. But the promised restitution had been publicly announced in both France and Spain, and he reiterated to Stair that he would be placed in the most unpleasant position if the English did not permit him to keep his word to the King of Spain. Stair remonstrated that England had never renewed the promise since the war began, and that Lord

35. Stair to Craggs, Feb. 22, 1720, S.P. 78:167. Craggs to Stair, Feb. 18/29, 1720, S.P. 104:31.

Stanhope had made no commitment when he visited Paris in January. The regent agreed that no promise had been made by Stanhope or anyone else, but said he had not realized that the English had altered their decision to surrender Gibraltar; and, believing that they were still willing to do so, he had given his renewed assurances to King Philip.[36]

The dispute over the restitution of Gibraltar really threatened to upset the harmony of the Anglo-French Alliance in February and March 1720. So far as any strategic considerations were concerned, the regent and DuBois probably cared little who held Gibraltar; but DuBois, while desiring to maintain the English alliance, was determined to arrange a reconciliation with Spain. The French still hoped to secure England's approval to the cession. Their chargé d'affaires, Destouches, had reported on February 15 that the triumph of the ministry in the South Sea affair had strengthened its position in Parliament, and Destouches felt that if the ministry sincerely desired to push through the cession it had the strength to do so.[37] It was therefore decided to send a special emissary to London to discuss the problem with Stanhope and Craggs.

The Comte de Senneterre, whom the regent chose for this mission, reached London early in March.[38] He found the English ministers obdurate. To overcome their opposition, he secretly assured them that the regent had the restitution of Gibraltar so much at heart that if it were a question of money to gain the support of the Commons,

36. Stair to Craggs, March 11, 1720, S.P. 78:167.

37. Destouches to the regent, Feb. 15, 1720, Cor. Pol., Angleterre, vol. 6 (Supplement), fols. 262–263.

38. Senneterre bore a letter of credence that clearly reflected the displeasure of the Duke of Orleans concerning the English attitude toward the Gibraltar question. Senneterre's mission, the letter stated, was made necessary by the "dangerous situation" created by England's refusal to give up Gibraltar after the regent had renewed his promise that he would obtain it for King Philip. England's refusal compromised his word of honor, and if she persisted in it the whole program for the pacification of Europe might be undone. The regent to the King of England, Feb. 23, 1720, in New York Public Library, Hardwicke Manuscripts (Schaub Papers), vol. 54. (Hereafter cited as N.Y.P.L., Hardwicke MSS.)

his Royal Highness would gladly meet the expense, no matter how much the sum might be. Senneterre reported that the opposition in Parliament had quieted down, although the ministry was still in difficulties there; in the Commons, he said, the question of Gibraltar was "more of an occasion than a subject." Some opposed the restitution merely to discredit the ministry, while others were angered at the king and his ministers for having taken steps toward restitution without consulting Parliament. Only a minority of the opposition really opposed the cession as contrary to the interests of the nation. In short, the opposition had taken up the point of Gibraltar principally to attack Stanhope and his administration. Senneterre believed that, had the ministry been willing, it could have "persuaded" a sufficient number of the opponents to push through a motion to part with Gibraltar; but the ministry, not willing to risk its position, was deaf to his offer of financial assistance. Furthermore, he soon became convinced that the ministry had no intention of pushing the question any further during the session of Parliament then in progress.[39]

The reports of the displeasure of the regent and DuBois over England's refusal to cede Gibraltar led Stanhope to believe not only that the cordial relationship with France was endangered, but also that the French were utilizing the pretext of Gibraltar to break off from England and effect a reunion with Spain.[40] Accordingly, the English minister decided to go to Paris and attempt to heal the breach. Arriving there on March 26, he was relieved to find that the displeasure of DuBois and his master was not so serious as had been reported. The regent denied vehemently that France wished to drop the English connection, and insisted that the dislike and rivalry between himself and the Spanish monarchs would make an entente with Spain impossible. The regent repeated his

39. Senneterre to the regent, March 7, 1720, and subsequent reports of March 14 and March 18, Cor. Pol., Angleterre, vol. 330, fols. 169 ff.

40. Craggs to Stair, March 10/21, 1720, S.P. 104:31. Lord Stanhope to Sir Luke Schaub, Paris, March 20/31, 1720, S.P. 78:167.

arguments about Gibraltar, but he agreed that the question should not be raised prior to an impending general congress.[41] At the congress, the regent asserted, he would feel obligated to use his offices to secure Gibraltar for Spain. Stanhope tried to persuade him to write to Madrid and urge that all discussion of Gibraltar be postponed until the congress, but was unsuccessful. Privately, Stanhope reported that the regent confessed to him his anger against King Philip because the latter had directly deceived him on some point of the negotiation. Stair and Penterridter, the Austrian minister at Paris, were both of the opinion that something must have occurred very recently in Madrid to modify sharply the regent's feeling on the Gibraltar question. At any rate, Stanhope's visit served to change the regent's tone in regard to Gibraltar. Whether the accusations of England, and the consequent fear of losing her support, was the reason; or whether some treachery on the part of the Spanish king had angered the regent, he agreed to drop his support of the restitution for the time being. Lord Stanhope returned to London well pleased with the results of his journey, and the French seem also to have been relieved that this temporary strain on Anglo-French relations had been removed.[42]

41. The Congress of Cambrai; see below, p. 72.

42. Lord Stanhope to Craggs, Paris, March 27, 1720; and Stanhope to Admiral Byng, March 28, 1720, S.P. 78:167. J. Robethon to M. de Schroder, London, March 22/April 2, 1720 and also Robethon to Lord Polwarth, April 5/16, 1720, *H.M.C., Polwarth MSS.,* II, 500, 514. DuBois to Senneterre, May 3, 1720, Cor. Pol., Angleterre, vol. 6 (Supplement), fol. 156. The imminence of a break in Anglo-French relations over the point of Gibraltar is described in the following extract from the journal of Lord Polwarth, ambassador to the Congress of Cambrai, the information being derived from the Austrian Baron Penterridter: ". . . [Baron Penterridter said] that the Regent while Laws was at Paris was on the point of breaking with the King of Great Britain in the matter of Gibraltar and had writt a very strong letter to the King upon that subject which had done the busyness but for the greatest accident in [the] world, that the courier who carryed the letters being by a storm drove to the coast of Holland and Lord Stanhope's arrival by accident to, and setting matters to rights, and so another courier was dispatcht befor the first could get to England with the letter; that the Regent had declared to Lord Stair that a positive promice had been given him that Gibraltar

Before returning to London in January 1720, Stanhope had appointed Luke Schaub British emissary to Madrid. Schaub reached the Spanish court early in February, and not until a month later did he hear of the parliamentary opposition to the restitution of Gibraltar and the
consequent embarrassment of the Stanhope ministry.
Thus, no other source is so clearly indicative of the true
intentions of the English secretary and his royal master
toward Gibraltar at the beginning of 1720 as the correspondence of Schaub during February and March. From
the outset, Schaub assumed that the English king intended
to arrange the cession at the first opportunity—not as a
quid pro quo for Spanish adhesion to the Quadruple Alliance, but as a step toward the improvement of Anglo-
Spanish relations and the security of England's commercial privileges in Spain and the Indies. In his first conferences with the Marquis Scotti, the Parmesan minister
who had engineered Alberoni's dismissal and who now replaced him, Schaub suggested that the matter might be
satisfactorily arranged in the approaching congress.
Schaub proposed as a suitable equivalent for the restitution of Gibraltar that the "King of Spain consent on his
part to regulate things in Minorca in such a manner as to
render the possession of it less inconvenient to the English
king, and give assurances of the execution of all that
[previous] treaties had stipulated in favor of our commerce."[43]

The news that the question of Gibraltar had been raised
in Parliament created new difficulties for Schaub. King
Philip suspected that the English ministry, in order to
avoid ceding the Rock, had resorted to the expedient of

should be restored and that he had given his word to the Court of Spain
for it, but that upon Lord Stanhope's laying out matters strongly to him
and to the Cardinal that matter was husht up; that Lord Stair was one
much in the Regent's confidence but in Laws time he was within an ace
of being ordered to quitt France in 24 hours." April 1, 1722. *H.M.C.,
Polwarth MSS.,* III, 101–102.

43. Schaub to Stanhope, Feb. 12, 1720, N.Y.P.L., Hardwicke MSS.,
vol. 56.

turning the decision over to Parliament and allowing that body to declare it an inalienable part of the realm of England. The Spanish monarch urged Schaub to return to England at once to explain Spain's attitude and determination to secure the fortress, but Schaub refused to do so until he was more fully informed of this new development.[44] King Philip then threatened to refuse to ratify his minister's signature of the Quadruple Alliance or execute his obligations thereunder, until the English promised to restore Gibraltar. Under the terms of Spain's adhesion to the Alliance, the Spanish were required to evacuate Sicily; and the English and French, Pensacola and the points in northern Spain seized during the late war. Now the Spanish wished to link the evacuations and the restitution of Gibraltar as a coincident reciprocal action. Schaub insisted that, in view of England's legal possession of Gibraltar and the obligation of Spain to carry out the terms of her unconditional acceptance of the Quadruple Alliance, the two questions could not be placed on an identical footing. Spain must carry out her obligations; points captured by the Allies would then be returned; and the cession of Gibraltar would be considered later at the congress.[45]

Fortunately for England, the position of principal minister at the Spanish court was now held by the weak and incompetent Marquis Scotti. Before long, Scotti succumbed to English flattery and bribery, accepting financial assistance and presents from the English in return for secret information and insinuations on their behalf in his audiences with the Spanish monarchs. Under such circumstances, Scotti did not want to press the Gibraltar question to extremities, and Schaub was sanguine of the future outcome of the problem. The English envoy felt certain that King George was "always of the same intention" about desiring to give up Gibraltar. "If the affair of Gibraltar turns out well in Parliament, of which I have

44. Schaub to Stanhope, March 4, 1720, N.Y.P.L., Hardwicke MSS., vol. 60.
45. Schaub to Stanhope, March 7, 9, and 13, 1720, S.P. 94:89.

no doubt," he wrote, "I will be able to make very good use
of it here, by drawing from this court such assurances
with relation to our commerce, that the [trade] conventions made before the rupture cannot be contested in any
manner in the congress."[46] Schaub felt the restitution to
be essential in order to combat French influence at Madrid. Should Parliament block the restitution, the English "would lose all manner of confidence [with the Spanish court] and we should meet with in the progress of the
negotiation such difficulties about our Commerce as the
Conservation of Gibraltar would certainly not make
amends for."[47] He reported that the recovery of Gibraltar
had become a matter of conscience to King Philip, and
that England would never be able to effect a reconciliation
with him without its restitution. Schaub even took it upon
himself to assure his Catholic Majesty "that Parliament
would leave Gibraltar to the king's disposition, and his
Majesty would not postpone unduly treating with the
King of Spain about it."[48] With the aid of Scotti, Schaub
finally succeeded in persuading the Spanish king to abandon his efforts to force the issue at the moment, and to
postpone the question of Gibraltar until the congress.[49]

Thus, by April 1720, a general understanding was
reached between England, France, and Spain that the
question of the restitution of Gibraltar should be post-

46. Schaub to Stanhope, March 9, 1720, S.P. 94:89.
47. Schaub to Stanhope, March 11, 1720, N.Y.P.L., Hardwicke MSS.,
vol. 56.
48. Schaub to Stanhope, March 27, 1720, S.P. 94:89.
49. A letter in the Schaub papers from Scotti to King Philip reveals
an interesting and rather naïve expedient that had occurred to the Spaniards as a means of pressing the restitution. Philip was contemplating an
expedition against the Moors, and Scotti suggested that England might
accept Orán, presumably to be captured by this expedition, as an equivalent for Gibraltar. Not only did Scotti think that the English would be
willing to make such an exchange, but he suggested that they might be
so eager to do so that they would (if King Philip demanded it) help to
defray the expenses of this African expedition of Spain. N.Y.P.L., Hardwicke MSS., vol. 60. This is the first notice of a suggestion made by the
Spanish on many subsequent occasions in the eighteenth century, that
England exchange Gibraltar for Orán.

poned until the forthcoming congress. It should be noted
that the English, while conveying this impression both at
Paris and Madrid, made no specific promise that the issue
of Gibraltar would be submitted to the congress. Once the
matter had been brought before Parliament, the Stanhope
ministry did not feel that it could commit England definitely. Yet Stanhope sincerely intended to arrange the
restitution when the tumult had quieted. Although Gibraltar was becoming a fetish in the popular mind, informed
opinion was against its retention. Those who led the opposition to the cession in Parliament in 1720 were the
same who had denounced Gibraltar as an incubus when it
was obtained under the Treaty of Utrecht.[50] Sir George
Byng, the commander of the Mediterranean fleet, wrote
that he wished "the House of Commons had come to some
resolution what should have been don with Gibraltar before the Quadruple Alliance was signed. I fear that place
will beget uneasiness and cost more than it is worth."[51] In
the ministry, only Craggs seems to have had some misgiv-
ings about parting with Gibraltar. In truth, the consummation of Stanhope's great dream, the establishment of a
permanent peace in Europe under the hegemony of English diplomacy, depended in part on the restoration of Gibraltar to Spain.

The Spanish king again opened the subject of Gibraltar to Sir Luke Schaub during an audience on June 2.
King Philip admitted that technically England was not
obligated to restore Gibraltar; but he held that Lord
Stanhope's promise in August 1718 and the subsequent
renewal of that promise by the regent, coupled with the
known disposition of the English king to part with Gibraltar, created a moral obligation to return it to Spain. The
king added, "I believe monarchs should hold as religiously

50. The French agent, Chammorel, who observed closely the sessions
of Parliament and noted the rising opposition there, made this comment
to the regent in his letter of Feb. 8, 1720, Cor. Pol., Angleterre, vol. 330,
fol. 79.

51. Byng to George Dodington, March 12, 1720, *H.M.C., Various Collections,* VI, 2.

to that which they promise by word of mouth as to that which they promise in writing." In reporting this conversation to Stanhope, Schaub expressed his conviction that, although Spain could not ask for Gibraltar "as a due," the English would be the greater losers by retaining it. "The King's heart is bent upon having it again," he wrote, "and as he knows it can be of no Service to us he will never trust nor be willing to oblige us as long as we keep it." In responding to King Philip, Schaub repeated the argument that circumstances had changed and that England was no longer bound to fulfill either Lord Stanhope's or the regent's promise. Nevertheless, he assured the Spanish monarch "that although circumstances were changed, the intentions of our Royal Master have not, and he [the English king] will do everything in his power to content his Catholic Majesty with regard to Gibraltar," a statement which certainly constituted a verbal promise on the part of the king and ministry in England to support the cession.[52]

King Philip, not content to let the matter rest, decided on his own initiative, and apparently against the advice of his ministers, to withhold the *cedulas*, or permits, for the South Sea Company's annual vessel and for the slave trade granted under the Asiento treaty, until Gibraltar had been secured or an effective guarantee of its cession had been delivered. A royal order to this effect was drawn up on June 14 and delivered to Schaub. The English envoy protested to the ministers Scotti and Grimaldo; and he was presently joined in his efforts by William Stanhope, who had returned to Madrid to assume the post of permanent minister. Their protests were unavailing. The king was determined to force a definite promise that Gibraltar would be returned. By withholding the *cedulas*, Spain could stop the legal trade of England with the Indies, and incidentally cripple the South Sea Company, whose fortune was then approaching its zenith. On June 30, the

52. Schaub to Lord Stanhope, Madrid, June 3, 1720, and *private* letter to Lord Stanhope of the same date, S.P. 94:89.

Spanish formally notified the English ministers that consideration of all unsettled matters, including the cession of Gibraltar, the granting of the *cedulas*, the other restorations, and the Italian settlement in Parma and Tuscany, must be postponed until the congress. Nevertheless, his Catholic Majesty agreed to dispatch the *cedulas* to England prior to the congress, and with great pleasure, if Gibraltar were restored. With great difficulty, Schaub and Stanhope persuaded the Spanish to draw up the *cedulas* and send them to England in the care of the newly appointed Spanish ambassador, Pozobueno, who was not to deliver them, however, until something had been arranged about Gibraltar.[53]

A new complication arose during August, when the Spaniards concentrated troops and supplies in Andalusia, especially in the vicinity of Gibraltar, with the ostensible purpose of sending an expedition across the Straits to attack the Moors. The nature of the preparations aroused the suspicions of both Stanhope and the garrison. Reports were dispatched to England stating that Gibraltar might possibly be attacked, and the Lords Justices lost no time in sending secret orders to the Mediterranean fleet to proceed to Gibraltar and do everything possible to sustain the place. Governor Kane at Minorca also received orders to proceed personally to Gibraltar with whatever reinforcements could be spared.[54] Gibraltar was in very poor condition to withstand an attack at this time, having on hand but five weeks' provisions, sixteen barrels of powder, and a force of 1150 men (whereas 3000 was considered the minimum number necessary to garrison the place).[55] Whether Spain had any real intention of attacking it in

53. Dispatches of Schaub and Wm. Stanhope, June 17, 24, July 8, 15, 1720; and Grimaldo to Wm. Stanhope, June 30, 1720; in S.P., 94:89. Schaub to [?], June 17, 1720, N.Y.P.L., Hardwicke MSS., vol. 54.

54. Wm. Stanhope to Craggs, Aug. 12 and Sept. 2, 1720, S.P. 94:90. "Resolution of the Lords Justices," Sept. 8/19, 1720, C.O. 91:1. Charles Delafaye to Colonel Kane, Sept. 8/19, 1720, S.P. 35:23.

55. Wm. Stanhope to Craggs, Sept. 2, 1720, S.P. 94:90. Stanhope's statement was based on the report of a Major Elrington, who passed through Madrid at this time on his way from Gibraltar to England.

1720 is uncertain; the arrival of a portion of Admiral Byng's fleet during the Spanish preparations may have dissuaded them from attempting it.[56] On several later occasions Spain was to threaten Gibraltar by military preparations in its vicinity at critical moments in diplomatic negotiations with England, with the evident purpose of forcing the issue. Perhaps this was the idea in 1720. If so, the effort failed miserably, for these Spanish preparations aroused resentment and suspicion in England among those who might otherwise have favored ceding the fortress.

Spain's attempt to force the restitution of Gibraltar by withholding the *cedulas* necessary to permit the resumption of England's commercial privileges roused the English ministry to action. When news of this turn in the negotiation reached England, Lord Stanhope was in Hanover with the king. His colleague Craggs, plainly irritated at the arbitrary and unreasonable position assumed by the Spaniards, instructed William Stanhope to continue his efforts to secure the delivery of the *cedulas;* but the English minister was unable to make any headway against the obstinacy of the Spanish king.[57] Craggs transmitted a full account of the situation to Lord Stanhope, with the remark that "which ever resolution the King takes about Gibraltar, I hope he will not yield to the manner in which the Court of Spain puts the matter."[58]

The suspension of England's trade to the Indies moved King George and his chief minister to consider anew the problem of Gibraltar. Stanhope did not relish the prospect of a general discussion of English commercial privileges at an international gathering. He decided that all

56. Lord Portmore to [?], Gibraltar, Nov. 18/29, 1720, C.O. 91:7. Portmore was convinced that Spain would have attacked Gibraltar if Admiral Byng's ships had not arrived. Some years later, the British minister at Paris, Horatio Walpole, secured secret information "that the armament made in Spain some years ago [1720], which was employed in a descent upon the Coasts of Africa, was first intended against Gibraltar, but by accident disappointed." Walpole to Benjamin Keene, March 29, 1728, Add. MSS. 32,755, fols. 32–33.

57. Wm. Stanhope to Craggs, Aug. 29, 1720, C.O. 95:3.

58. Coxe, *Robert Walpole,* II, 188.

matters in dispute between England and Spain, including Gibraltar and the trade treaties, must be settled before the congress. For this purpose he drew up a project for a new treaty on the following terms: Article 1 renewed all former treaties of peace and commerce; Article 2 provided that British merchants in Spain should pay no *other* or *higher* taxes than had been in force during the reign of Charles II; Article 3 required Spain to abandon all claims to the Newfoundland fisheries, and to recognize England's right to cut logwood in the Bay of Campeche; Article 4 provided that this treaty was to take effect as soon as signed and ratified, but that the terms were to be kept secret until after the conclusion of a general peace in the forthcoming congress; Article 5 concerned the cession of Gibraltar, and read:

His Britannic Majesty, to show the sincere friendship which he bears toward his Catholic Majesty, and the ardent desire which he has that the peace which is so happily reëstablished with him shall last always and be cemented more and more, and also to testify his recognition of the accommodations that his Catholic Majesty has contributed to the present treaty, and above all to the third article of it, will restore to his Catholic Majesty the city and fortress of Gibraltar immediately after the publication of this present treaty, reserving to himself nevertheless the liberty to draw out beforehand from this place all provisions of war and of commissary, and all the artillery that was not there before Great Britain took possession of it.

Stanhope transmitted this draft to Secretary Craggs with instructions "to forward it in such a manner as you think best"; in his opinion, if Spain would accept these terms, "not only Gibraltar would be well given but that if a sum of money were necessary to get it signed without leaving any interest of ours to be discussed at the Congress it would be well bestowed."[59]

59. N.Y.P.L., Hardwicke MSS., vol. 55 (treaty draft) and vol. 56 (Stanhope's letter to Craggs, July 20/31, 1720, with his supporting

Although expressing his general approval of Stanhope's projected treaty with Spain, Craggs hesitated to present the matter to the Lords Justices. Agitation against the restitution seems to have increased rather than abated during the summer of 1720; as Craggs put it, "there is an aversion with the generality of mankind to give it up which is terrible." Therefore he implored Stanhope to compose a new letter that would summarize all the arguments in favor of the cession as projected in the treaty draft and express them as the unanimous opinion and will of King George, Stanhope, and Sunderland. With such a document in hand, Craggs felt confident that he could persuade the Lords Justices to approve the terms suggested by Stanhope. Lord Stanhope himself would then go to Madrid to complete the negotiation of the treaty.[60] Responding to Craggs' appeal, Stanhope wrote a long letter setting forth in detail his opinion of the international situation and the reasons in favor of the cession of Gibraltar as a means of effecting a reconciliation with Spain. If the King of Spain would admit that he could not claim Gibraltar as a right, England ought to take advantage of Philip's ardor and secure in return for the Rock a proper equivalent in the form of commercial concessions. All arguments in favor of the utility of Gibraltar should be weighed not only against this equivalent but also "against the almost certainty, that by means of this restitution we will be able to prevent for a long time to come the union of Spain with France, in order jointly with her to make war on us." The voluntary return of Gibraltar to Spain, free from French auspices, would be the surest way to keep Spain and France separated, and to permit England

arguments in favor of the terms as outlined, including the above quotations). Both are originals, and to the author's knowledge their existence has never before been disclosed. Stanhope in his letter instructed Craggs, in case this project was not followed up, to burn both the draft and the supporting letter. Instead, they fell into the hands of Sir Luke Schaub and have been preserved in his papers.

60. Craggs to Lord Stanhope, Sept. 16/27, 1720, N.Y.P.L., Hardwicke MSS., vol. 56.

to maintain a balance of power between the two. Further, a settlement of all outstanding Anglo-Spanish issues in advance of the impending congress would be highly desirable. All things considered, the king recommended to the Lords Justices that they approve the restoration of Gibraltar to Spain in return for a suitable equivalent, such as that suggested in the treaty project drafted by Stanhope in July.[61]

In order to understand the fate of the Stanhope project for an accommodation with Spain, we must first consider other aspects of the negotiation. The bursting of the South Sea Bubble in September threw England into confusion and diverted the attention of the ministry from foreign affairs to the domestic crisis. Under such circumstances, Stanhope was forced to return from Hanover (with the king and Sunderland) and devote his full attention to saving England from bankruptcy and complete financial chaos. His several projects for the pacification of Europe, both north and south, had to be shelved for the time being. He had to give up the idea of going to Madrid. The financial crisis and ensuing public indignation influenced the outcome of the Gibraltar negotiation in another manner. The entire ministry, with the exception of Stanhope, had been involved in the wave of speculation that had swept England in the summer of 1720. Even Stanhope was suspected of participation. After the collapse, the fury of public resentment directed itself against the leaders of the administration. By October an attempt to push through such an unpopular and delicate measure as the cession of Gibraltar would have been suicidal.[62]

Furthermore, before Stanhope's proposed solution to

61. Lord Stanhope to Craggs, Oct. 1/12, 1720, in Mahon, *History of England,* II, appendix, liv–lix.

62. See B. Williams, *Stanhope,* chap. XV. Thomas Gordon contributed an unveiled threat of the dire consequences that would befall the ministry if it proposed the cession of Gibraltar at this critical juncture, in his "Reasons to prove that we are in no Danger of losing Gibraltar," *Cato's Letters* . . . (London, 1733), I, 1–5. No. 1, dated Nov. 5, 1720, and composed during October.

the Gibraltar question could hope to succeed, it was necessary to persuade the King of Spain to abandon his arbitrary tactics and agree to grant an equivalent for Gibraltar. After Schaub returned from Madrid, he maintained a secret correspondence with Scotti in an effort to convince the marquis that Spain must modify her tone and procedure; he insisted that Parliament would never sustain the restitution of Gibraltar if made under any shadow of duress. Lord Stanhope also took advantage of an offer made by the Duke of Parma to exert his influence at Madrid (so strong with the queen and Scotti) in the direction of a modification in the Spanish position. Under such pressure, the Spanish agreed in September to give for Gibraltar any reasonable equivalent that England might suggest as satisfactory to King George and his Parliament.[63] For Spain, this was a concession. Previously King Philip had claimed Gibraltar as his due for signing the Quadruple Alliance. By consenting to grant an equivalent, the Spanish king admitted that England was not obligated to surrender Gibraltar without a new consideration.

When Craggs presented to the Lords Justices the proposed settlement with Spain as outlined in Stanhope's letter of October 1, he met with far stronger opposition than either he or Stanhope had anticipated. Craggs had felt certain that the king's authorization given in that letter would be sufficient to overcome the opposition of certain ministers, notably Lord Townshend.[64] His forecast proved incorrect. Townshend did not dare directly to disapprove of Stanhope's project. He even professed to be largely of the same opinion. He insisted, however, that an equivalent

63. Schaub to Scotti, Aug. 24/Sept. 4, 1720, N.Y.P.L., Hardwicke MSS., vol. 55. Lord Stanhope to Sir Robert Sutton, Sept. 8/19, 1720, C.O. 95:3, and Sutton to Stanhope, Nov. 9, 1720, S.P. 78:169. Wm. Stanhope to Craggs, Sept. 20 and 23, 1720, S.P. 94:90.

64. In his letter to Stanhope of Sept. 16/27, Craggs had assured him that "Lord Townshend, who is the only person that can debate this matter amongst us, will probably consider his situation and when he knows all your minds not subject it to some new alteration." N.Y.P.L., Hardwicke MSS., vol. 56.

in territory be demanded for Gibraltar, and that nothing else would satisfy Parliament. Probably the information previously received from William Stanhope, that Spain was now willing to grant an equivalent that would satisfy both king *and* Parliament, encouraged Townshend and others to stand out against Stanhope's proposal. Then too, the critical domestic situation made any immediate solution of the Gibraltar question impracticable. Townshend suggested that Spain be asked to give for Gibraltar either Florida or the eastern part of Santo Domingo. His opinion carried the meeting. On November 17, William Stanhope was instructed to sound the Spanish on these proposed equivalents. On the same date, Schaub wrote Scotti that the crisis in England made a postponement of the restitution practically mandatory; he insisted that Spain must agree to a restoration of England's commercial privileges in advance, and rely on the good faith of the English ministry for a subsequent procurement of Gibraltar as soon as the crisis had passed.[65]

William Stanhope did not receive the instructions of November 17 until January 6; he then discussed the whole problem of Gibraltar with King Philip and his ministers. As a result of his conversation with Andrés de Pez, secretary of state for the Indies, Stanhope reported that he was convinced that the Spanish would be unwilling to surrender either Florida or eastern Santo Domingo. Indeed, the Spanish answered Stanhope's approaches with a new ultimatum: that Gibraltar be restored within a specified period of one year, or that the Asiento be annulled.[66] The progress of secret Franco-Spanish negotiations, presently to be reviewed, had stiffened the resolve of Spain to refuse any other equivalent for Gibraltar than the restoration of England's commercial privileges in the Spanish Indies.

65. Schaub to Wm. Stanhope, Nov. 17/28, 1720, in Mahon, *History of England,* II, appendix, lix–lx. Schaub to Scotti, Nov. 17/28, 1720 (two letters), N.Y.P.L., Hardwicke MSS., vol. 55.

66. Wm. Stanhope to Schaub, Jan. 18, 1721, N.Y.P.L., Hardwicke MSS., vol. 55.

The foreign policy of DuBois had for its principal objectives the maintenance of the Anglo-French Alliance, and at the same time a rapprochement and an alliance with Spain, in order to insure peace and stability to France and to safeguard the regent's position. Some preliminary overtures for an alliance with Spain were conducted in conjunction with the Duke of Parma; but the duke's ambition lay in driving the Austrians out of Italy, and an alliance between France, Spain, and Parma might have precipitated another war, which France did not want. DuBois, therefore, determined to negotiate with King Philip independently. For that purpose he sent the Marquis de Maulevrier as emissary to Spain in September 1720. Maulevrier's instructions enjoined him to maintain, if possible, a discreet silence upon the point of Gibraltar. If the question were raised, he was to assure his Catholic Majesty that the regent intended to continue his active offices in favor of the restitution.[67] Maulevrier's instructions and the subsequent negotiation leading to the secret treaty of March 27, 1721, do not seem to have been unfriendly to England. Indeed, DuBois and Stanhope were pursuing the same objective—to settle their differences with Spain before the approaching congress—and the secret treaty of March served as a basis for the public triple alliance of June 1721.[68]

In answer to the French overture, the Spanish king demanded that the regent agree to continue his active offices for the restitution of Gibraltar, even that he consent to follow any proposal Spain might make as to the means of forcing Great Britain to make the restitution. Philip was not averse to bringing England into the proposed alliance, but wanted the regent to show how this could be done. In any event, the restitution of Gibraltar must be a *sine qua*

---

67. "Mémoire pour servir d'instruction au Marquis de Maulevrier . . .," Sept. 9, 1720, in *Recueil des instructions,* XII, *Espagne,* II, 378–381.

68. For further details of the Franco-Spanish negotiation of 1720–1721, see Baudrillart, *Philippe V et la cour de France,* II, 403–468, and Bourgeois, *La diplomatie secrète au XVIIIe siècle,* III, 211–261.

non of the negotiation.[69] In response to the draft submitted by Spain, the regent answered that France would
be willing to support all the pretensions of Spain which
did not conflict directly with the Quadruple Alliance. As
to Gibraltar, he would continue his good offices; but he
would not commit himself in advance to support any line
of action Spain might think fit to adopt to force the restitution. Indeed, the regent attempted to exclude all mention of Gibraltar in the proposed treaty, but Spain would
not negotiate on such a basis.[70]

In view of the fact that the French failed to communicate to England the secret treaty of March 1721, it might
seem that its negotiation was an act of duplicity on the
part of France toward her English ally, especially since
France bound herself by treaty to attempt to secure Gibraltar from England. Yet there was no essential difference of opinion between Stanhope and the regent on the
Gibraltar question. In a conversation on January 20,
Lord Stanhope assured Destouches:

If the King of Spain gives us time to breathe and to draw
ourselves out of the financial tangle where we now are, I
guarantee to him that inside of a year we will return Gibraltar to him for the most feeble equivalent, or even for the
shadow of an equivalent. For I am always of the same opinion, that not only is that place useless to us, but even that it
is a charge. The opinion of the king my master is the same
as mine and I swear to you by all that is most sacred that if
the thing depended only on him and his ministers, Gibraltar
would be returned to Spain within a fortnight. But at present, if I engage the king to it, I can not do it without losing
it [for Spain], and without risking my own position. . . .
In a word, we will make war on the emperor on behalf of

69. The Spanish demand in regard to Gibraltar is quoted in a memorandum of instructions for Maulevrier, dated Jan. 18, 1720, Cor. Pol.,
Espagne, vol. 300, fol. 185.

70. Maulevrier to the regent, Jan. 6, 1721; and the regent to Maulevrier, Jan. 21 and Jan. 28, 1721, Cor. Pol., Espagne, vol. 300, fols. 19–56.

Spain, if he breaks his engagements, provided that Spain desists from the article of Gibraltar before the opening of the congress, which she can do with good grace and without injuring either her glory or her interests, since it is certain that within a year we will return that place to her, without requiring her to purchase it by any equivalent that can be a charge to her.[71]

The regent sent the report of this conversation to Maulevrier so that he might use it both to convince the Spanish king of the necessity of postponing the issue for the moment and to indicate that England sincerely intended to make the restitution at an early date. On the basis of Lord Stanhope's statement, the regent assured the Spanish court that, if Spain would give England time, Gibraltar "will infallibly be obtained without its even costing an equivalent of any moment."[72]

King Philip insisted, however, that the regent guarantee to force the restitution within a specified time limit, which should be one year. Several exchanges between Madrid and Paris followed, with this the only real point left to be settled. The regent persisted, stating that he had no doubt of the success of the issue, provided Spain consented that the King of England should not be forced to propose the restitution to Parliament "at a time when it would certainly be refused to him and they would place it outside his power to bring the matter up again."[73]

The Spanish finally consented to a draft article proposed by France; and it was included in the secret treaty of March 27, 1721, in the following form:

71. This is a translated excerpt from a memorandum written by Lord Stanhope and given to Destouches, the French chargé d'affaires in London. It was enclosed in Destouches' letter to the regent of Jan. 20, 1721, quoted in Baudrillart, *Philippe V et la cour de France*, II, 447–449.

72. The regent to l'Abbé de Mornay (an assistant of Maulevrier at Madrid), Feb. 4, 1721, Cor. Pol., Espagne, vol. 300, fols. 89–90.

73. The regent to Maulevrier, Feb. 25, 1721, Cor. Pol., Espagne, vol. 300, fol. 152.

ARTICLE TWO

His Most Christian Majesty will continue to exercise without interruption his most pressing offices to engage the King of Great Britain to return Gibraltar and its dependencies as soon as it shall be possible to the power of his Catholic Majesty, and he will never desist from that demand, until his Catholic Majesty has obtained entire satisfaction on that point, either by the effective return of the said place into his power, or by assurances that shall satisfy him, that it will be returned within a fixed and determined time.[74]

This was the first of a succession of Franco-Spanish treaties in which France promised to attempt to secure the fortress for Spain. It also marked the first step, though a halting one, toward the Family Compact.

The existence of the treaty of March 27 was kept secret from the British until long after its signature, although many of its terms were included in the joint treaty with England negotiated in the following June. Why was England kept in the dark about this treaty? The answer lies in the sudden deaths of Lord Stanhope (February 5) and Secretary Craggs (February 16).[75] The friendship and support of Stanhope had been the strongest link in the Anglo-French connection, and he had also dominated the

74. Translation, from the "Projet des Articles Secrets" sent to Maulevrier on March 13, 1721, Cor. Pol., Espagne, vol. 300, fols. 233–234. This article was included in the treaty without change.

75. When the memorandum delivered by Lord Stanhope to Destouches was sent to Maulevrier on February 4, the French ambassador was authorized to explain to Wm. Stanhope the French position on the point of Gibraltar, although he was not to go into detail with him on the other subjects of the pending Franco-Spanish treaty negotiations. Cor. Pol., Espagne, vol. 300, fol. 84. But before Maulevrier had opened himself on the subject, Lord Stanhope died, and Wm. Stanhope was at once instructed to inform the Spanish that England would never cede Gibraltar, or so Maulevrier reported in his letter to the regent, Madrid, March 3, 1721, Cor. Pol., Espagne, vol. 301, fol. 9. Judging from the French correspondence, from the beginning of the secret Franco-Spanish negotiation until the death of Lord Stanhope, the entrance of England into the secret treaty was anticipated by France, if the matter of Gibraltar could be settled; and Lord Stanhope's frank statement to Destouches seemed to give assurance that it would be.

administration at home. He was the principal exponent of the cession of Gibraltar, and it might well have been that if he had lived the Rock would have been returned to Spain within the year, as he had forecast. Although his death wrought no profound change in the course of English policy, it removed the confidential interchange between London and Paris. Apparently, the French did not dare to inform the new ministers of their commitment in regard to Gibraltar.

As the French feared, the new English ministers had no desire to fulfill Lord Stanhope's virtual promise that Gibraltar would be restored to Spain. Lord Townshend, who assumed leadership in the direction of foreign affairs, had been the chief opponent of Stanhope's projected settlement in the fall of 1720. But Townshend could not completely disavow his predecessor's commitments. A few days before Stanhope's death, King George, acting on a suggestion of the Duke of Parma, had agreed to write a letter to the King of Spain promising to settle the Gibraltar issue at a more suitable time, on the basis of an exchange for a satisfactory equivalent and subject to the consent of Parliament. The British king's willingness to write such a letter had been made known to DuBois, who communicated it to the Spanish.[76] Townshend instructed William Stanhope to tell the Spanish that England could never admit that the resumption of her trading privileges in the Spanish Indies was in any way contingent upon the restoration of Gibraltar to Spain; but, realizing that the Spanish would probably refuse to renew those privileges unless England promised something on Gibraltar, he admitted that King George might have to write a letter to King Philip along the lines mentioned above.[77]

76. Bourgeois, *La diplomatie secrète au XVIIIe siècle*, III, 248 ff.

77. I have been unable to find all of the English correspondence dealing with the background of King George's letter on Gibraltar, February–April 1721; but the gist of the negotiation can be found in the following: Schaub to Wm. Stanhope, March 6/17, 1721, N.Y.P.L., Hardwicke MSS., vol. 55. Lord Carteret to Sir Robert Sutton, March 16/27, 1721, Add. MSS. 22,515, fols. 24–25. Wm. Stanhope to Lord Townshend,

Immediately after the signature of their secret treaty
with France, the Spanish delivered a new ultimatum to
William Stanhope, declaring that Spain would neither deliver the *cedulas* necessary for the resumption of the Indies
trade nor enter into any treaty with England until the
English pledged themselves to restore Gibraltar, either by
a public announcement of King George that he would do
so, or by the transmission of a private letter, to be held in
the greatest secrecy, certifying that the restitution would
be made.[78] Stanhope forwarded this ultimatum to London,
with the observation that the least that would possibly satisfy Spain would be a private letter assuring the restitution for an equivalent, whenever the king should find Parliament in a mood to give its consent. Lord Carteret, the
new secretary of state for the Southern Department,
voiced the opposition of the ministry to putting in writing
any promise relating to Gibraltar; but he agreed that a
secret letter, on the above basis, would be sent if Spain insisted.[79]

In mid-April, the Spanish king himself suggested that
the problem of Gibraltar be solved by a secret letter. Stanhope responded that he had no authority to promise such
a letter (though privately he knew that the ministry would
approve it), but that he would write to England and see
what could be done. In the meantime he urged that negotiations be carried on to draft a particular treaty that
would renew prior treaties and arrange all outstanding
differences (aside from Gibraltar) in preparation for the
signature of a triple alliance with France. After some argument, the Spanish king agreed to let the negotiation
proceed without waiting for a response from England,

April 7, 1721, Add. MSS. 22,520, fol. 62. Wm. Stanhope to Sir Luke
Schaub, April 23, 1721, Add. MSS. 22,521, fols. 16–25. Also the correspondence in the French archives, Cor. Pol., Espagne, vol. 301, fols. 65–
218, especially the regent's letter to Maulevrier of April 2, 1721.

78. Grimaldo to Stanhope, March 30, 1721, Add. MSS. 22,520, fol. 60.

79. Stanhope to Townshend, March 31, 1721, Add. MSS. 22,520, fols.
58–59. Carteret to Sir Luke Schaub, April 3/14, 1721, Add. MSS. 22,515,
fol. 42. Carteret to Stanhope, April 4/15, 1721, Add. MSS. 22,515, fol. 47.

with the understanding that if a satisfactory letter on
Gibraltar were not delivered, the treaty would not be ratified. Stanhope agreed to this expedient.[80]

Accordingly, a letter with the king's signature was
drawn up and sent off to Madrid on April 29/May 10. It
was sent by way of Paris so that it might be shown to the
regent and DuBois, both of whom expressed approval of
it and the belief that the Spanish king ought to be satisfied
with such a document. Lord Carteret himself thought the
letter sufficiently innocuous, believing that it might be
produced before Parliament "without any inconveniency,
if that Step should by future conjunctures become necessary."[81] But King Philip refused to accept the letter in its
original form. He could not recall that he had ever promised to accept a letter specifying an equivalent, and he insisted that the words *sur le pied d'un equivalent* be eliminated; he also demanded that the word *restitution* be
inserted to clarify the meaning. After much argument,
Stanhope agreed to request a new draft embodying these
changes. The British minister noted that, while the elimination of the requirement of an equivalent might seem a
retraction, an equivalent would certainly be demanded if
and when the matter came up before Parliament for its
consent; and thus England did not stand to lose anything
by the change. A similar comment was made independently by DuBois when he saw the new draft.[82]

The second and official letter, dated June 1/12, 1721,
is quoted below in full, following a translation made in
1729 from the original French:

Sir, My Brother. I have learn't with great Satisfaction by
the Report of My Ambassador at your Court, that your
Majesty is at last resolved to remove the obstacles that have

80. Stanhope to Schaub, April 23, 1721, Add. MSS. 22,521, fols. 16–25.
81. Carteret to Sutton, April 29/May 10, 1721, Add. MSS. 22,515, fols.
77–78.
82. Stanhope to Townshend, May 29, 1721, Add. MSS. 22,520, fols.
103–109. Schaub to Carteret, June 7, 1721, Add. MSS. 22,521, fols. 156–
158.

for some time delayed the entire Accomplishment of our Union; Since from the Confidence that your Majesty expresses towards me, I may look upon the Treatys, which have been in question between us, as reestablished, and that accordingly the Instruments necessary for the carrying on the Trade of my Subjects will have been delivered out. I do no longer balance to assure Your Majesty of my Readiness to satisfy you with regard to your Demand touching the Restitution of Gibraltar, promising you to make use of the first favorable opportunity to regulate this article with the Consent of my Parliament. And to give Your Majesty a further proof of my Affection, I have ordered my Ambassador, as soon as the Negotiation with which he has been charged, shall be finished, to propose to Your Majesty new Engagements to be entered into, in concert and jointly with France, suitable to the present Conjuncture of Europe. Your Majesty may be persuaded that I, on my part, will shew all the facility imaginable, promising Myself that You will do the Same for the mutual benefit of our Kingdoms.—being most perfectly, etc.[83]

A new triple alliance between Great Britain, France, and Spain was signed on June 13. On the same day, Stanhope and the Spanish ministers signed a particular Anglo-Spanish treaty, confirming and renewing England's trading privileges in the Spanish Indies. Neither of these treaties mentioned Gibraltar, but two separate acts signed on the same day did concern the fortress. Unbeknownst to the British, Grimaldo and the French minister Maulevrier in a secret declaration renewed all the terms of the Franco-Spanish treaty of March 27, including the French pledge

83. "Translation of His Late Majesty's Letter to the King of Spain, dated June 1st 1721," S.P. 94:90. Stanhope was instructed to obtain the return of the first letter, "lest hereafter any chicane be formed at the Spanish Court upon account of our having consented to leave out the word *Equivalent* in this Second letter," and he remitted the first draft the following September. Carteret to Stanhope, June 1/12, 1721, Add. MSS. 22,520, fol. 157; Stanhope to Townshend, Sept. 8, 1721, Add. MSS. 22,520, fol. 267.

to work for the restitution of Gibraltar.[84] And as King George's letter on Gibraltar, the *quid pro quo* for which Spain had consented to sign a treaty renewing England's commercial privileges, had not yet been received, Stanhope and Grimaldo signed a separate agreement stating that if the letter were not delivered in the form agreed upon, the particular Anglo-Spanish treaty would be considered null and void.[85] Thus it can be said that the renewal of England's trading privileges was the equivalent granted by Spain, not indeed for the *restitution* of Gibraltar, but for the promise by the King of England to "make use of the first favorable opportunity to regulate this article with the Consent of my Parliament."

Suspicion that France and Spain had bound themselves by some secret agreement of their own, with a provision referring to Gibraltar, was voiced by Lord Carteret to Schaub in August 1721. Schaub doubted that an actual treaty had been signed, but thought something might have passed between the two powers on Gibraltar. But DuBois and the regent assured Schaub, truthfully, that they would not promise more than good offices to the Spanish king. Schaub also observed that if the regent had actually promised something stronger, the Spanish king would not have been so insistent on a letter from King George.[86]

In summary, at the end of 1721 the British king and ministry had agreed to bring the question of the restitution of Gibraltar before Parliament at the earliest opportune moment. The letter of King George having been a *quid pro quo* for the signature of the particular treaty

84. Baudrillart, *Philippe V et la cour de France*, II, 465.

85. A. del Cantillo (ed.), *Tratados, convenios y declaraciones de paz y de comercio . . . 1700 hasta el dia* (Madrid, 1843), p. 200. Stanhope to Townshend, June 9, 1721, Add. MSS. 22,520, fols. 116–129, enclosing a draft of the agreement providing for the nullification of the treaty if the English king's letter were not delivered.

86. Carteret to Schaub, Aug. 6/17, 1721, Add. MSS. 22,515, fol. 226. Schaub to Carteret, Aug. 30, 1721, Add. MSS. 22,521, fols. 411–412.

with Spain, England could hardly allege that she was not obligated to fulfill this promise. But the disposition to cede Gibraltar had faded with Stanhope's death, and it is rather obvious that the new ministers had no intention of forcing the cession through Parliament. England was determined that neither the matter of Gibraltar nor any other dispute with Spain be brought up at the prospective congress.

In Spain, King Philip must have felt that his chance of obtaining the return of Gibraltar at an early date was excellent. He had bound France to support his pretension, and he had secured from England a promise that the question would be presented to Parliament, with the implication that the English king and ministry would do all they could to secure parliamentary support for the cession. Spain had not obligated herself to refrain from bringing the subject before the congress, and subsequent events indicate that she intended to do so if England did not settle the matter in advance. Furthermore, Spain had renewed the English trade treaties only on the condition that the question of Gibraltar be considered in the near future. If King George failed to keep his word, Spain might with a degree of right again withhold the *cedulas* for the trade to the Indies.

France, although she had promised King Philip her unremitting good offices, nonetheless does not appear to have been anxious to push the question. The French hoped that the matter could be avoided at the congress, so that the Spanish would not be in a position to call for their support. To achieve and maintain DuBois' policy of good relations with both Spain and England, the French had to maneuver between the two on the question of Gibraltar. They insisted to England that the regent felt himself bound to exercise his promise of good offices only if and when the issue was precipitated; to Spain, they continued to pledge their unremitting efforts to persuade England to part with Gibraltar. Yet the French never pressed the question at London or upon the British emissaries at Paris after the signature of the secret treaty of March 1721.

The signature of a triple alliance between the three nations might seem to have augured well for the future. But the underlying antagonisms still remained; and it was evident that, without the return of Gibraltar, the alliance between Spain and England was scarcely worth the paper on which it was written.

III

THE ILLUSION OF THE BRITISH "PROMISE"

THE British promise to present the question of the
restitution of Gibraltar to Parliament proved illusory in the succeeding decade. By means of that
promise, England secured the restoration of her commercial privileges in the Spanish dominions. Nevertheless, the
new ministers of George I were loath to fulfill the obligation that had developed out of the assurances given by the
Stanhope administration that England would consider the
return of Gibraltar at an appropriate time. Regardless of
obligation, Stanhope's successors were determined to avoid
the unpleasant consequences that might ensue from an attempt to re-open the question. As we shall see, the Walpole ministry, amid the complications of European diplomacy, succeeded in eluding Spanish demands that it carry
out the engagement implied in the royal letter of 1721.

Immediately after the conclusion of hostilities with
Spain in 1719, an international congress had been projected to settle the differences among the powers of southern Europe on the basis of the Quadruple Alliance and
previous treaties. Spain's defeat forced her to accept unconditionally the terms laid down by Lord Stanhope and
DuBois, but the details of the settlement in Italy and
other points in conflict between the emperor and King of
Spain remained to be worked out. England and France
patched up their own differences with Spain in the secret
triple alliance and particular treaties of June 1721, and
accepted the rôle of joint mediators between Austria and
Spain in the forthcoming congress. The delegates to the
congress, held at Cambrai out of respect to DuBois,
started to gather in the spring of 1722, but the congress
did not officially convene until two years later. As a device
to effect an Austro-Spanish settlement and the pacifica-

tion of southern Europe, the congress was a fiasco. Neither France nor Austria desired to grant the extension of Spanish power in Italy contemplated in the Quadruple Alliance. With one of the mediators cold to the projected settlement, the Imperialists managed to equivocate and postpone a fulfillment of their obligations in a manner that effectively sabotaged the work of the congress.[1]

The fact that the English were prepared to give far stronger support than the French to Spanish pretensions in Italy pushed the problem of Gibraltar into the background during the period of the Congress of Cambrai. Spain could not afford to risk the loss of English support by attempting to force a fulfillment of the British promise to present the question to Parliament. The Spanish king repeatedly pressed William Stanhope to urge the British ministry to comply with their obligation, only to be told that insistence on this step might lead to the withdrawal of British support for Spanish claims at the congress.[2]

One of the Spanish envoys to Cambrai, the Duke of Veraguas, approached Stanhope on the Gibraltar question in the fall of 1722 before his departure from Spain. Stanhope, "by way of conversation," suggested that if Spain would give Spanish Santo Domingo, or part of it, as an equivalent for Gibraltar, something might be done. He justified this proposal on the ground that this equivalent was one of the two mentioned to him two years previously. Both Veraguas and Stanhope believed the exchange of Gibraltar for Spanish Santo Domingo feasible if France did not object; and Veraguas intended to seek French support for it when he reached Paris, by pointing out the facility which the scheme presented for relieving the regent of his engagements on Gibraltar.[3]

The English ministry was in no mood to consider the

1. On the Congress of Cambrai, see Basil Williams, "The Foreign Policy of England under Walpole," Part II, *English Historical Review,* XV (July 1900), 479–494.

2. Stanhope to Carteret, Jan. 10, 1723, S.P. 94:92.

3. Stanhope to Carteret, Nov. 25, 1722, C.O. 95:3.

exchange of Gibraltar for Spanish Santo Domingo or any other equivalent. Sir Luke Schaub, now at Paris, received secret instructions to forestall any attempt Veraguas might make to secure French backing. Carteret directed Schaub to inform the regent and DuBois that the disposition of Parliament was such that there was no possibility of obtaining its consent to the cession of Gibraltar, no matter how advantageous the equivalent that might now be offered. Similarly, Carteret warned the English plenipotentiaries to the congress, Lords Polwarth and Whitworth, to avoid any discussion of the matter with Veraguas. Schaub answered that DuBois had agreed to give no encouragement to Veraguas, and that the French ministers at Cambrai would be instructed to act in unison with the British to prevent the subject of Gibraltar from being raised at the congress.[4] To Stanhope, Carteret sent a mild rebuke for even mentioning a possible equivalent for Gibraltar and instructed him to avoid any further discourse with the Spanish ministers on the subject. In response, after insisting that his conversation with Veraguas had been of an entirely private nature, Stanhope correctly forecast that he would be able to convince the Spanish that the presentation of the subject to Parliament must be postponed to a more propitious time.[5]

Spain again attempted to revive the subject of Gibraltar in the fall of 1724. The Duke of Newcastle, who had succeeded Carteret, informed the new British envoy at Paris, Horatio Walpole, that the ministry was not disposed to re-open the question. Wrote Newcastle: "Whenever this matter is again mentioned between you, you will continue to convince him of the rashness of the Spaniards mentioning it in any manner whatsoever either at Cam-

4. Carteret to Schaub, Dec. 5/16, 1722, Add. MSS. 22,518, fols. 70–73. Carteret to Lords Polwarth and Whitworth, Dec. 7/18, 1722, *H.M.C., Polwarth MSS.*, III, 212. Schaub to Carteret, Jan. 2, 1723, *H.M.C., Polwarth MSS.*, III, 219.

5. Carteret to Stanhope, Dec. 6/17, 1722, Add. MSS. 22,518, fols. 73–74. Stanhope to Carteret, Jan. 10, 1723, S.P. 94:92.

bray or elsewhere, and to insist that no further notice be taken of it."[6]

The first symptom of a renewal of Spanish hostility toward England appeared in connection with a rupture in Franco-Spanish relations in the spring of 1725. The Duke of Bourbon, DuBois' incompetent successor as first minister of France, outraged the Spanish monarchs by annulling a marriage compact between the young French king and a younger Spanish Infanta and returning the child to her parents. The Spanish promptly severed diplomatic relations with France. England offered her mediation, which both France and Spain accepted, the latter with obvious reluctance. The Duke of Newcastle discovered the insincerity of Spain's acceptance in the usual eighteenth-century course of intercepting the dispatches of the Marquis de Pozobueno, the Spanish envoy at London. Pozobueno had urged his government not to accept England's mediation; rather, he suggested that the Franco-Spanish reconciliation be made at English expense by the immediate demand of Gibraltar, which France was bound by treaty to support.[7] Newcastle was about to demand Pozobueno's recall, when news of a far more serious threat to the recent comparative harmony in Anglo-Spanish relations reached London.

After its belated opening, the work of the Congress of Cambrai resolved itself into a fruitless effort on the part of France and England to arrange an understanding between King Philip and the emperor. Seemingly the latter two were as much at odds as ever, but secretly the Spanish monarchs had sent a confidential agent, a Dutchman

6. Sept. 29/Oct. 10, 1724, in L. G. W. Legg (ed.), *British Diplomatic Instructions,* IV, *France, 1721–1727* (London, 1927), p. 88. The Spanish monarchs had sent an emissary, Monteleon, to Paris with instructions to seek a new alliance with France and Great Britain in opposition to the emperor. But Monteleon was also required to secure the restitution of Gibraltar in the projected treaty, and the British peremptorily refused to have any dealings with him. This rebuff helped to persuade their Catholic Majesties to attempt a direct settlement with Vienna.

7. Newcastle to Stanhope, April 29/May 10, 1725, S.P. 94:96.

named Ripperda, to seek a direct settlement at Vienna. On April 30, 1725, a public treaty between Austria and Spain was signed, to the great surprise of the other powers, for the terms accorded to Spain were less favorable than those already offered to and rejected by her at Cambrai.[8] This private settlement between Spain and Austria brought the Congress of Cambrai to an abrupt end.

The terms of the first Treaty of Vienna as publicly announced seemed so inequitable to Spain that the English at once suspected the existence of secret articles, among them a pledge of Austrian good offices on the Gibraltar question. William Stanhope soon confirmed this suspicion by reporting that one of the secret articles promised the emperor's mediation for the restitution of Gibraltar, "if not further engagements on his part upon that head."[9] The English were highly incensed at this proposed meddling of Austria. Lord Townshend believed that the emperor hoped to stir up trouble between Spain and England in order to strengthen his diplomatic position, with the intention of exacting as the price of his mediation the guarantee of his succession. He instructed Stanhope to protest and refuse this suggested mediation in no uncertain terms. If Spain, on the strength of her new alliance, persisted in raising the issues of Gibraltar, Port Mahón, and English commerce, Townshend declared that "his

8. On Ripperda and the background and progress of the Spanish negotiations with Austria, see G. Syveton, *Un cour et un aventurier au XVIIIe siècle* (Paris, 1896). The Treaty of Vienna should not have been a complete surprise to the English. Four and a half years earlier, William Stanhope had learned from the Marquis de Scotti that "the Emperor is now endeavouring by all the means imaginable to make a separate Allyance with Spain for the ruine, both of France and England: that he offers such advantages that nothing but the Piety of the King of Spain could resist . . . [Scotti] hinted to me that amongst other things a double marriage was projected between the Emperors two Daughters and the Sons of the Queen." Stanhope to Craggs, Nov. 18, 1720, S.P. 94: 90.

9. Newcastle to Stanhope, May 4/15, 1725, S.P. 94:96. Stanhope to Townshend, June 22, 1725, S.P. 94:93. In negotiating, Ripperda represented to the emperor that King Philip would not sign a treaty without this provision; to the Spanish king, Ripperda reported that the emperor had voluntarily offered his mediation.

Catholic Majesty may be sure that the King and his people cannot but look upon such ill treatment as a breach of the faith of treatys, and done with a view of coming to an open rupture, and [England] will in such case take measures accordingly."[10]

King Philip told Stanhope on June 21 that the emperor had offered his mediation on the Gibraltar affair. The English minister, after hearing from Townshend, informed the Spanish monarch that England would not countenance Austrian mediation. He complained to King Philip that Ripperda, at Vienna, had publicly stated that in case Gibraltar was not forthwith restored, Spain would look upon all her engagements with England—particularly those relating to commerce—as void. At an audience on July 11, King Philip protested that Ripperda's pronouncements were unauthorized, and insisted that there would be no interference with English commercial privileges even though Gibraltar were not returned. On the following day a courier reached Madrid with news of the ratification of the Austro-Spanish treaty. The Spanish abruptly changed their conciliatory tone. The Spanish minister Grimaldo delivered an ultimatum to Stanhope that Spain would maintain the English alliance and commercial privileges only in the event that Gibraltar was immediately restored.[11]

In answer to the Spanish ultimatum, Stanhope informed the Spanish monarchs that there was no possibility of considering the restitution of Gibraltar at this time. He pointed out that nothing could be done without the consent of Parliament, which would not meet until the following year. To this the queen replied: "Let the King your

10. Townshend to Stanhope, The Hague, June 20, 1725, S.P. 94:93. In a letter to Thomas Robinson, English envoy at Vienna, of July 21, 1725, Townshend remarked: "I dare say the Emperor meant no more by offering that Mediation, than by getting the Affair of Gibraltar by that means under his direction, to bring us to guarantee his Succession." Add. MSS. 38,502, fol. 213.

11. Grimaldo to Stanhope, July 13, 1725; and Stanhope to Townshend, July 14, 1725, British Museum, Stowe MSS. 256, fols. 6, 18–21.

Master return presently into England and call a Parliament expressly for this purpose, it being no more than we might expect from his friendship for us, and I am assuredly and positively informed that the matter once fairly proposed, would not meet with one negative in either House, let but this short argument be once made use of, either give up Gibraltar or your trade to the Indies and Spain, and the matter (I will answer for it) wont admit of a moment's debate." Both the king and queen insisted that the cession must be made immediately in order to avoid a rupture. Stanhope noted that, far from being discouraged by his response to their ultimatum, the Spanish monarchs were highly confident that they could coerce England into ceding Gibraltar.[12]

When news of this peremptory Spanish demand reached London, orders were at once given for the strengthening of the Rock. Stanhope was instructed to tell the Spanish that any molestation of English trade or other act of force would be met by force, and that England was determined to defend her treaty rights to the best of her ability. Lord Townshend lost no time in informing the French of the situation and in demanding their vigorous support.[13]

Stanhope found the Spanish monarchs more tractable after they learned that the British ministry was unmoved by their threats and resolved "to meet force with force." In any case, they did not dare to risk a breach with England until they had concluded a new and more binding treaty with the emperor. At an audience on September 2,

12. Stanhope to Townshend, Aug. 6, 1725, Stowe MSS. 256, fols. 38–43.
13. Townshend to Stanhope, Aug. 4, 1725, S.P. 94:93. Townshend to Horatio Walpole, Aug. 4, 1725, Add. MSS. 38,502, fols. 283–284. At this same time, Walpole (English ambassador at Paris) reported that the Pope had offered his mediation in the Franco-Spanish rupture and that the Spanish were trying to persuade the French to accept Papal, in lieu of English, good offices. Walpole realized the danger to England if affairs between France and Spain were patched up without English assistance while the Gibraltar issue remained unsettled. He secured a pledge from the French not to accept any other mediator in the Franco-Spanish dispute. The French, moved more by enmity toward Austria than toward Spain, decided to stand by their English ally. Walpole to Townshend, July 26, 1725, Add. MSS. 38,502, fols. 220–223.

Philip protested to Stanhope that he did not desire to break with England, and he no longer insisted on the immediate restitution of Gibraltar. The English minister, anxious to discover the true intentions of Spain, pursued the issue with the Marquis de la Paz, one of the Spanish secretaries. The Marquis suggested that his master might be willing to drop his pretensions until the meeting of Parliament. Stanhope retorted that there was scant probability of Parliament's being in a mood to consider the matter when it did meet. Asked to suggest some acceptable equivalent for the Rock, the Englishman answered that, although he was absolutely unempowered to make such a suggestion, he might hint, by way of conversation, two or three things: permission to cut logwood on the Bay of Campeche; settlement of the South Sea Company's trade upon a better footing; and extension of the term of the Asiento contract. The Marquis reported these suggestions to King Philip, who promised to take them under consideration.[14]

The Austro-Spanish reconciliation of 1725 was a direct consequence of the domination exercised by Elizabeth Farnese over her husband, and thus over Spanish policy. King Philip, on his own account, would never have come to terms with the emperor, his personal enemy. Queen Elizabeth's paramount objectives were to secure a settlement in Italy, and advancement for her sons. The prospect of the marriage of one or both of them to the emperor's daughters, even though not mentioned in the first treaty with Austria, was the principal attraction of an Austrian alliance for the ambitious queen. She had no interest in the recovery of Gibraltar; but to secure Philip's assent to her projects she needed to humor his prejudices and interests, and nothing was closer to the king's heart than the recovery of the fortress, "that thorn in my side," as he termed it.

The first Treaty of Vienna was but an introduction to a grand scheme concocted by the irresponsible Ripperda

14. Stanhope to Townshend, Sept. 4, 1725, S.P. 94:93.

for an attack on France and the maritime powers. His projects assumed their most concrete form in the second Treaty of Vienna of the following November. This offensive alliance not only arranged for the double marriage compact sought by the Queen of Spain, but also forecast a general offensive against England and France. It provided for the partial dismemberment of France if she were defeated in a war, a general expansion of imperial control in Germany, and an assault on Britain's Mediterranean strongholds of Gibraltar and Minorca. Beyond the formal treaty terms, Ripperda's schemes included aid for the Pretender and a general holy war on Protestantism. The indiscreet and loquacious Dutchman spread the impression that the Vienna compacts were far more inimical to England than they actually were on paper. The English became convinced that Spain and Austria had specifically agreed to attempt to overthrow the Hanoverian dynasty, and that the threat to their Mediterranean possessions and Indies trade was far more real than actually seems to have been the case. In fact, the sincerity of Austria in the whole negotiation is very doubtful. By playing upon the ambition of the Spanish queen, and vaguely promising handsome advantages to Spain, the emperor secured a very favorable settlement of his own interests, including Spanish support for the Ostend Company and the payment of large subsidies in money, which replenished the empty coffers of Austria.[15]

The hostile intentions of the Austro-Spanish coalition, illuminated by the high-handed manner in which the Spanish king sought to force the restitution of Gibraltar, roused the English ministers to action. At Hanover, Lord Townshend negotiated a new alliance, headed by England and France, to oppose the Vienna allies.[16] In London, five of the principal ministers held an important secret conference on September 8/19 at the home of Sir Robert

15. See Syveton, *Un cour et un aventurier*, pp. 78 ff.; and J. F. Chance, *The Alliance of Hanover* (London, 1923), especially pp. 37–40.

16. Signed on September 3. For the details of its negotiation, see Chance, *The Alliance of Hanover*, pp. 57–75.

Walpole. At this meeting Walpole and Newcastle described the danger of the situation. In brief, Austria had seized the opportunity of the rupture between France and Spain to gain the ascendancy over the Spanish queen, who had the sole direction of the government. Newcastle characterized her as "an ambitious, passionate woman, excited on the one hand by the excessive thirst of Revenge against France and on the other led away by the flattering prospect of the high pitch of power and glory to which her family might possibly be raised by the match of Don Carlos with the oldest Archduchess." With Spanish support and the probable break between England and Spain over Gibraltar, which would divert English strength, the imperial court hoped to bring the whole Empire under its arbitrary power and direction and secure by pressure the English guarantee of the settlement of the succession in the emperor's family, even before it was made known what that settlement would be. The assembled ministers heartily approved the firm tone which had been used toward Spain, were unanimous against giving up Gibraltar, and even considered that Stanhope had gone too far in making suggestions of an equivalent for the Rock. The conferees decided to hold fast to their French alliance; and, if Spain should attempt to seize British vessels or interfere with British trade, to institute reprisals immediately.[17]

The Alliance of Hanover seems to have checked effectively the designs of the Vienna allies, whatever they may have been. Although Ripperda signed another treaty two months later, the Austrians at least did not dare to proceed unless they could break the new Hanoverian alliance. Under pressure from the emperor, Prussia was induced to withdraw her signature from the Alliance of Hanover. This check was more than offset by the winning of Sweden, accomplished by copious bribery, to the Hano-

17. Newcastle to Townshend, Sept. 10/21, 1725, in Coxe, *Sir Robert Walpole*, II, 474–476. The rough draft of this letter, dated Sept. 9/20, 1725, which contains the description of Queen Elizabeth quoted in the above paragraph, and other information not included in the letter in its final form, is in Add. MSS. 32,687, fols. 155–159.

verian cause.[18] The adhesion of Sweden helped deter the
Russians from aiding the Vienna allies, and the evenness
in strength between the two opposing coalitions prevented
the outbreak of a general European war.[19]

In accordance with the decision of the ministers in London, Secretary Townshend instructed Stanhope to refrain
from any further mention of equivalents for Gibraltar.
The English secretary asserted that those mentioned by
Stanhope were too illusory to be satisfactory in any event,
and that the idea of returning Gibraltar to Spain for an
equivalent must be abandoned. Townshend even insisted
that the offers of Lord Stanhope in previous years had
been made without the king's orders, and contrary to English opinion at that time. As to the obligation incurred by
the royal letter of 1721, Townshend stated that "the behaviour of the Spanish Court since they entered into
measures with that of Vienna, has been such that it is impossible they themselves can think his majesty any longer
under the least obligation of laying this demand before the
Parliament."[20] Stanhope responded by insisting (as in
1723) that what he had proposed had been by way of conversation only, and that it in no way obligated England.
He expressed surprise at Townshend's statement that the
English king no longer felt himself under the least obligation to present the question of the restitution of Gibraltar
to Parliament; he asserted that he would not dare to make
such a statement to the King of Spain.[21]

18. Great Britain, France, and Prussia were the original signatories
of the Alliance of Hanover; subsequently Holland, Portugal, Denmark,
and Sweden were induced to join, offsetting the defection of Prussia.
Such a coalition thwarted the imperial design of attack in Germany, for
it left the Austrian Netherlands exposed to attack on all sides.

19. Townshend to Horatio Walpole, Oct. 5, 1725, and subsequent cor-
respondence in Add. MSS. 38,503. Chance, *The Alliance of Hanover*.
Williams, "The Foreign Policy of England under Walpole," Part III,
Eng. Hist. Rev., XV (Oct. 1900), 696–698.

20. Townshend to Stanhope, Sept. 26, 1725, S.P. 94:93.

21. Stanhope to Townshend, Nov. 5, 1725, S.P. 94:93. Spanish ingrati-
tude in making the compact with Vienna may partially be excused by
the fact that in four years the English ministry had never evinced the
slightest intention of ever fulfilling its Gibraltar pledge. Since the *quid*

After receiving Townshend's new instructions, Stanhope tried to obtain a definite statement from the Spanish as to what course they proposed to follow with respect to Gibraltar. The Spanish evaded his solicitations for several weeks, for they wished to leave the question in suspense until they concluded their new treaty with Austria which would bind the emperor to aid Spain in the event of a rupture. Finally, as a reward for Stanhope's persistence, Grimaldo stated that he had been instructed by King Philip that no action would be taken by Spain until the meeting of Parliament in January. The English minister at once declared this concession to be valueless, for there appeared to be no possibility that Parliament would be willing to approve the cession for some time to come. No further commitment could be extracted from the Spanish; and Stanhope concluded that they would continue to avoid any repetition of the open declaration that the continuance of Spanish friendship and English commercial privileges depended on the return of Gibraltar, in order to keep the matter open and have a pretext for declaring war as soon as circumstances were favorable.[22]

In December, Horatio Walpole urged Lord Townshend to present the question of Gibraltar to Parliament as soon as it convened in January. Walpole strongly favored the retention of Gibraltar; he argued that Parliament would certainly refuse to restore it to Spain, yet at the same time the English could clear themselves of their obligation to bring the matter before Parliament. Such a procedure might avoid the risk of a rupture with Spain, and it certainly would undeceive the Spanish king and all others who had claimed that Parliament would favor the cession. Walpole insisted that a parliamentary decision would

pro quo for the renewal of England's commercial treaties in 1721 had been the promise to present the question of Gibraltar to Parliament with ministerial support, an English declaration that they no longer considered themselves bound to do so certainly would have given Spain some justification for a new suspension of England's commercial privileges.

22. Stanhope's letters to Townshend, Oct. 11 and Nov. 5, 1725, in S.P. 94:93; and Nov. 19, 1725, in Stowe MSS. 256, fols. 50–51.

"take away all handle and pretext for making the restitution of that place a condition of a reconciliation [with Spain], which France so earnestly desires, and would purchase almost at any rate," a prophetic forecast, for such was the circumstance of the first Family Compact. Lord Townshend approved Walpole's proposal, but it struck a snag somewhere; and no further mention is to be found of it.[23]

In the meantime, Ripperda had negotiated the second Treaty of Vienna, dated November 5, 1725, an offensive alliance to cover the contingencies of a general European war with the allies of Hanover.[24] In the treaty of April 30, the emperor had agreed to furnish Spain with thirty thousand men if both powers were drawn into a war. Now he promised that this aid would be furnished for the reduction of Gibraltar and Minorca if Austria went to war with England; in the meantime, he would continue his good offices to secure the restitution of those two places. After the conclusion of this treaty, the Dutchman Ripperda hastened to Spain, where he was showered with honors by the queen and given the post of first minister.

After his return to Madrid, Ripperda tried to convince Stanhope that the King of Spain did not really intend to break with England over the Gibraltar question. The English minister continued to press for some definite statement from Spain, for even though no formal break had occurred between the two nations, English trade had been

23. Walpole to Townshend, Dec. 2, 1725; and Townshend to Walpole, Dec. 19, 1725, Add. MSS. 38,504, fols. 113–116, 166–167.
24. For terms and details of its negotiations, see Syveton, *Un cour et un aventurier,* pp. 142–159. Stanhope subsequently reported that Ripperda asserted that a collateral project, between Spain, the emperor, and the Pretender, had been agreed to but never signed. In this projected treaty the Pretender promised to restore Gibraltar and Minorca to Spain, and guarantee to open all the colonies of England to the trade of the Ostend Company. Although there is no doubt that Ripperda, the Spanish monarchs, and the emperor privately favored the Catholic cause in general, there is no evidence to corroborate Ripperda's statement that a specific treaty project in favor of the Pretender had actually been drafted. See Chance, *Alliance of Hanover,* pp. 316–317.

seriously curtailed because of the fear that Spain would suddenly confiscate English vessels and merchandise. Ripperda finally announced that King Philip would no longer insist on the restitution during January, but would grant England an extension of three months. Not satisfied by this, Stanhope demanded to know what Spain would do if Gibraltar were not returned within the three months granted. Ripperda confidentially replied that the Spanish king undoubtedly could be persuaded to extend the period almost indefinitely, and he promised in the strongest terms that Spain would not go to war with England over Gibraltar. Stanhope was more than suspicious of Ripperda's sincerity; his promise of friendship and amity had been accompanied by the remark that before he left Vienna the emperor had agreed to support Spain with all his forces in the event that the Spanish became involved in a war over Gibraltar.[25] Stanhope was convinced that the Spanish were merely playing for time in order to get home their fleets from the Indies, for until they arrived Spain would not have sufficient resources to support a war; and he stated that Spanish equivocation on the subject of Gibraltar was sufficient proof that they only awaited a favorable occasion to break with England upon that affair.[26]

Anglo-Spanish relations hung in a balance for the remainder of Ripperda's ministry. Ripperda reiterated to Stanhope that Spain would never go to war over Gibraltar and would not require that it be restored within a defi-

25. Stanhope to Townshend, Dec. 27, 1725, S.P. 94:93.
26. Stanhope to Newcastle, Jan. 21, 1725, S.P. 94:94. The Spanish at this time tried to induce Holland to assume the rôle of mediator in the Gibraltar dispute, probably with the hope of creating friction between the Dutch and English and thus eliminating a prospective English ally. Of course, the English refused to accept the idea of Dutch mediation. To this and every other suggestion of a settlement of the question, Newcastle instructed Stanhope to give a categorical negative: "His Majesty cannot on any account, think of doing anything with relation to the Restitution of Gibraltar, and therefore . . . the Repitition of those Demands will always meet with the same answer from the King." Stanhope to Newcastle, Jan. 7, 1726, S.P. 94:94. Newcastle to Stanhope, Jan. 13/24, 1726, S.P. 94:96.

nite time. In February he asked Stanhope to re-open negotiations on the basis of an exchange, and assured the
English minister that Spain would give an equivalent that
would be entirely satisfactory to the king and nation.[27]
Subsequently he proposed that a general congress be convened to discuss all matters in dispute. The English turned
a deaf ear to these overtures; Newcastle refused to consider the exchange of Gibraltar for any equivalent whatsoever, and he looked upon Ripperda's proposals merely
as expedients to gain time.[28] As the year progressed, Stanhope became convinced that there was a good deal of sincerity in Ripperda's efforts to avert a clash.[29] The Austrians, despite their treaty obligations, openly declared
that they would not join Spain in a war over Gibraltar;
and there was too much evidence that if Spain started a
war she would be left alone. Ripperda realized that Spain
was in no condition to sustain a war by herself, yet so bitter were the Catholic monarchs against France and England and so confident were they in the pledges of Austria
that Ripperda could retain their grace only by pushing
matters to extremities. His unwillingness to do so, and the
whisperings of the Austrians, who were now anxious for
his removal, brought his downfall.[30]

Even before the fall of Ripperda, the English took steps
to prevent the arrival of the treasure fleet in Spain, an
event which might have precipitated hostilities. Admiral
Francis Hosier led a fleet to the West Indies in April
1726, with orders to bottle up the galleons; this step was
taken both to prevent King Philip from receiving the necessary resources to sustain a war and to safeguard the interests of British, French, and Dutch nationals, to whom
much of the contents of the fleet belonged. In truth, Spain
was practically bankrupt in May 1726, and Philip would
have had to seize more than the royal portion of the fleet's

27. Stanhope to Newcastle, Feb. 28, 1726, S.P. 94:94.
28. Newcastle to Stanhope, March 10/21, 1726, S.P. 94:96.
29. Stanhope to Newcastle, April 11, 1725, S.P. 94:94.
30. Baudrillart, *Philippe V et la cour de France,* III, 243–246. Coxe,
Kings of Spain, III, 137–146. Armstrong, *Elisabeth Farnese,* pp. 193–198.

cargo merely to meet the demands of the Austrian subsidy.[31]

After his dismissal, Ripperda took refuge in the house of the British minister at Madrid. There is no evidence that this was done by pre-arrangement; but Walpole in Paris, before news of the event arrived from Madrid, expressed the hope that some sort of refuge would be found for Ripperda, and that information could be extracted from him about the Spanish engagements with Vienna.[32] The Spanish finally seized and imprisoned Ripperda, despite the asylum opened to him by Stanhope. But in the interim Stanhope had extracted from his guest the full details of Spain's negotiations with the emperor. This information he secretly dispatched to London, where it confirmed the worst of the ministry's suspicions, and furnished rather ample justification, albeit a bit tardy, for the expedition of Admiral Hosier.[33] The refuge granted to Ripperda increased Spanish ire against England, for the Spanish correctly suspected that the ex-minister had divulged all their secrets.

Austrian dominance over the queen and Spanish policy increased rather than diminished after Ripperda's downfall. Count Konigsegg, the imperial envoy, became virtually first minister at Madrid. The Spanish secretaries were mere figureheads. But the Austrians had come to

31. Chance, *The Alliance of Hanover,* pp. 350–356.

32. Horatio Walpole to Newcastle, May 28, 1726, Add. MSS. 32,746. Stanhope was absent from Madrid at the time that Ripperda took refuge at his home, and always publicly contended that the asylum was not pre-arranged. However, Walpole's letter suggests that he may have secretly advised Stanhope to grant asylum to Ripperda in order to extract information from him. Stanhope was a past master at extracting information, by fair means or foul; and it may well have been that Ripperda was granted asylum as a *quid pro quo* for his disclosures, which he made through fear, and most reluctantly.

33. Stanhope did not dare to send the details of Ripperda's disclosures to England by mail; instead, he sent Benjamin Keene, then consul-general at Madrid, to London to report them in person. Finally, on July 30, 1726, Stanhope wrote to Newcastle a full account of the secret Austro-Spanish treaties as disclosed by Ripperda, the letter being sent via an obscure British merchant, who managed to get it out of Spain without being detected. Add. MSS. 32,747, fol. 35.

realize the financial weakness of their Spanish ally. They were probably equally impressed by their absolute failure to break the bonds between France and England, and the consequent growth in the strength of the Alliance of Hanover. They continued to stir the hopes of the queen by the enticement of the marriage compact,[34] and to draw what subsidies they could wring from impoverished Spain. Nevertheless, as the year progressed, it became increasingly evident that the Austrians had no intention of embarking upon their grand project, and they attempted to dissuade the Spanish from launching a premature attack on Gibraltar.[35]

The Spanish king at last determined to assert himself. During the fall of 1726 he pushed preparations for a siege of Gibraltar. Count Konigsegg tried to check him, but in vain. It is probable, especially when the subsequent conduct of the attack is considered, that the Spanish monarchs were resolved to drive the emperor into a war with England and France by taking the first step at Gibraltar. The hitch in the proceedings was the refusal of the Austrians to follow King Philip's lead. England meanwhile had strengthened the fortifications of the Rock, and the English were supremely confident that Spain would be the only loser in the impending attack.[36]

34. In the second Treaty of Vienna, the emperor gave his qualified consent to the marriage of his two younger daughters and the sons of Elizabeth Farnese. Although he probably never intended to fulfill this promise, the lure of this marriage compact kept the Queen of Spain under the emperor's dominance for nearly four years.

35. Baudrillart, *Philippe V et la cour de France,* III, 273. Newcastle to Stanhope, Feb. 6/17, 1727, S.P. 94:96.

36. Newcastle to Stanhope, Dec. 1/12, 1726, and Dec. 22/Jan. 2, 1726/ 1727, S.P. 94:96. Spain formally broke off diplomatic relations with Great Britain in September, following a note delivered by the Marquis de Pozobueno to Newcastle. Pozobueno justified Spain's severance of relations by citing England's failure to fulfill her Gibraltar promise. He also charged that the original cession had been nullified by England's failure to conform to the terms of the Treaty of Utrecht—by extending the fortifications beyond the stipulated limits of the fortress, by permitting Jews and Moors to reside at Gibraltar, and by harboring a contraband trade ruinous to Spain. Pozobueno to Newcastle, Dec. 21, 1725,

The siege of Gibraltar begun in December 1726 continued during the following year until the signature of a truce at Paris at the end of May. Before the attack on the Rock had been effectively launched, the imperial court, prompted by the French, proposed on February 16 the following terms for a preliminary peace: (1) a reconciliation to be effected between France and Spain, and those powers to be mediators in the dispute over the Ostend Company between the emperor, England, and Holland; (2) the emperor and France to be mediators between England and Spain in the current hostilities; (3) the King of Spain to withdraw his troops from before Gibraltar, and to desist from all hostilities; and (4) the English fleets to be recalled from the coasts of Spain and America. King Philip accepted these propositions with the reservation that if Gibraltar should be taken before the signature of the preliminaries he should not be obliged to restore it immediately, but the matter should be left open for further consideration. The English, supported by Cardinal Fleury,[37] took exception to this reservation and insisted that the siege must be stopped unconditionally, and that the possession of Gibraltar must not be the subject of a future mediation. After the exchange of several counter-projects, the Hanover allies finally accepted a new set of proposals, to which the Spanish ambassador at Vienna had agreed. The essential features, from the standpoint of this study, were the guarantee by Spain to England of all her possessions and commercial privileges as established by treaties entered into before the year 1725, and the calling of a general European congress to discuss and settle

in James S. Dodd, *The Ancient and Modern History of Gibraltar* (London, 1781), pp. 65–67.

37. The septuagenarian Fleury, tutor of Louis XV, supplanted the Duke of Bourbon as first minister of France in 1726. Fleury had an active hand in forestalling the precipitation of a general European war following the Spanish attack on Gibraltar. For a detailed account of his policy and the background of the preliminaries of May 31, see A. M. Wilson, *French Foreign Policy During the Administration of Cardinal Fleury, 1726–1743* (Cambridge, Mass., 1936), especially chap. IV.

other differences among the powers. The preliminaries
were signed at Paris on May 31, and the ratifications were
finally exchanged on July 30.[38]

The Spanish king found the terms of the agreement of
May 31 most unpalatable, and was loath to confirm it.
The Spanish siege of Gibraltar had been vigorous; although the English defense was successful during the period of the attack, the British commander, Lord Portmore, had been apprehensive for the fate of the fortress if
the siege had continued. Portmore stated that the siege
had been stopped only by diplomacy, not by the bad condition of the attacking force, nor by any feeling of hope-
lessness among the Spanish. The Spanish army, Portmore
asserted, was in excellent shape when hostilities were suspended.[39] In truth, the diplomatic efforts of the emperor
had nipped in the bud Spain's attempt, by an attack on
Gibraltar, to start a European war on the bases forecast
by the Treaties of Vienna.

Despite their ratification of the preliminary agreement
of May 31, the Spanish refused to execute their obligations thereunder until England recalled her navy from
the West Indies and from the coasts of Spain. Gibraltar

38. This paragraph and some of those following are based partly on
material in S.P. 103:109, a chronological outline of the diplomatic developments from June 1726 until January 1728. Although the terms of
the preliminaries of May 31 apparently confirmed Britain's possession
of Gibraltar, the agreement to recognize the British position on the basis
of treaties entered into prior to 1725 actually furnished a loophole for
continued Spanish pretensions to the Rock. France had agreed, in the
secret treaty of March 1721, to render her continuous good offices to
Spain for the recovery of Gibraltar; and the renewal of England's
commercial privileges in the treaties of June 1721 had been made contingent upon the promise of George I to present the question of Gibraltar to Parliament. The Spanish felt that these treaties, antedating 1725,
still gave them a just claim to the consideration of the restitution of Gibraltar.

39. Portmore to Newcastle, June 25/July 6, 1727, C.O. 91:4. See also
a report in the Newcastle Papers, Add. MSS. 33,005, fol. 456. As previously stated, the preliminaries were initiated at Vienna on Feb. 16,
1727—before the Spanish trenches at Gibraltar had been completed and
the main attack begun—and the progress of the siege seems to have had
little or no influence on the course of the diplomatic negotiation.

continued in a state of blockade, even though actual hostilities ceased. The Spanish monarchs refused in any case to restore the *Prince Frederick*, the South Sea Company's vessel seized in the harbor of Vera Cruz, prior to the congress and to the consideration of British contraband trade in the Indies. Indeed, the Spanish even advanced their posts before Gibraltar closer to the town and fortifications, with the obvious intention of denying to Britain any territorial jurisdiction outside the fortified area. Naturally the English were unwilling to recall their fleet or diminish the garrison at Gibraltar unless Spain would execute her obligations simultaneously. Rottembourg, the new French ambassador at Madrid,[40] tried to solve this tangle, but he was far more interested in improving his position with the Spanish court than in working for what he confidentially termed "the petty interests of England."[41] He accepted on December 3 a declaration regulating the execution of the preliminaries on terms that were directly contrary to his instructions in regard to the *Prince Frederick*. Benjamin Keene, the new British emissary to Spain, and Vander Meer, the Dutch minister, reluctantly acquiesced in the declaration; but at the insistence of the English ministry, Cardinal Fleury promptly disavowed Rottembourg's action.[42]

40. The efforts of Cardinal Fleury to effect a reconciliation with Spain had succeeded in August 1727, when letters from the French king congratulating the Spanish monarchs on the birth of a son were accepted at Madrid. The French then sent as ambassador to Madrid Count Rottembourg, and entrusted him with the task of cementing this reconciliation between the two branches of the House of Bourbon. Rottembourg was accompanied by Benjamin Keene, who was destined to fill William Stanhope's place as British minister at Madrid, but whose activities were unofficial until his presentation at the Spanish court at the end of December. During the period of hostilities, English and French interests had been represented by the Dutch minister Vander Meer. The ensuing negotiation relating to the execution of the preliminaries of May 31 was handled jointly by these three emissaries. Baudrillart, *Philippe V et la cour de France*, III, 345 ff. Coxe, *Kings of Spain*, III, 188–203. Also material in S.P. 103:109.

41. Coxe, *Kings of Spain*, III, 193.

42. Baudrillart, *Philippe V et la cour de France*, III, 378–384. Sir Richard Lodge, "The Treaty of Seville, 1729," in *Transactions of the*

The disavowal of the settlement negotiated by Rottembourg almost caused another rupture with Spain. Newcastle instructed Lord Portmore on no account to execute
any orders from Keene at Madrid for reducing the garrison of Gibraltar or sending home the protecting fleet;
and additional armaments were sent to the fortress. Both
the Duke of Newcastle and Lord Portmore entertained
suspicions of Spanish treachery; they thought that, although the Spanish were attempting to persuade the English to send away their fleet and weaken the garrison,
Spain had no intention of executing her own obligation to
withdraw from Gibraltar, but intended to deliver a surprise attack upon the garrison as soon as it became weakened. Portmore was cautioned against any negotiation
with the local Spanish commander about withdrawal of
troops or regulation of the jurisdiction of the place. In
response, the governor firmly asserted that he would do
nothing until he received further orders from England.[43]
At Madrid, the queen seriously considered the resumption
of hostilities; but several factors served to curb her thirst
for revenge against England. King Philip's health took a
sudden turn for the worse early in 1728, and the queen
dared not risk a war until his condition improved. Though
Elizabeth was still under the domination of the Austrian
emissary, and hoped for the fulfillment of the alluring
promises of the Vienna treaties, the reluctance of the Austrians to be dragged into a war, and their diplomatic efforts to prevent one, were obvious. In addition, Spanish
finances were still in a precarious state; and the Spanish
minister Patiño assured the queen that resources were sufficient to support a defensive war only, and for Spain

Royal Historical Society, 4th Series, XVI (London, 1933), 22–24. Keene's
acceptance of this declaration, though unofficial, greatly irritated the
Duke of Newcastle. This initial blunder aroused suspicion in London of
Keene's acumen and ability, and for several years letters from Newcastle reflect a lack of confidence in him. This may explain in part the
subsequent neglect that England exhibited toward one of her most able
diplomatic representatives of the century.

43. Newcastle to Portmore, Dec. 27/Jan. 7, 1727/1728, C.O. 91:1. Portmore to Newcastle, Feb. 13/24, 1728, C.O. 91:4.

alone. In other words, no subsidies could be expected for Austria.[44]

Under these circumstances, the Spanish were induced to capitulate, and a new agreement was signed at the Pardo on March 6, 1728. Among the articles, it was agreed "to raise at once the blockade of Gibraltar, by withdrawing the [extra] troops to their quarters, by withdrawing the cannon, leveling the trenches, and destroying all of the other works erected in connection with the siege, so that everything should be restored on both sides in conformity to the Treaty of Utrecht."[45] The Spanish began to withdraw their troops and cannon even before the signature of the Pardo Act. The Convention of the Pardo set the stage for the Congress of Soissons.[46]

The Congress of Soissons represented a new effort to arrange a peaceful settlement of the affairs of southern Europe under the auspices of an international gathering. The unsolved problem of Gibraltar helped to frustrate this effort. The agenda of the congress, while based on the preliminary agreement of May 31, 1727 and the subsequent Pardo Act, did not specifically exclude the question of Gibraltar's restitution.[47] The English were determined if possible to prevent its consideration, while the Spanish

44. Baudrillart, *Philippe V et la cour de France,* III, 383–384. Coxe, *Kings of Spain,* III, 217.

45. Cantillo, *Tratados de paz y de comercio,* p. 244.

46. See chap. V, below, for the subsequent acrimonious controversy over the territorial jurisdiction of Gibraltar and other local problems. Even after the signature of the Convention of the Pardo, the English entertained suspicions of Spanish treachery. During March and April the Spanish concentrated a large force near Málaga. Newcastle and Horatio Walpole feared that Spain contemplated a surprise attack on Gibraltar. The garrison was duly warned to be on its guard. This incident illustrates the underlying and mutual distrust which characterized the negotiation. In point of fact, the Spanish soon dispersed these troops. It is entirely possible that they, as on previous and subsequent occasions, made this show of force to back up their diplomatic representations on the question of the restitution of Gibraltar. Horatio Walpole to Keene, March 29, 1728; Keene to Walpole, April 10, 1728; Keene to Newcastle, May 3, 1728; in Add. MSS. 32,755, fols. 32–33, 266, 344.

47. The English did agree to submit the issue of the territorial jurisdiction of Gibraltar to the congress. See chap. V, below.

were equally resolved to place the matter before the congress. In fact, the demand for the restitution headed the list of instructions for the Spanish plenipotentiaries. They insisted that the English pledge of 1721 be carried out, since the commercial advantages enjoyed by England had been renewed only on the promise that Gibraltar would be restored.[48] Spain counted on both French and Austrian support for her pretension, in fulfillment of their obligations under the treaties of 1721 and 1725. Of course, the fundamental question for the congress to solve was the old one of an Italian settlement between the emperor and Spain. Despite the Austro-Spanish Alliance, there was no real agreement between the two as to what that settlement should be.

The official British position at the congress with regard to Gibraltar was that there was no ground whatsoever for considering its restitution; and the British plenipotentiaries were instructed on no account to consent to the discussion of the question.[49] The Duke of Newcastle plainly stated the English position in the following extract from a letter to Walpole:

. . . Spain itself has not any shadow of foundation for making that pretention [i.e., for the restitution of Gibraltar], since there neither is, nor ever was any treaty or convention for the giving it up to Spain; on the contrary several [have been] made even since the first demand of it, wherein the possession of that place, as well as of all others is confirmed and preserved to His Majesty; and as to the late King's letter, there is no pretence that it contained any further promise than that of laying it before the Parliament in a proper time; and it was never insisted upon by his Catholic Majesty or anybody for him, that the late King should so much as

48. It should be borne in mind that the Spanish always interpreted the letter of 1721 as a promise to restore Gibraltar; whereas the letter promised only to present the question to Parliament.

49. Instructions for William Stanhope, Horatio Walpole, and Stephen Poyntz, plenipotentiaries to the congress to be held at Soissons, April 30/May 10, 1728, in *British Diplomatic Instructions,* VI, *France, 1727–1744,* 29.

lay this affair before the Parliament, till after the offensive
engagements were entered into between the Emperor and
Spain; and then Mr. Stanhope was told in form, that the
continuance of the performance of our treaties with Spain
depended upon the immediate giving up of Gibraltar . . .
after such a declaration the court of Spain did even proceed
to open hostilities and endeavoured to take that place by
force. This behaviour on the part of Spain toward England
has certainly cancelled all obligations, it might be imagined,
the late King was under by his letter, to lay this affair before
the Parliament. . . . And had there been any foundation for
it, which there was not in the least, the Preliminary Articles
and the Act signed at Madrid . . . [have] directly precluded the court of Spain from renewing any attempt of this
kind at the Congress.[50]

The thread of this argument is faulty in at least one important particular: Between 1721 and 1725, Spain had
repeatedly pressed the British ministers to present the
matter to Parliament, and they had refused to do so.

The English sought the support of Cardinal Fleury in
their attempt to prevent the Spanish from introducing the
Gibraltar question at the congress. The cardinal, with evident sincerity, gave manifold promises of unqualified
French support for England's possession of the Rock if
the question were raised by Spain. He even permitted the
English to redraft the instructions for the French plenipotentiaries on the subject, but he would not consent absolutely to deny Spain the right to present her claims to
the congress in writing. Fleury agreed that the promise
made by the Duke of Orleans in the secret treaty of March
1721 (which the cardinal averred had only recently become known to him) was outweighed by the repeated and
subsequent guarantees given by France to England respecting her possession of Gibraltar, and he insisted that
the united stand of the English and French envoys would

50. Newcastle to Walpole, March 14/25, 1728, Add. MSS. 32,754, fols.
498–500.

be sufficient to nullify any demand by Spain for restitution.[51] A refusal by France to admit the presentation of Spanish claims to Gibraltar probably would have upset the recent reconciliation between the Bourbon powers, and Fleury was determined to nourish the new understanding with Spain. He urged the Austrians, however, to use their influence at Madrid to dissuade the Spanish from making any demand for the restitution; and he reiterated to Count Sinzendorf that subsequent French guarantees to England superseded the promise of good offices made to Spain in 1721.[52] Privately, Walpole reported to Newcastle that he had no reason to suspect the cardinal's sincerity; and, although England might have to bow to the inevitable and permit the subject to be mentioned at the congress, he was convinced that in view of the solid front presented by France and England "both the Spanish and Imperial ministers despair of doing anything in it."[53] Under the circumstances, the English envoys were authorized not to insist on the absolute exclusion of any demand for the restitution at the congress.[54]

Despite their public opposition to any demand for reopening the question of the restitution of Gibraltar, English diplomatists still favored parting with the Rock if

51. Horatio Walpole and Waldegrave to Newcastle, March 30, 1728, Add. MSS. 32,755, fols. 43–47. The plenipotentiaries to Newcastle, May 17, 1728, Add. MSS. 32,755, fols. 491–492. The plenipotentiaries to Newcastle, May 29, 1728, and enclosed draft of instructions for the French plenipotentiaries at the Congress of Soissons, Add. MSS. 32,756, fols. 15–27.

52. Stanhope to Newcastle (private letter), May 30, 1728; and Walpole to Newcastle, June 4, 1728, Add. MSS. 32,756, fols. 32–34, 85–87.

53. Walpole to Newcastle (private letter), June 10, 1728, Add. MSS. 32,761, fol. 150. Walpole accidentally dated this letter *1729* instead of *1728,* and so it was bound with the Newcastle Papers for the wrong year.

54. The English and French finally agreed that, if the Spanish did present a formal demand for Gibraltar, the following joint response should be made to it: "That His Majesty's Right to that Place is so clearly and unalterably established by the Treaty of Utrecht, and by several other Treaties antecedent to the Year 1725, and confirmed by the Preliminarys, of which Treatys His Most Christian Majesty is Guarantee, that it can never be called in question." Newcastle to the plenipotentiaries, June 3/14, 1728, Add. MSS. 32,756, fols. 153–154.

that could be accomplished without loss of prestige. Both William Stanhope and Benjamin Keene realized that no solid reconciliation with Spain would be possible without the restoration of Gibraltar. Even Lord Townshend, who since the death of Lord Stanhope had been the chief opponent of restitution, indicated, in response to a letter from Stephen Poyntz,[55] that he personally favored returning it to Spain. Early in June, Poyntz wrote to the secretary that though England probably could prevent the question from being raised at Soissons, Spain would leave no stone unturned to distress English commerce in retaliation. Poyntz remarked, "the Catholic king and the true Spaniards are animated against us by this single consideration," and urged that if Spain could be induced to desist from her peremptory demands and attitude, and present the matter in an amicable fashion on the basis of a satisfactory equivalent, it would be to England's advantage to accept such terms. In reply, Townshend stated:

What you propose in relation to Gibraltar, is certainly very reasonable, and is exactly conformable to the opinion, which you know I have always entertained concerning that place. But you cannot but be sensible of the violent and almost superstitious zeal, which has of late prevailed among all parties in this kingdom, against any scheme for the restitution of Gibraltar upon any conditions whatsoever. And I am afraid, that the bare mention of a proposal, which carried the most distant appearance of laying England under an obligation of ever parting with that place, would be sufficient to put the whole nation in a flame.[56]

Such a statement indicates that Britain's position in this negotiation was influenced chiefly by the fear of political opposition at home, rather than by any enhanced estimation of the value of Gibraltar.

55. One of the British emissaries to the Congress of Soissons.
56. Poyntz to Lord Townshend, June 9, 1728; and Townshend to Poyntz, June 3/14, 1728. In Coxe, *Sir Robert Walpole,* II, 627–629, 630–632.

The situation in Spain at this time was more uncertain than ever. The king, too ill to participate in affairs, was completely dominated by the queen. Nothing could satisfy Elizabeth but the Austrian marriage of her son. All her maneuvers, including her constant prodding of the king on the point of Gibraltar, were designed to maintain the animosity of the Spanish toward France and England in order to safeguard the Austrian alliance. The British felt that no concession England might make—neither the cession of Gibraltar nor the rectification of the Asiento difficulties—would mollify Queen Elizabeth if her Italian ambitions and the Austrian marriage were not achieved. On the other hand, if her true objectives could be obtained with French and English approval and support, "all other things would be made easy." France secretly opposed the Austro-Spanish marriage project, and probably hoped, as England did, to check the queen's endeavors and break the Austro-Spanish Alliance.[57] Keene reported that the British refusal to give up Gibraltar had created a rising tide of resentment toward England in Spain, so that hardly a trace remained of the traditional Anglo-Spanish friendship. Yet advisors were not lacking at the Spanish court who thought that the Spanish demand for Gibraltar should be postponed to a more propitious time.[58]

The delegates to the congress assembled at Soissons in June. By that time, for a variety of reasons, the British, French, and Austrians were all opposed to a general discussion and settlement of the troubled affairs of Europe by an international gathering. Among the particular obstacles to such a settlement, Gibraltar again stood out. Sensing that the British and French would refuse even to discuss their demand for the restitution of Gibraltar, the

57. The private letters of Wm. Stanhope to Newcastle, July 1, 1728, Add. MSS. 32,756, fols. 356–358; and of Horatio Walpole, July 24, 1728, Add. MSS. 32,757, fols. 146–148, are especially interesting and illuminating on the general situation. Keene wrote a brilliant and detailed description of the situation at the Spanish court to the Duke of Newcastle on May 16, 1728, Add. MSS. 32,755, fols. 439–447.

58. Keene to Stanhope, Aug. 14, 1728, Add. MSS. 32,757, fols. 495–496.

Spanish refrained from presenting any demands to the congress whatsoever.[59] Only the Dutch sincerely desired to use the congress as a vehicle for the negotiation of a permanent European peace.[60]

After much parrying, the delegates attempted to draft a new provisional treaty, in which all possessions of the signatory powers would be guaranteed as of the treaties in effect before 1725. No mention was to be made of Gibraltar; but since the Spanish claim to that place antedated 1725, the British correctly suspected that Spain would not consider this treaty a surrender of her claims to the Rock.[61] The Spaniards tried to insert into the provisional treaty a clause specifying that the territorial guarantee would not affect any *pretensions* which Spain might base on treaties prior to 1725. Spain finally agreed to sign the provisional treaty without any reference to pretensions, if England would agree to submit the questions of commerce and Gibraltar to the congress; the English refused. In turn, the English proposed an additional article to the projected treaty, declaring that within three months after its signature, England and Spain would appoint commissioners to meet at Madrid and settle their remaining difficulties. They insisted, however, that this settlement must not involve any question concerning the possession of Gibraltar, and that the article providing for the Madrid conference must be drawn so that the Spaniards could not base any such pretension on it. The French wholeheartedly supported this proposal, and agreed that Madrid was the only proper place to settle Anglo-Spanish

59. Probably the Spanish delegates were secretly authorized to dispense with the demand for Gibraltar if absolutely necessary. Stanhope and Walpole to Newcastle, July 20, 1728, Add. MSS. 32,757, fol. 124. Also Add. MSS. 33,006, fol. 87.

60. For the general attitude of the powers toward the congress, see Wilson, *French Foreign Policy,* chap. VI. The Dutch position and belief that Gibraltar was a great obstacle to a permanent settlement are described in great detail in A. Goslinga, *Slingelandt's Efforts Toward European Peace* (The Hague, 1915), especially pp. 267 ff.

61. Stanhope to Newcastle, Aug. 9, 1728, Add. MSS. 32,757, fols. 311–312.

commercial disputes. After much quibbling, the Spanish finally accepted the English proposal *ad referendum*, agreeing that only questions relating to *commerce in America* might be brought into discussion; and this project was transmitted to Madrid.[62]

The suggested Anglo-Spanish conference at Madrid brought no response from the Spanish court. The queen still hoped to obtain the fulfillment of the marriage alliance with Austria. She was loath to abandon the pretension to Gibraltar, as it furnished a medium for preventing a reconciliation with England and France. Keene enlisted the aid of the Marquis de Brancas, the French minister at Madrid, in an effort to persuade the queen to drop the question. To Brancas the queen replied that if she did so the Spanish would consider that she had sacrificed the interests of Spain to her own ambitions, and this would increase her unpopularity. Brancas then begged her to present the matter openly to her Spanish councillors, stressing the impossibility of forcing England to restore Gibraltar under the existing circumstances; it was necessary, he told her, to await a more favorable opportunity to present the question, and "as there was once a time when England would have parted with it for a sum of money, perhaps another favourable occasion might offer." According to Brancas' report to Keene, the queen "did not seem to dislike" this advice.[63]

Keene reported late in November that he had learned on good authority that the Spanish monarchs had determined to remain silent on the affair of Gibraltar, but intended also to reduce England's trading privileges to the bare limit of the treaty of 1713, nullifying all subsequent con-

62. Résumé of the English plenipotentiaries' correspondence concerning the discussion of Gibraltar at Soissons, June–October 1728, Add. MSS. 33,006, fol. 87. Stanhope and Walpole to Newcastle, Sept. 12, Oct. 5, and Oct. 19, 1728, Add. MSS. 32,758, fols. 1, 268–275, 349–356. Stanhope and Walpole to Keene, Oct. 4, 1728, Add. MSS. 32,758, fols. 232–233.

63. Keene to Newcastle, Oct. 25, 1728, Add. MSS. 32,758, fol. 432. See p. 21 above.

cessions. "By these means," wrote the British minister, "they are to cramp the annual ship, postpone the sale of her effects 'till the Indies are supplied with goods by the Flota and Galleons, embarrass our trade as much as they possibly can, in hopes to exasperate the [English] Nation, and endeavour to make them sensible that it is Gibraltar, which is the cause of the interruption of their commerce, and to induce them [the English] to think differently upon our possession of that place to what their general sentiments are known to be at present."[64]

The efforts of the Congress of Soissons to arrange a general peace came to a standstill by the end of 1728, primarily because of the refusal of Spain to accept any peace which did not leave some opening for renewing her claim to Gibraltar, and because of the indifference of the Austrians toward any solution of their problems. Fleury repeated his assurances that France would not permit the question of Gibraltar to be raised anew in the general negotiation, but Stanhope and Walpole do not appear to have been as firmly convinced of the cardinal's sincerity as they had been earlier in the year.[65] Benjamin Keene expressed the opinion that the Spanish queen's objections to a settlement had no relation to Gibraltar and the Asiento trade, "any further than as those two Articles served as a pretext, 'till she could gain her own Views and Designs, and induce the King and Spanish Nation to come into her Schemes." So far, however, the Viennese court had always found means "to stave off her Instances and amuse her," and thus to continue the deadlock.[66] Queen Elizabeth still hoped to draw the emperor into a war against England and France, but the Austrians no longer had any desire for such an undertaking. They sought to assure the continuance of their subsidies from Spain by humoring the Spanish queen and preventing the consummation of a set-

64. Keene to Newcastle, Nov. 22, 1728, Add. MSS. 32,759, fols. 205–206.

65. Stanhope and Walpole to Newcastle, Nov. 17, 1728, Add. MSS. 32,759, fol. 121.

66. Keene to Stanhope and Walpole, Dec. 20, 1728, Add. MSS. 32,759, fol. 405.

tlement; but Count Waldegrave, the British envoy at Vienna, wrote Keene:

. . . 'tis the common opinion that notwithstanding the assurances this Court may have given their Catholic Majesties to stand by and support Them in their refractory ways, all is still but Grimace to veil and cover their Design of getting their Mony and then leaving Them in the Lurch of which the Spaniards have had a very fresh and memorable Example in the late Troubles.[67]

Thus, while the point of Gibraltar had been an important cause for the failure of the Congress of Soissons to arrange a general settlement, the underlying factors were: on the one hand, the domination of Queen Elizabeth over Spanish policy and her continued faith in the emperor's fulfillment of his promises; and on the other, the efforts of the imperialists to stave off a settlement as long as possible, in order to obviate the necessity of fulfilling their promises to the Spanish queen, and at the same time to prevent a reconciliation between Spain and the Hanoverian allies.

Spain showed no disposition to break the deadlock in Anglo-Spanish relations as the new year opened. The Duke of Richmond, returning from Spain in February, reported that the Spaniards unanimously favored war unless Gibraltar were given up, and would accept no peace without it.[68] But the queen still hoped for aid from Austria before precipitating a struggle. King Philip was a pitiful figure. After recovering from his late illness, which had been both mental and physical (the latter from overeating and over-indulgence), he had actually been kept a prisoner at San Ildefonso for some time in order to prevent his abdication. There is every evidence that, disappointed and thwarted in his quest for Gibraltar and his desire for a reconciliation with France, he would have ab-

67. Vienna, Jan. 5, 1729, Add. MSS. 32,759, fols. 477–478.

68. Lady A. Irwin to Lord Carlisle, London, Feb. 22/March 5, 1729, *H.M.C., Carlisle MSS.*, pp. 57–58.

dicated if he had been permitted to see his ministers and council. When he had so far recovered that confinement was no longer possible, the queen decided to get him away from Madrid, and thus isolate him from his council, which alone could act on an announcement of abdication. A "progress" through southern Spain was begun by the Spanish monarchs in December 1728, and continued for some years, during which the king was not permitted to return to his capital.[69]

The English, fearing that the close approach of the Spanish monarchs to Gibraltar might revive the desire of King Philip to launch a sudden attack on it, took measures to warn and strengthen the garrison. Secret intelligence reached London in February of a new scheme for obtaining Gibraltar: the Spanish minister, Patiño, who was gaining the ascendancy over the other ministers of their Catholic Majesties, proposed that a sudden attack be launched against Jamaica, which he thought could easily be captured; once taken, it could be exchanged for Gibraltar. According to the report, this project was actually agreed to, and was to be undertaken as soon as the galleons reached Spain from the Indies.[70] This report certainly indicates the absence of any Spanish desire for a reconciliation or pacific settlement with England at the beginning of 1729. Such feelings were reciprocated. The English commercial classes were demanding war against Spain for the protection of English commerce with the Indies, and a project for intercepting the galleons was under consideration.

The question of Gibraltar and of the royal letter of

69. Keene's secret dispatches during the winter of 1728–1729 give a clear picture of the situation. In a letter to Wm. Stanhope and Horatio Walpole, from Badajoz, Jan. 20, 1729, he pithily summed up the situation by remarking: ". . . the true state of affairs here is that the Queen has the absolute direction of them." Add. MSS. 32,760, fol. 30.

70. "Intelligence in M. Poyntz to Mr. Stanhope, Feb. 15, 1729," in Add. MSS. 32,760, fols. 190–191. Newcastle to Poyntz, Feb. 18/March 1, 1729, S.P. 78:193. Governor Clayton to Newcastle, Gibraltar, March 16/27, 1729, C.O. 91:9. Newcastle to Keene, April 1/12, 1729, Add. MSS. 32,760, fol. 321.

1721 was raised in Parliament in March 1729. In the previous December, it had been rumored in London that the forthcoming Parliament might move that Gibraltar and Minorca be formally annexed to the realm of England. The object of this step would be either to assure their retention, with the apparent certainty that this measure would force the ministry into war with Spain; or to place the question under the jurisdiction of Parliament, so that the restitution and its terms would be made by Parliament and not by the ministry.[71] After the opening of Parliament, the opposition seized the question as an opportunity to embarrass the ministry and as a means to force the pacific administration of Robert Walpole into a war against Spain in defense of English commercial privileges. The opposition succeeded in raising the issue in the House of Lords, and on February 27/March 10 the Lords requested that a copy of the late king's letter be laid before them.[72] On March 18/29, the opposition attempted to force through a resolution requiring the king to obtain a specific renunciation from Spain of all claims to Gibraltar and Minorca in the treaty then under consideration, that is, the provisional treaty drawn up by the Congress of Soissons. After warm debate, this proposal was defeated by a substantial majority, and a similar motion was defeated in the Commons three days later. With ministerial support, a more moderate resolution was adopted, with the concurrence of both houses, in the following terms:

Resolved, by the Lords Spiritual and Temporal and Commons in Parliament assembled, That they do entirely rely upon His Majesty, that He will, for the maintaining the Honour, and securing the Trade of this Kingdom, take ef-

71. Wm. Stratford to Earl of Oxford, Dec. 15/26, 1728, *H.M.C., Portland MSS.,* VII, 471.

72. The idea of the formal annexation of Gibraltar and Minorca by Parliament was not new; it had been agitated for the past decade. Likewise, an attempt had been made previously, on Feb. 6/17, 1727, to force the king to lay before the Commons the letter of June 1, 1721; but the motion had been defeated. See the *Journals of the House of Commons,* XX, 733; and Cobbett's *Parliamentary History,* VIII, 548.

fectual Care, in the present Treaty, to preserve His undoubted Right to Gibraltar and the Island of Minorca.

In response, King George solemnly promised to preserve his rights to those possessions; and the matter was dropped.[73] But the agitation for war against Spain increased, and England undertook active preparations to decide her differences with Spain by force of arms.

With an Anglo-Spanish war almost certainly in prospect, a new factor entered into the situation. The Queen of Spain, who for so long had been confident that the emperor would fulfill his engagements, particularly that to unite Don Carlos and an archduchess in marriage, now began to realize that the emperor had been deceiving her and that there was little prospect of fulfilling her Italian schemes with Austrian acquiescence. When she learned that the emperor had made secret overtures to France and England, promising to withdraw all support from Spain in return for the guarantee of his succession, Austrian influence at the Spanish court rapidly waned. By the end of May, Queen Elizabeth apparently had decided that the only way to secure the succession of Don Carlos in Italy would be to obtain the support of France and England, with whom a reconciliation was therefore necessary. So far as England was concerned, she persuaded her husband that the question of Gibraltar must be passed over in silence.[74]

Progress toward an understanding between Spain and the Hanoverian allies was slow, due to the natural tendencies of the Spanish court, to the opposition of certain Spanish ministers who still favored reliance on Vienna, and to the machinations of the imperialists themselves. Tension during the summer of 1729 was at the breaking

---

73. *Journals of the House of Lords,* XXIII, 336–377. *Journals of the House of Commons,* XXI, 272, 285. *A Collection of the Parliamentary Debates in England* . . . (London, 1740–1749), IX, 423–428. Also Poyntz to Keene, April 12, 1729, Add. MSS. 32,760, fol. 326.

74. Keene to Newcastle, Cádiz, April 5, 1729, Add. MSS. 32,760, fol. 317. Keene to Newcastle, Seville, May 12, 1729, S.P. 94:100. Keene to Newcastle, May 26, 1729, Add. MSS. 32,761, fol. 120.

point, with the commercial classes of England and Holland clamoring for war. By June 1729, a considerable fleet of both English and Dutch vessels had been assembled at Portsmouth, in preparation for a general attack on the West Indies and the Spanish coast. Keene was instructed to inform the Spanish court of England's earnestness in pushing through her military preparations. The sailing of the fleet was deferred, pending a final effort at an accommodation with Spain; but the English ministry had "resolved to come to a sincere reconciliation or to an open rupture with Spain," and would countenance no further delay in the negotiation.[75]

The foundation for a successful negotiation with Spain was laid on June 26, when Keene and Brancas formally notified their Catholic Majesties that the Hanoverian allies would permit and support the establishment of Don Carlos in Parma and Tuscany, under the protection of Spanish garrisons, provided that Spain reëstablish British commercial rights and make amends for all violations, on the basis of treaties in effect prior to 1725, and also guarantee the possession of all English territories secured by treaties prior to 1725. The latter provision was intended, of course, to safeguard Gibraltar. Keene's explicit instructions followed the language of the March parliamentary resolution: "You are to lay it down for a rule that no Treaty can be admitted that does not preserve His Majesty's undoubted right to Gibraltar."[76] Lord Townshend authorized Keene's declaration respecting the Spanish garrisons in Italy on June 11/22 in a secret letter to the English ministers at Paris.[77] The latter had already assumed the responsibility of authorizing Keene to take such a step in concert with the French minister. Wil-

75. Townshend to the plenipotentiaries, Hanover, June 23, 1729, S.P. 78:193. Stanhope and Walpole to Keene, July 4, 1729, Add. MSS. 32,761, fol. 257.
76. The plenipotentiaries to Keene, June 14, 1729, Add. MSS. 32,761, fol. 158.
77. Townshend to the plenipotentiaries, June 11/22, 1729, Add. MSS. 32,761, fols. 208–209.

liam Stanhope wrote the Duke of Newcastle that this had
been done because they felt it was the only basis on which
the Spanish queen would settle, and they considered an
Anglo-Spanish settlement almost imperative. Stanhope
was suspicious not so much of the sincerity as of the timid-
ity of Cardinal Fleury; he asserted that England should
and could no longer depend upon France as her chief ally,
and that a Spanish reconciliation was therefore necessary.
Furthermore, a Spanish settlement would isolate the emperor, who would be forced to come to terms and acquiesce.[78]

Keene received full authority to conduct the negotiation
from the plenipotentiaries at Paris on July 26. His instructions concluded with the "particular and material
caution" that no expression must be included in the forthcoming treaty which might directly or indirectly bring
into question in the future England's right to, and possession of, Gibraltar; if any such expression were proposed
by the Spanish, it was to be refused absolutely and was
not even to be received *ad referendum*. Keene was told that
the project which Spain was expected to present must be
clear, precise, and ready for immediate signature without
further quibbling and without any further reference to
the Congress of Soissons, which was considered at an end.
His instructions included an unveiled threat "that at this
Season of the year, we nor indeed any of our allies are to
be trifled with."[79]

Before these instructions reached Keene, the Spanish
had delivered to him a project for a treaty, which he had
forwarded to Paris on August 2. In this project, the
Spanish king had insisted on the insertion of a clause stating that the omission from the project of sundry points
and claims could not derogate from or prejudice any right
or pretension that his Catholic Majesty claimed by virtue

78. Stanhope to Newcastle, June 17, 1729, Add. MSS. 32,761, fols. 199–
202.
79. The plenipotentiaries to Keene, July 26, 1729, Add. MSS. 32,761,
fols. 431–432.

of the treaties and conventions antecedent to 1725.[80] Keene
accepted the Spanish project under some protest. Even
stronger criticism followed its reception at Paris and London. It was immediately stated that the project would
never be accepted in the form submitted by Spain; only
the general feeling that Spain sincerely desired a reconciliation prevented a rupture in the negotiations. Reports
received in Paris indicated that the Spanish queen had
had a very difficult task in persuading her husband to omit
the claim to Gibraltar from the treaty. Despite their
strong stand, the British ministers believed that it would
be impossible to secure a specific retraction from King
Philip of his pretensions to the Rock.[81] The English and
French redrafted the treaty project and returned it, with
the suggestion that if the Spanish king insisted on retaining in the treaty a statement concerning his pretensions
based on treaties antecedent to 1725, those pretensions
must be specifically enumerated and must not include anything which could be construed as preserving a claim to
Gibraltar.[82] At the same time, Keene was instructed to inform the Spanish that the Anglo-Dutch fleet in Portsmouth harbor was prepared to assist immediately in the
transportation of Spanish troops to Italy, if Spain were
disposed to agree to the project as laid down by the Allies. This notification implied, of course, that if Spain
were *not* so disposed, the fleet was being kept in readiness
for entirely different purposes.[83]

To facilitate the conclusion of the new treaty, the English ministry sent William Stanhope to Spain to supplement Keene's efforts. Stanhope was loath to undertake the

80. A copy of the project was enclosed in Keene's letter to Townshend,
sent via Paris, Aug. 2, 1729, Add. MSS. 32,762, fol. 27.

81. Horatio Walpole and Poyntz to Townshend, Aug. 13, 1729; and
Poyntz to Mr. Tilson (an aid of Townshend), Aug. 13, 1729, S.P. 78:192.
The plenipotentiaries to Keene, Aug. 15, 1729, Add. MSS. 32,762, fols.
150–151.

82. The plenipotentiaries to Keene, Sept. 10, 1729, Add. MSS. 32,762,
fols. 398–400.

83. The plenipotentiaries to Keene, Sept. 11, 1729, Add. MSS. 32,762,
fol. 483.

journey. He had but slender hopes for the success of the negotiation, and felt that its failure might injure his ambition for advancement into the ministry. Only the secret promise that he would be raised to the peerage immediately after his return finally persuaded Stanhope to undertake the mission. He was highly regarded by the Spanish monarchs; and it was hoped that he might persuade King Philip to make some secret declaration renouncing all claim to Gibraltar, and even that he might procure the return of the embarrassing letter of the late king. He succeeded in neither of these objectives. Indeed, before Stanhope left Paris, the English seemed to have abandoned any intention of extracting a specific renunciation from the Spanish king. Both the Dutch and French urged the English to refrain from such a demand. Walpole still had confidence, however, in the assurances of the French that they would continue to insist with England that Spain accept the Allies' project without any alteration that could be construed "to effect in any way His Majesty's interests and possessions."[84] Before Stanhope reached the Spanish court at Seville, Keene and Brancas had almost concluded the negotiation with the Spanish ministers; the latter postponed any final agreement until the arrival of Stanhope, hoping that he would be empowered to make new concessions. But Stanhope carried no new proposals or concessions, save only the promise of specific naval and military aid by the Allies to support Don Carlos' descent upon Italy, in lieu of the aid already promised in general terms. Stanhope reached Seville on October 26, and within a fortnight the Treaty of Seville was signed on the basis which England had already indicated would be satisfactory; that is, complete silence on the point of Gibraltar, with no reservation by the Spanish king of claims or pretensions based on the treaties antecedent to 1725.[85]

84. Horatio Walpole to Newcastle, Oct. 26, 1729, Add. MSS. 32,763, fol. 442.

85. Correspondence in the Newcastle Papers, Add. MSS. 32,763, 32,764; also in S.P. 78:192 (France, General Correspondence). Also the reports

The success of England in securing by implication in the Treaty of Seville a renunciation of Spanish claims to Gibraltar was a surprise to the English themselves. A few weeks before, it had been generally agreed that no sort of threat would ever get King Philip to give up that treasured objective. When, on November 24, Horatio Walpole forwarded to London the good news of the signature of the treaty, he expressed his "fullest satisfaction of a treaty . . . which I think our enemys may read with envy," and whose terms were "beyond expectation."[86]

Why had Spain renounced her claims and concluded a treaty so favorable to England? Why had King Philip virtually abandoned his hope of securing a fulfillment of the promise given by the English king and ministry to make a sincere effort to induce Parliament to approve the restitution of Gibraltar? Several explanations may be advanced. The open threats of England to go to war rather than agree to any treaty not preserving her possession of

of M. Brancas, the French minister at the Spanish court, Sept. 1 and Sept. 15, 1729, Cor. Pol., Espagne, vol. 364, fols. 179, 341. For the text of the Treaty of Seville, see F. G. Davenport (ed.), *European Treaties Bearing on the History of the United States* . . . (Washington, 1917–1937), IV, 46–49.

An interesting sidelight on the Seville negotiation was the disclosure in 1739 of the text of a secret article alleged to have been attached to the treaty and signed on Nov. 23, 1729. This article provided for the absolute restoration of both Gibraltar and Minorca within six years; the British king was to secure the consent of his Parliament to this step within three years; and Spain was not to be bound to execute her obligations under the Treaty of Seville until the consent of Parliament had been obtained for the above restorations. A copy of this spurious article, written in Italian, was forwarded to Paris by Polignac, the French minister at Rome, on Feb. 16, 1730, and bears the marginal notation: "This article has been suspected at Rome." Thus, it is evident that this article had been concocted shortly after the signature of the Treaty of Seville, for some undisclosed purpose. Its authorship is likewise unknown, but a comparison of the English and Italian versions makes it apparent that the former was a translation from the Italian. Such a secret article, if genuine, would furnish a happy explanation of the willingness of King Philip to sign a treaty which made no mention of his favorite objective; but there is no evidence to indicate that it was not fraudulent. Add. MSS. 35,589, fols. 346–347. Cor. Pol., Espagne, vol. 365, fol. 257.

86. Horatio Walpole to Charles Delafaye, Nov. 24, 1729, S.P. 78:192.

Gibraltar and securing a complete resumption of her Indies trade probably had something to do with Spain's decision. Spain, too weak to sustain such a war by herself, had been deserted by her Austrian ally. Furthermore, eight years of futile attempts to persuade the English to comply with their promise must have convinced even the obstinate Philip that there was no hope of achieving his cherished objective through the usual channels of Anglo-Spanish diplomacy. Then, too, Queen Elizabeth—not her husband—had been responsible for the sudden shift in Spanish policy that led to the Treaty of Seville. The queen thought only of the marriage alliances and the establishment of her son Carlos in Italy; as soon as she was convinced that there was no longer any chance of attaining those objectives under the Austrian alliance, she was perfectly willing to sacrifice Gibraltar and the Indies trade to secure English friendship and assistance. The final reason for Philip's apparent surrender on the Gibraltar question would have considerably dampened the enthusiasm of the English for the Treaty of Seville if they had been aware of it. During the negotiation of the treaty, France secretly agreed to give Spain a declaration promising her continued good offices on behalf of the recovery of Gibraltar. The promise of this declaration marked the first step in secret negotiations which culminated in the Family Compact of 1733. To these Franco-Spanish negotiations, made possible by the festering British thorn of Gibraltar in the side of Spain, we must now turn.

IV

GIBRALTAR AND THE ORIGIN OF THE FAMILY COMPACT

FRANCE sought to arrange a private reconciliation between the Bourbon courts for almost a decade prior to the Treaty of Seville. Cardinal DuBois and the regent took the first positive step in that direction by negotiating the secret Franco-Spanish treaty of March 1721. DuBois' successors, the Duke of Bourbon and Cardinal Fleury, pursued the same goal. The Treaties of Vienna checked progress toward an understanding; but those treaties failed to effect a real settlement between Spain and Austria. During the period of the Congress of Soissons, France exerted every effort to break down the Austro-Spanish Alliance, coöperating wholeheartedly with Great Britain to achieve that end. These efforts succeeded when, in the spring of 1729, the Spanish queen was at last convinced that the emperor had no intention of fulfilling his engagements, and that she could not secure an establishment for her son in Italy without the aid of France and England. Through personal appeals to the Queen of Spain, Cardinal Fleury helped persuade the Spanish monarchs to sign the Treaty of Seville, but only by secretly promising to renew the pledge of French support for a subsequent negotiation to arrange the restitution of Gibraltar.[1]

1. Two of Fleury's letters to Queen Elizabeth, and a general survey of Franco-Spanish engagements on Gibraltar, 1729–1733, are contained in a "Mémoire historique sur Gibraltar," written by one Gauthier de la Ceyronie, composed in November 1782, in M.A.E., Mémoires et Documents, Espagne, vol. 208, fols. 123–148.

In the summer of 1728, shortly after the opening of the Congress of Soissons, Walpole and Stanhope informed Newcastle of their suspicions that France intended to give Spain just such a declaration. To quote: "We apprehend from some Dark Expressions that have fallen as well from the Cardinal as Count Sinzendorf that altho' it is really intended

The draft of a secret declaration on Gibraltar was forwarded to the French minister Brancas on September 13, 1729. It stated that, though the French king considered himself bound by his several guarantees sustaining England's possession of the Rock, France did not want to see King Philip lose the advantage he had gained through the letter of King George I. On the bases of that letter and the previous pledge of good offices in the secret treaty of March 1721, the French king promised "to continue to employ without interruption his most pressing offices to engage the King of Great Britain to restore as soon as it shall be possible Gibraltar and its dependencies to the power of His Catholic Majesty," and that he would "never desist from that demand until His Catholic Majesty had obtained entire satisfaction on that point."[2]

The declaration as drawn did not satisfy the Spanish king, who wanted to eliminate any reference to the French guarantees of Gibraltar to England. His objections prevented its formal delivery until long after the Treaty of Seville had been signed. Yet the knowledge that France was willing to renew in strong terms her promise of good offices respecting Gibraltar, coupled with the beginnings of a close confidential relationship between the Bourbon courts, was undoubtedly an important factor in securing Philip's assent to the Treaty of Seville and to its silence with regard to Gibraltar.[3]

This secret interchange between the French and Spanish courts during the fall of 1729 provided the germ for

that His Majesty should have a full and effectual Confirmation and Guaranty of all his Possessions, according to former Treaties, yet France, in order to manage Spain in some measure, and to make them more easy and save their own honour, on account of the private Treaty which the D. of Orleans concluded with that Crown in Mar. 1721, may have a Design to give secretly, without our knowledge or Intervention, Spain to understand that the promise of good offices with regard to Gibraltar will still subsist. . . ." Cypher letter to Newcastle, July 20, 1728, Add. MSS. 32,757, fol. 125.

2. "Projet de declaration sur Gibraltar, envoyé au Marquis de Brancas le 13 Septembre 1729," Cor. Pol., Espagne, vol. 365, fol. 326.

3. Correspondence in French archives, especially Chauvelin to Brancas, Paris, Dec. 14, 1729, Cor. Pol., Espagne, vol. 365, fols. 331–335.

the negotiation of the first Family Compact, concluded four years later. Nearly two years were to pass, however, before the Bourbon powers made any further progress in their efforts to conclude a family alliance. The principal obstacle to a closer union was the execution of the Italian settlement provided by the Treaty of Seville, a treaty that had been a compromise unsatisfactory to all parties. Under the terms of the treaty, an Italian expedition on behalf of Don Carlos, to obtain for him the investiture of the duchies of Parma and Tuscany, was to be undertaken within six months of ratification. France and Great Britain agreed to supply ships to help convey and support this expedition, and also approved the introduction of Spanish troops to protect Don Carlos. If the emperor resisted the expedition by force, Spain was assured of military aid by the Seville signatories. Despite continuous negotiations, nothing was done during the year 1730.

Since the period following the Treaty of Seville marked the turning point in the previously existing European relationships, a brief review of the situation may properly be inserted here. The most important trend during 1730 was the rift between England and France. Signs of a rift in their close diplomatic alliance had not been wanting for several years past, but the real break in friendship between the two nations came after the signature of the Seville treaty.

Following the ratification of the Treaty of Seville, the British continually asserted their willingness to execute their obligations thereunder, but in so doing they did not want to become involved in a general European war, which might threaten Hanover. Prussia was on the verge of war with England, and it was feared that a clash of arms with the emperor might lead to such a general war. Furthermore, England was not disposed to support the Italian venture until Spain had stopped her depredations on the ships of the South Sea Company, and had delivered up the effects of foreign merchants from the recently arrived galleons. But if France had shown a real willingness to exe-

cute the treaty, it could have been performed within the
agreed time by Britain.

France disliked the treaty because privately she opposed the establishment of Spanish power in Italy in any
case, and because she too dreaded a war. Since the prime
objective of Cardinal Fleury at this time was to conciliate
Spain and perfect a Bourbon union, he could not risk giving offense to the Queen of Spain by directly opposing the
Italian expedition. Fleury, therefore, did the opposite; he
proposed and encouraged plans for a grand offensive war
against the emperor, the primary scene of which would be
staged in Germany. He well knew that the British would
not support such a proposal, and by suggesting a campaign in the Austrian Netherlands he estopped Dutch
support of the project. When her allies refused to back
such a grandiose scheme, France insinuated to Spain that
it was the English and Dutch who were blocking the execution of the treaty. By such diplomatic finesse, France
hoped to stay out of a war. At the same time, France
aimed to conciliate Spain and to break up the new reconciliation between Spain and Britain.

Spain continued to protest against the failure of France
and England to execute the Treaty of Seville. Her protests were especially bitter against the English, although
Patiño and the Spanish ambassador at Paris privately admitted on several occasions that Britain had been much
more sincere in her overtures than France. Actually the
rancor against Britain was chiefly owing to the old sores,
Gibraltar and trade. The pro-French party at the Spanish court was gaining in strength; only Patiño and the
queen seem to have favored England, and they not for
love, but because the British fleet was needed to support
the Italian venture. In reality, as several private reports
from Spain showed, the Spanish themselves were not prepared for the Italian expedition; Spain probably could
not have undertaken it in 1730 even if Great Britain and
France had been ready.

The emperor, who opposed the entry of Spanish garrisons into Italy, might have used force to prevent their introduction even though they were accompanied by a joint Anglo-French supporting expedition. Since his chief worry concerned his succession, however, there seemed to be a strong possibility that he would settle the Italian questions as Spain desired, if the powers would guarantee the Austrian succession to his daughter. In September 1730 the British minister at Vienna was instructed to open negotiations with the emperor for a settlement on this basis.[4] Although England attempted to conceal this move from France and Spain, the Bourbon powers suspected that such a negotiation was in progress; these suspicions were not calculated to improve the existing relations between Great Britain, France, and Spain.

By the end of 1730 diplomatic relationships in Europe were drifting back into the traditional channels, with Britain and the Empire approaching a reconciliation and Franco-Spanish ties being strengthened. This new alignment definitely upset the precarious balance of 1718–1730, in which a close Anglo-French union had been the chief ingredient.[5]

The year 1731 opened inauspiciously for Anglo-Spanish relations. France had appointed as her *ministre de famille* Count Rottembourg, who had previously served in Spain. Rottembourg's written instructions were sketchy, but it is probable that he carried with him authority to initiate the negotiation of a new family alliance. He reached the Spanish court on January 13, and soon after his arrival formally delivered the confidential declaration on Gibraltar which had been substantially agreed to at the time of the signature of the Treaty of Seville. In addition, Rottembourg was at once granted special privileges in audiences with the Catholic monarchs.[6] Shortly thereafter,

4. Coxe, *Sir Robert Walpole,* III, 33–39.

5. This review is based principally upon correspondence in S.P. 78: 194, 195 and S.P. 94:103, 104, 105. See also Williams, "The Foreign Policy of England under Walpole," Part VI, *Eng. Hist. Rev.,* XVI (July 1901), 439–451.

6. Baudrillart, *Philippe V et la cour de France,* IV, 65–68.

on January 28, the Spanish minister at Paris, Castelar, announced that because of the failure of Britain and France to execute their obligations under the Treaty of Seville, his master considered himself no longer bound by it.[7] Despite these developments which threatened to nullify the Anglo-Spanish accord that had silenced the question of Gibraltar for the time being, other factors entered into the diplomatic tangle in the ensuing two years and prevented the complete undoing of the Seville negotiation. During this period, the English and French waged a keen duel for Spanish favor. Though the French won eventually, their victory was a rather empty one. Both Keene and Rottembourg were instructed to sow seeds of discord in Spain against their rival governments. In June, Rottembourg frankly expressed French distaste for the Treaty of Seville, and hinted to the Spanish that it might not be safe for them to entrust the passage of Don Carlos to a British fleet, for he might be held as a hostage for the performance of British commercial servitudes upon Spain. In the month following, Newcastle wrote Keene that there were movements of French troops toward the Atlantic coast apparently threatening an invasion of England; proper steps had been taken, however, to forestall any such attempt. So far had relations between the late and still nominal allies been strained![8]

The English negotiations with the emperor produced a new Treaty of Vienna, signed on March 6, 1731, that provided for the execution of the Italian provisions of the Treaty of Seville, as well as for a new general accord between Britain and Austria. This treaty was promptly communicated to Spain, with the result that on June 6 Spain and England signed a joint declaration at Seville, renewing in full force all portions of the Seville treaty between the two nations. Shortly thereafter Spain herself

7. Cantillo, *Tratados de paz y de comercio*, pp. 257–258.
8. Newcastle to Keene, March 26/Apr. 6, 1731, S.P. 94:109. Keene to Newcastle, June 29, 1731, S.P. 94:107. Newcastle to Keene, July 2/13, 1731, S.P. 94:109.

acceded to the new Treaty of Vienna.[9] As a result of this negotiation, the establishment of Don Carlos in Italy was undertaken with the assistance of a British fleet in the fall of 1731. Anglo-Spanish relations appeared to have improved, although Spain delayed the settlement of the trade controversies.

At the same time, apparent bitterness marked the negotiations between Spain and France, despite the efforts of Rottembourg. Queen Elizabeth expressed her hostility toward the French in no uncertain terms because of their opposition to the execution of the Seville treaty; and she was ably seconded by Patiño, who, though no friend of England, had an equal distaste for France.[10] A further check on the Franco-Spanish entente during 1731 and 1732 was the constant ill health and melancholia of the Spanish king, which made future Spanish policy unpredictable. Despite the apparent and actual distrust between the two Bourbon courts, their projected alliance gradually took shape. In August of 1731, Keene reported his suspicion that a declaration on the subject of Gibraltar had been made by France.[11] Actually, after the British had given the necessary aid to the Italian expedition in the fall of 1731, their utility to the Spanish court ceased, and Spanish goodwill toward England correspondingly decreased.

During the following year, France pushed the negotiation of the projected alliance with all her powers of persuasion. It had practically assumed its final form by the end of 1732. By August of that year Keene was convinced that an entente between the Bourbon powers was taking shape, and that the French were using every pretext to get themselves into the good graces of the Spanish court and to break up the recent Anglo-Spanish harmony.[12] Keene correctly forecast that the result of the negotiation

9. Cantillo, *Tratados de paz y de comercio*, pp. 258–271.

10. Keene to Newcastle, July 13 and Sept. 2, 1731, S.P. 94:108.

11. Keene to Newcastle, Aug. 23, 1731, Add. MSS. 32,774, fol. 170.

12. Keene to Newcastle, Aug. 19, 1732, S.P. 94:112. Keene to Lord Harrington (Wm. Stanhope), Aug. 29, 1732, S.P. 94:112.

would be largely negative. "Their [the French] business then," he wrote, "is only to separate Spain from Us, and do nothing for them [the Spanish] afterwards, of which Patiño appears as much convinced as I am."[13]

At the close of 1732, one of the few unsettled points in the proposed compact was that relating to Gibraltar. France in her draft had already promised to use force if necessary to aid in the recovery of Gibraltar for Spain. To this promise, King Philip attempted to add a clause stipulating that this force should be provided whenever the Spanish king thought the situation in Europe favorable for undertaking an attack on the fortress, or whenever some special occurrence, especially that of the launching of a joint war by the two powers, might offer itself. This clause, which would have left the initiative in the hands of the capricious Spanish king, was termed by Chauvelin "neither decent nor tolerable" for France.[14] Indeed, France would have preferred to renew only her empty promise of continued good offices for the restitution of the Rock; but the French realized that King Philip would not enter into an alliance without a stronger stipulation on Gibraltar. Rottembourg in July 1733 temporarily convinced the Spanish that the provision for aid by force should be limited by the words "lorsque les circonstances seroient jugées favorables," but this clause was subsequently dropped.[15] It is most evident that France had neither the intention to carry the article regarding Gibraltar into immediate execution, nor the expectation ever to use more than the good offices promised in the first portion of the article. This article, in its final form in the treaty signed on November 7, 1733, reads as follows:

His Most Christian Majesty will employ without interruption his most pressing offices to engage the King of Great

13. Keene to Charles Delafaye, Oct. 31, 1732, S.P. 94:112.
14. Marginal notation on the Spanish reply to the French draft of January 1733, Cor. Pol., Espagne, vol. 403, fol. 323.
15. Rottembourg to Chauvelin, July 26, 1733, Cor. Pol., Espagne, vol. 405, fol. 386.

Britain to restore as soon as it shall be possible to the power of his Catholic Majesty the town and dependencies of Gibraltar and he will never desist from this demand until his Catholic Majesty has obtained entire satisfaction on this point, either by the effective restitution of this place to his power, or by assurances which shall be satisfactory to him that it will be restored to him within a fixed and determined time, his Most Christian Majesty even promising to use force if it shall be necessary.[16]

The signature of the Treaty of the Escurial, or first Family Compact as it has been termed, had been delayed through most of 1733 by the continued illness of King Philip, by the mutual distrust still existing between the French and Spanish courts and ministers, and especially by the opposition of Patiño. Its conclusion was finally precipitated by the hostilities between France and the emperor over the Polish succession.[17] When it was finally signed, the French and Spanish governments were looking forward to a general campaign against the imperial forces, both in Germany and Italy. Perhaps Spain hoped that Britain would be embroiled in this general war on the side of the emperor, and that an excuse would accordingly be furnished for a joint and immediate attack on Gibraltar. The maritime powers, however, refused to be drawn into the war; and no move against Gibraltar was undertaken. The result of the campaigns in 1734 included the conquest of southern Italy by Spanish troops and the subsequent

16. Translation from copy in the French archives, Cor. Pol., Espagne, vol. 408, fol. 42.

17. On the death of Augustus II, Elector of Saxony and King of Poland, France championed the claims of Stanislaus Leszczinski, the father-in-law of Louis XV. Russia and Austria supported the son of Augustus. Hostilities began in the fall of 1733. France and Spain, concerting their military activities even before the signature of the Family Compact, decisively defeated the Austrians in Italy, and France captured Lorraine from the imperial dominions in Germany. The subsequent conflict between France and Spain over the division of the spoils in Italy did much to nullify the effectiveness of the first Family Compact; for, regardless of the Bourbon alliance, France followed her traditional policy of opposition to the extension of Spanish power in Italy.

elevation of Don Carlos as King of Naples. Another result, more important for Anglo-Spanish relations, was renewed distrust and discord between the allies France and Spain; so that the Family Compact remained largely nominal in its effectiveness.[18]

Keene's reports to his government during 1733 left no doubt that a Franco-Spanish entente was in progress. Keene had purchased the services of a clerk in the Spanish secretary's office, close to the secret channels of information. At Paris, the British minister Waldegrave was continually assured by the cardinal and Chauvelin that no negotiation with Spain was on foot, and the French attempted to deny the existence of the Escurial treaty for some time after its signature. The resourceful Keene was successful in securing a substantially accurate copy of the secret alliance only a few weeks after its signature, and Newcastle and others at London were at once convinced of its genuineness.[19] The British ministers were greatly agitated by this discovery; steps were at once taken to place the navy on guard against a Franco-Spanish attack, and also to warn and strengthen the garrison at Gibraltar. Newcastle also attempted to secure a confirmation of Keene's information through Waldegrave at Paris. As late as April 1734, Cardinal Fleury categorically assured Waldegrave "that France was not engaged with them [the Spanish] directly or indirectly against any of His Majesty's Dominions, and of himself he named particularly Gibraltar and Port Mahon without putting me to the trouble of sifting it out of him."[20] Waldegrave doubted the cardinal's sincerity, but the ministers at London had no uncertainty whatsoever. They were even more strongly

18. My remarks upon the general situation during 1733 and 1734 are based upon the correspondence in the Newcastle Papers, Add. MSS. 32,782–32,784; and in the Record Office volumes, S.P. 94:116–118.

19. Keene to Newcastle, Nov. 19, 1733, with enclosures. The original of this letter is in Add. MSS. 32,783; and copies are to be found in Add. MSS. 35,883, fols. 164–167, and in S.P. 103:111.

20. Waldegrave to Newcastle, April 29, 1734, Add. MSS. 32,784, fol. 409.

convinced of the existence of the Bourbon alliance and of its provisions against Gibraltar, and the French attempts to deceive in the matter only widened the breach in Anglo-French relations.

The execution of the first Family Compact concluded an epoch in the diplomatic history of Gibraltar. It marked the overthrow of the preceding pattern of England's continental diplomacy—the Quadruple Alliance, the Anglo-French Alliance, and the recently renewed friendship between England and Spain. Despite the Treaty of Seville, Philip of Spain did not consider that he had relinquished to England his "pretensions" to Gibraltar; and he certainly had not relinquished his hopes of recovering the fortress. He now based those hopes on the good offices and military aid of France, rather than upon direct negotiations with Britain. At the very time when France was promising such aid, reports were not lacking that the French secretly preferred that both Gibraltar and Minorca remain in English possession, not only because they kept alive Spanish resentment toward England and increased Spanish dependence upon France, but also because Spanish resentment over British possession of those places had decreased British trade to Spain and thereby increased that of France.[21] In the Escurial treaty, Gibraltar was the "bait" to lure Spain into French arms;[22] the French promise on Gibraltar was a decisive factor in overcoming Spanish reluctance to a family alliance with France.

21. Secret report, dated Feb. 13, 1734, drawn up at Paris and sent by Horatio Walpole to the Duke of Newcastle, Add. MSS. 32,784, fols. 355–356.

22. A copy of Keene's translation of the treaty of Nov. 7, 1733, in the Hardwicke Papers (Add. MSS. 35,883, fols. 164–167) bears the following marginal note: "This came from a clerk in Patiño's office. . . . It is the first draft of the Family Compact which ever fell my way. It appears that Gibraltar was the constant *Bait*." The author of this note was probably Philip Yorke (1720–1790), 2nd Earl of Hardwicke.

V

LOCAL PROBLEMS AT GIBRALTAR
1728–1734

THE preliminary agreements that terminated the brief siege of Gibraltar in 1727 apparently restored Great Britain's possession of the Rock to the *status quo* in effect prior to 1725, as defined in Article Ten of the Anglo-Spanish Treaty of Utrecht. After the Treaty of Seville, Spain abandoned for the time being her effort to regain Gibraltar through direct diplomatic negotiations with England. With the execution of the first Family Compact, the Spanish pinned their hopes for the recovery of the fortress on French aid. Nevertheless, because of the survival and intensification of disputes over local problems, Gibraltar continued to be an active and irritating ingredient in Anglo-Spanish diplomatic relations.

The most serious controversy that arose in 1728 concerned the territorial jurisdiction of Gibraltar. During the siege of 1727, the Spanish advanced their lines on to the narrow neck of land connecting the Rock and the mainland. In the Convention of the Pardo, the Spanish agreed to raise their siege works, withdraw their troops (presumably to their old lines), and "restore" the situation existing before the siege began.[1] Even before the Convention of the Pardo was signed, the Spanish began to execute these steps; and in turn the English withdrew their blockading force and the extra troops sent to bolster the garrison.[2] But instead of withdrawing all their troops to their old positions, the Spanish insisted on keeping a skeleton force of 130 men at a distance of six hundred *toises*

1. See above, p. 93.
2. Keene to Newcastle, Feb. 27, 1728, Add. MSS. 32,754, fols. 316–317. Newcastle to Portmore, March 9/20, 1728, C.O. 91:1.

(1260 yards) from the foremost English fortifications. Lord Portmore, the governor, assumed that Keene at Madrid had negotiated an agreement limiting the territorial jurisdiction of Gibraltar to that distance. Keene promptly denied that he had entered into any such arrangement. He agreed with Portmore that, although the Treaty of Utrecht did not grant the English any territorial jurisdiction beyond the base of the Rock, the safety of the fortress and common practice among nations required that there be no military occupation by the Spanish within cannon-shot of the fortifications. The Duke of Newcastle assured Keene that this was the correct viewpoint, and that the British assumed that the Spanish had always accepted it, as they had never previously posted troops within cannon-shot of the fortifications during English possession.[3]

To resolve this dispute, the British, French, Austrian, and Spanish ministers at Paris drafted a *minute* late in March 1728 to clarify the provision of the Pardo Convention governing the local situation at Gibraltar. This new agreement stipulated that the Spanish should withdraw all of their troops to the lines occupied before 1725 as soon as the English reduced the garrison to its peace-time status, with the understanding that the proper limits of the British and Spanish lines would be settled at the Congress of Soissons. This *minute* was forwarded to Keene, with instructions to insist that Spain at least agree to postpone any discussion of the territorial jurisdiction of Gibraltar until the Congress of Soissons, and in the meantime withdraw all troops to their old lines. The Spanish court approved this *minute* on its receipt at Madrid.[4]

When Spain was frustrated in her effort to bring the question of Gibraltar's restitution before the congress, that body made no attempt to settle the problem of territorial jurisdiction. Actually, the Spanish refused to with-

3. Newcastle to Keene, March 7/18, 1728, Add. MSS. 32,754, fols. 432–433.

4. Horatio Walpole to Keene, March 26, 1728; Newcastle to Keene, March 25/April 5, 1728; Walpole to Newcastle, April 5, 1728; Keene to Newcastle, April 10, 1728; Add. MSS. 32,755, fols. 6–14, 74, 97, 155–160.

draw to their old lines as a preliminary to a boundary settlement, and continued to maintain a skeleton line within
three-quarters of a mile of the British guns. Keene delivered a sharp protest to the Spanish Secretary de la Paz
about this violation of the Pardo Convention and subsequent *minute*. The Spaniard retorted that it had only been
agreed not to "break ground" within the disputed area.[5]
This controversy over territorial jurisdiction remained in
abeyance during the Congress of Soissons and the Seville
negotiation, only to be revived two years later when it became a contributory factor in disrupting the Anglo-Spanish reconciliation of 1729.

Another vexing problem concerned the interchange of
goods and supplies between Spain and Gibraltar. On the
eve of the Congress of Soissons, Spain cut off all communication between Gibraltar and the Spanish mainland,
both by land and by sea, in direct contravention to the
terms of the Treaty of Utrecht. On May 28, 1728, a
Spanish edict prohibited all communication between Spain
and the Barbary states, allegedly because of the danger of
infection from the plague. Since Gibraltar by necessity received supplies from Barbary, Spain proceeded to forbid
all intercourse with Gibraltar, the prohibition being based
on the above order. At this very time, the British ministry
made an effort to propitiate Spain by sending orders, via
Keene, for the eviction of all Jews and Moors from Gibraltar. This naturally pleased the Spanish; but when
they showed no disposition either to withdraw from their
advanced lines or to permit supplies to reach Gibraltar
from the adjacent country, Keene withheld the execution
of these orders. When Keene informed the governor that
he had received such instructions, Clayton advised that he
felt the continuance of communication with Barbary for
supplies to be necessary, and preferable to relying on
Spanish sources even if available. The eviction of the
Moors and Jews would probably have disrupted relations

5. Newcastle to Keene, May 17/28, 1728, Add. MSS. 32,756, fols. 11–
12. Keene to Newcastle, May 24, 1728, Add. MSS. 32,755, fols. 541–543.

with the Barbary states and cut off that source of supply.[6] The policy of quarantining Gibraltar, initiated in the summer of 1728 on the ground that trade with Barbary threatened to introduce the plague into Spain, continued to be a standing pretext of the Spanish throughout the century for not permitting the intercourse between the fortress and Spain provided for by the Treaty of Utrecht.[7]

The Spanish continued to occupy posts within 1260 yards of the British garrison and to prevent all communication between Gibraltar and Spanish territory until 1730. In the fall of that year, when English preparations were under way to assist the Spanish occupation of the Italian duchies, the Spanish issued orders to re-open communication by land so that the garrison might be supplied with provisions from Spain. At this time three British regiments, intended for participation in the Italian expedition on behalf of Spain, were quartered at Gibraltar; Spain could scarcely refuse to allow local provisions to reach them. Despite the above order the Spanish on various pretexts practically nullified its execution, permitting only two shipments of cattle to reach the garrison by land. After that, Gibraltar's communication with the mainland was again absolutely severed.[8]

6. Newcastle to Governor Clayton, April 16/27, 1728, C.O. 91:1. Newcastle to Keene, May 17/28, 1728; and Keene to Newcastle, May 31, 1728, Add. MSS. 32,756, fols. 11–12, 41–42. Governor Clayton to Keene, July 1/12, 1728; and added note of Keene in transmitting this letter to Newcastle, July 26, 1728, Add. MSS. 32,757, fols. 164–165. Newcastle to Keene, July 29/Aug. 9, 1728, Add. MSS. 32,757, fols. 317–318. Townshend to Keene, Aug. 15/26, 1728, Add. MSS. 32,757, fol. 468. Keene to Newcastle, Sept. 15, 1728, Add. MSS. 32,758, fol. 19.

7. In 1787, when Floridablanca composed a long treatise on the proper course of Spanish policy, he advocated the continuous use of this pretext of quarantine to cut off all trade between Gibraltar and the Spanish coast and thus help to make Gibraltar commercially useless. See D. Andrés Muriel (ed.), Gobierno del rey Carlos III, ó instrucción reservada . . . (Paris, 1838), No. 339, pp. 372–373.

8. Keene to Newcastle, Sept. 4 and Nov. 17, 1730, S.P. 94:104. Newcastle to Keene, Oct. 5/16 and Nov. 30/Dec. 11, 1730, S.P. 94:105. General Joseph Sabine to Newcastle, Nov. 21/Dec. 2, 1730, enclosed in Keene's letter to Newcastle, Dec. 8, 1730, Add. MSS. 35,883, fols. 71–79. The origi-

With the improvement of Anglo-Spanish relations in view of the impending Italian expedition, the English seized their opportunity once more to press the Spanish to withdraw out of cannon-shot of the English fortifications. When Keene applied to the Spanish ministers, he found them not only determined to prevent any more Spanish supplies from reaching Gibraltar, but also as unwilling as ever to withdraw to their old lines. According to Keene, Patiño had promised verbally, at the time of the signature of the Treaty of Seville in the previous year, and in the presence of both Keene and Stanhope, that Spain would withdraw her troops from the disputed area. Patiño apparently felt himself under no obligation to fulfill this verbal agreement, and he protested to Keene that any mention of the question of Gibraltar to the king might upset all the engagements between the two nations.[9]

Spain now decided to settle the dispute over territorial jurisdiction in her own behalf by undertaking the construction of permanent fortifications a little to the rear of the temporary line that the Spanish had been holding, and slightly under a mile (1640 yards) from the English outposts. Keene protested to Patiño, insisting that the *minute* arranged in connection with the Pardo agreement obligated the Spanish to withdraw to their old lines. The French and Austrian ministers, who had helped draft that agreement, subsequently had disagreed on its interpretation. Rottembourg had asserted that this understanding implied that the Spanish should withdraw to their ancient posts, which were distant about a cannon-shot fired *à toute volée*, a distance then reckoned to be about five thousand yards. Konigsegg, however, had held that the Spanish need only retire to the distance of a cannon-shot fired *de point en blanc*, or about 450 yards. Spain had naturally adopted Konigsegg's opinion, which had certainly never

nal of Keene's letter is in S.P. 94:104, in which the correct date, Dec. 8, is given; in the Hardwicke Papers it was copied as of Oct. 8.

9. Keene to Newcastle, Nov. 17, 1730, S.P. 94:104.

been accepted by Britain; and Patiño told Keene that his Catholic Majesty had every right to construct whatever works he chose on land that was his.[10]

General Joseph Sabine, who had recently replaced Clayton as governor of Gibraltar, immediately ordered a survey of the new Spanish works and their possible threat to the fortress. In his report to Newcastle he stated that the principal result of the new works would be to cut off all communication by land with the fortress and to prevent any sallies from the garrison in time of war. Secondly, the new Spanish batteries commanded the safest anchoring places before the town and might seriously hinder its communication by sea. Fire from the Spanish batteries could reach a good portion of the British fortifications. Lastly, the Spanish could prevent the English from making any use of the peninsula of level land connecting Gibraltar with the mainland, and could cut off communication with the back of the mountain.[11]

The construction of the new Spanish fortifications within easy range of the cannon of the fortress thoroughly aroused the British government. Keene worked hard to get the Spanish to discontinue these works, but to no avail. Patiño would agree only to an experiment of a cannon-shot, to be fired point blank, which would, of course, have fallen far short of the Spanish lines.[12] To settle the question Keene was authorized, in January 1731, to negotiate with the Spanish in regard to the territorial jurisdiction of Gibraltar, on the basis of complete demolition of the new fortifications and withdrawal of the Spanish lines beyond the furthest range of the artillery of the British fortifications.[13] Shortly thereafter, Newcastle wrote Keene to insinuate to the Spanish, in the strongest manner, that they could not expect England to perform her engage-

10. Keene to Newcastle, Dec. 8, 1730, S.P. 94:104.
11. Sabine to Newcastle, Dec. 4/15, 1730, enclosing the report of Captain Jonas Moore, an engineer at Gibraltar, C.O. 91:9.
12. Keene to Newcastle, Jan. 10, 1731, Add. MSS. 35,883, fol. 107.
13. Newcastle to Keene, Jan. 1/12, 1731, S.P. 94:109.

ments in favor of Spain (that is, aid to the Italian expedition) unless and until Spain discontinued her hostile works before Gibraltar.[14] Before Keene could communicate to the Spanish his new authority to negotiate, their minister at Paris announced that Spain no longer felt herself bound by the Treaty of Seville; and all that the Spaniards would agree to do was to level the earthwork batteries erected during the late siege, which were between the new permanent fortifications and the British lines. Keene carried his threats so far as to tell the Spanish ministers that he "could not answer for what the Governor [of Gibraltar] might do for the defense of the Place, if They continued their Works."[15]

When Newcastle transmitted a copy of the Anglo-Austrian treaty of March 6 to Keene, he enclosed the draft of a declaration on Gibraltar. This declaration proposed that the Spaniards demolish all their works and withdraw to a distance of 4500 to 5000 yards, this being better than "to leave room for a Dispute about what is a Canon Shot; and it is generally allowed that the Random Shot of a Canon is about that Distance." The declaration also specified that all other matters concerning Gibraltar be returned to the status as regulated by Article Ten of the Treaty of Utrecht, including the granting of constant provision by sea from Spanish ports, and emergency provision by land, when that by sea was impossible. Keene was instructed to tell the Spanish that a renewal of England's obligations under the Treaty of Seville was contingent upon the acceptance of this declaration, but it does not appear that such acceptance was to be made a *sine qua non* of the negotiation.[16]

The Spanish ministers were entirely willing to renew the Treaty of Seville, and to arrange all other matters in dispute with Britain save those regarding Gibraltar,

14. Newcastle to Keene, Jan. 14/25, 1731, S.P. 94:109.
15. Keene to Newcastle, Feb. 18 and March 3, 1731, S.P. 94:107.
16. Newcastle to Keene, April 15/26, 1731, and enclosed declaration, S.P. 94:109.

"which could not be touched upon," as Keene reported. Privately, Patiño told Keene that there was no possible hope of getting King Philip to give up the new works before Gibraltar, for they "kept Gibraltar itself out of his Sight and Thoughts." If England attempted to insist on the acceptance of the declaration outlined above, Patiño asserted, the result would be "to break off all sort of Negotiation, and even friendship with the Catholic King, who would let himself be cut to pieces rather than consent to desist from those Works." Keene himself despaired of any amicable settlement on the basis of the declaration.[17]

Keene's further instances to the Spanish ministers finally elicited a formal reply from the Spanish minister de la Paz on May 25. In answer to the argument that the cession of any fortress implied the control of all territory within cannon range, de la Paz insisted that Gibraltar had not been obtained by England either by inheritance or by conquest, but by grant from the King of Spain in the Treaty of Utrecht. England could claim only what had been accorded her by that grant, which included no territorial jurisdiction whatsoever beyond the town and fortifications. Not only were the new Spanish works on Spanish territory, but also Spain might properly claim title to all of the land outside the English fortifications. De la Paz asserted that Spain would adhere to the strict interpretation of the Utrecht treaty on the matter of communication between Gibraltar and Spain; land communication would be permitted in case of necessity—and since the judgment of necessity remained with Spain, she could always refuse it—and communication by sea would not be interrupted except when it was necessary to restrict it to prevent infection from the plague. This latter exception, which the Spanish had already adopted as an excuse to prevent trade by sea between Spanish ports and Gibraltar, was not mentioned by the Treaty of Utrecht, and was a clear evasion of Spanish obligations. Finally, de la Paz insisted that if Great Britain continued to press Spain on the

17. Keene to Newcastle, May 2, 1731, S.P. 94:107.

question of the works before Gibraltar, not only would this disrupt all relations between the two nations, but also the Spanish king would feel justified in reviving and pressing his former demands for the restitution of the fortress.[18]

Shortly before the above reply had been delivered, Patiño, whose relations with Keene were friendly and almost confidential at this time, had privately urged the British minister to drop all mention of Gibraltar. To continue such a demand would drive the Spanish king to a French alliance, an eventuality that Patiño was as anxious to avoid as were the British. Patiño repeated the same arguments to the Dutch minister, Vander Meer, urging him to try to persuade Keene to abandon all mention of Gibraltar in the negotiation then in progress to revive the terms of the Seville treaty.[19]

Under the circumstances, Keene felt that there was nothing to do but to drop the demand for a declaration about Gibraltar, and he therefore notified the ministry at London that he had done so. Newcastle approved this step; but he urged Keene to continue his offices, although not making them contingent upon the main negotiation, to secure some written promise to destroy the siege works which still remained between the Spanish and English fortifications, and a statement from Spain that the new line was solely for defensive purposes and for the prevention of contraband trade.[20] The latter statement was never made, but a satisfactory agreement for the demolition of the temporary siege works was reached by the end of the year.[21]

The question of the territorial jurisdiction of Gibraltar was left unsettled, and remained so for nearly a century afterward. It had threatened to disrupt the negotiation for the acceptance by Spain of the Treaty of Vienna, and the revival of the Anglo-Spanish terms of the Treaty of

18. Keene to Newcastle, May 26, 1731, Add. MSS. 35,883, fols. 150–153.
19. Keene to Newcastle, May 20, 1731; and Keene to Charles Delafaye, May 20, 1731 (private letter), S.P. 94:107.
20. Newcastle to Keene, May 31/June 11, 1731, S.P. 94:109.
21. Keene to Sabine, Dec. 25, 1731, S.P. 94:108.

Seville. The British withdrew their demand for a declaration about Gibraltar, not because they were convinced of the justice of the Spanish position—indeed, they were highly incensed at the action of Spain in refusing to negotiate a reasonable settlement[22]—but because they desired to maintain the improved Anglo-Spanish relations of 1731, and feared that further insistence might revive demands for Gibraltar's restitution and abet French efforts to negotiate a Bourbon alliance. In addition, former Governor Clayton and Sir Charles Wager testified, at a special meeting of the Privy Council called to consider the question, that the new Spanish works would be of no service to Spain in case of an attack on Gibraltar, and that they were not a real hindrance to the garrison. Orders were sent to Governor Sabine not to interfere with the Spanish unless they attempted to advance their lines.[23]

The British defenses at Gibraltar were in good order by 1730; but the town had suffered greatly in the late siege, and most of the buildings were in a deplorable condition. The civil population numbered less than eight hundred, of whom the majority were Genoese, Moors, and Jews. The military garrison consisted of six regiments, totaling about thirty-one hundred men and officers. The soldiers were reported to be very restless, and much given to desertion. Keene, who visited Gibraltar in November 1730, wrote that "the Houses are so very bad and the poor Troops so ill accommodated, that I could wish for their

22. Keene in particular was deeply chagrined at the outcome of this negotiation over the territorial jurisdiction of Gibraltar. The following extract epitomizes Keene's feelings about his negotiations with the Spanish court; while not referring specifically to Gibraltar, it might well be applied to the several negotiations concerning that place. (By "We," Keene means the Spanish ministry.) "For here We do what We think proper without conculting Treaties till the work is over, and then We set about chicaning to prove what We have done to be agreeable to Treaty, and when We can't make it out We content ourselves with swearing it is so, as you must have seen in a thousand answers to the Offices that have been passed since the Treaty of Utrecht." Keene to Delafaye, Aug. 12, 1732, S.P. 94:112.

23. Minute of the meeting of the Privy Council, May 25/June 5, 1731, C.O. 91:1.

sakes that some of them were removed to Port Mahon."[24] The Spanish economic blockade of the town not only prevented the garrison from receiving any fresh supplies from Spain, but also stopped the dispatch of mails overland to England; letters sent by sea sometimes had to wait several months for a boat. The new governor, General Sabine, recommended the eviction of the Moors and Jews, in order to conciliate the Spaniards; but, as we have already seen, Spain's determination to continue to harass and isolate Gibraltar prevented this measure from being carried through.[25]

It is difficult to estimate the volume of trade and shipping at Gibraltar at this time. The town was a free port, and no customs or other records were kept of ships that entered. Governor Kane, in answer to a questionnaire sent to him by the Board of Trade and Plantations in December 1728 asking the number of ships annually visiting the port and their nationality, responded: "It is not possible for any person to resolve this . . . but it is to be observed that the Numbers are very great, and the number of British much more than those of all other Nations Joynt." Shortly before this, a letter from Gibraltar mentioned that for ten days past no ships had been in the harbor, an almost unprecedented situation.[26] That Gibraltar was extensively utilized as a stopping place for British shipping entering the Mediterranean was doubtless true, though the town offered scant facilities either for repairing or for provisioning vessels. The Spanish "quarantine" of Gibraltar after 1728 undoubtedly greatly reduced its trade and use as a way-station for British Mediterranean trade.

A new source of friction arose early in 1733, when the Spanish registered complaints with Keene that the governor of Gibraltar had permitted three Moorish armed vessels (really corsairs) to take refuge at Gibraltar, contrary to the terms of the Treaty of Utrecht. Governor

24. Keene to Delafaye, Nov. 24, 1730, S.P. 94:104.
25. Sabine to Newcastle, June 15/26, 1730, C.O. 91:9.
26. C.O. 91:4.

Sabine assured Keene that the vessels had been driven in under stress of weather, that it would have been inhumane to refuse them shelter, and that they were immediately forced to leave when the weather had moderated. This the Spanish did not deny, but they insisted that under the Treaty of Utrecht England could not give shelter to armed Barbary vessels on any pretext, since the knowledge that such shelter was available would encourage the Moors to cruise along the Spanish coast when they otherwise might not dare. Privately, Keene sympathized with the Spanish position, asserting that if the Moors "may take a Pretext from every Gust of Wind to take shelter under our Canon, Spain will not have a fishing boat left from Barcelona to San Roque, nor shall we have a Genoese or Spaniard to bring us a Sallad to Gibraltar." But the ministry at London thought differently, and upheld Sabine's action. Several cases arose at this time in which vessels traveling between Barbary and Gibraltar and carrying provisions for the fortress were stopped and seized by the Spanish. Keene was instructed to make a strong protest, and to demand that the trade by sea with Gibraltar, as secured by treaty, be unmolested by Spain.[27] These grievances, not significant in themselves, are indicative of Spanish intentions to annoy and frustrate the English in their possession of Gibraltar.

When the Spanish assembled an expedition for an undetermined purpose during the spring of 1732, the British had some suspicion that they might try to attack Gibraltar. Keene wrote to General Sabine to be on his guard, and the following significant note was addressed to the Admiralty in London:

As to the present Armament people here are in the dark, tho' generally it is asserted for Oran, but I am humbly of Opinion that some English Ships of War at Gibraltar would not

27. Correspondence between Keene and Newcastle and Delafaye, Jan. 1733, S.P. 94:116, 118.

be an Imprudent Expense, tho' they were only Spectators of
the Debarkment at Oran.[28]

Two years later, following the signature of the Franco-
Spanish alliance, various reports of secret Spanish schemes
for a surprise attack on Gibraltar were in circulation.
These reports do not seem to have caused any great apprehension, though Sabine was warned about them. Sabine
was entirely confident that, considering the excellent state
of the defenses, Gibraltar could withstand any attack
which Spain might attempt.[29] Much as King Philip may
have yearned to attack and capture the fortress, his ministers realized that it was virtually impregnable as long as
its protection and communication by sea remained unin-
terrupted. It is very unlikely that any serious consideration was given to an attack on Gibraltar until much later
in the century.

The disputes over the territorial jurisdiction of Gibraltar, over the new Spanish works before the fortress, and
over other local problems added to the conflict between
England and Spain, a conflict founded primarily on England's failure to fulfill her promise to consider the restitution of Gibraltar and on the inroads of English commerce upon the Spanish trade monopoly in the Indies.
The new Spanish fortifications at Gibraltar, standing face
to face with the British defenses, symbolized the armed
peace that characterized Anglo-Spanish relations in the
brief interval before hostilities actually began in 1739.
Fortunately for England and for the English possession
of Gibraltar, Spain was on the downward path. A weak
king and capricious queen, neither of whom had endeavored to support the true interests of the Spanish nation,
had sapped the vigor of their adopted country and rele-

28. John Crookshanks (secretary to the English commissioners engaged in administering the Treaty of Seville) to Sir Charles Wager,
April 18, 1732, S.P. 103:111.

29. Newcastle to Sabine, March 30/April 10, 1734; and Sabine to Newcastle, July 15/26, 1734, C.O. 91:10.

gated it to the rôle of a satellite in the orbit of French diplomacy. Henceforth, the fate of Gibraltar rested primarily in the hands of France. We shall see in succeeding chapters how France utilized Gibraltar, on the one hand to hold Spain and on the other to prevent her reconciliation with Great Britain.

VI

GIBRALTAR AND THE WAR OF THE AUSTRIAN SUCCESSION

THE conclusion of the first Family Compact between France and Spain did not immediately alter the course of Anglo-Spanish diplomacy. The distrust and hatred of France generally prevalent in Spain,[1] the clash of Franco-Spanish interests in Italy, and the independent policy of the chief Spanish minister, Patiño, all tended to prevent harmonious relations and a close understanding between the Bourbon courts. On the other hand, continued British possession of Gibraltar and Minorca, as well as the disputes arising out of English trade with the Spanish Indies, made a genuine reconciliation between England and Spain equally impossible. Though Spain ceased to press her claims to Gibraltar, the failure to recover the fortress rankled, and continued to be a fundamental obstacle in her relations with Great Britain.[2]

The English never ceased to fear that Spain only

1. On this feeling of hatred for France, see the mémoire by M. Favier in *Politique de tous les cabinets de l'Europe pendant les regnes de Louis XV et de Louis XVI* (Paris, 1802), II, 281–285. Of fundamental importance in preventing coöperation between the Bourbon courts at this time was the personal dislike of Queen Elizabeth for Cardinal Fleury. See Armstrong, *Elisabeth Farnese*, p. 366.

2. The following extract, from a paper written in the spring of 1739, probably by one of the Spanish ministers, epitomizes Spanish resentment over the status of Gibraltar: "Your houses of parliament, that make such loud complaints against the Spaniards, and impute several crimes to them that never can be proved, why do they forget the just pretensions of Spain, and the promises of his Britannic majesty? Does the usurpation of Gibraltar and Port Mahon, continued for so many years, give less motives of complaint than the pretended losses of your merchants? Are the damages they have suffered greater than those caused by that usurpation? There never can be a solid and durable peace between Spain and England as long as Gibraltar and Port Mahon are under the British dominion. . . ." From Coxe, *Sir Robert Walpole*, III, 531.

awaited an opportune moment again to attempt to recover
Gibraltar by force. Keene correctly forecast that the differences between France and Spain would prevent the execution of the article in the Family Compact of 1733 relative to the recovery of Gibraltar,[3] but the British ministry
repeatedly warned the governor to be on his guard. In response to such a warning, Governor Sabine wrote in 1735
that, while the Spaniards were in no condition at the time
to threaten the fortress, "they will ever be ready to Snap
at it when a Convenient Opportunity offers, for which
Reason I shall always have a Watchfull Eye to any attempt that may be made to Surprise us."[4]

The strength and independence of Spanish diplomacy
suffered a severe blow on the death of Patiño, in November
1736. For the previous decade Patiño had exercised an increasingly strong hand in the direction of Spanish policy.
He had promoted with great ability the improvement of
Spanish trade and administration in the Indies, and it was
probably due to his inspiration that the conflict with England over that trade came to a head in 1739. Patiño had
aimed to make Spain independent of all entanglements in
her foreign relations. Though unable to prevent the signature of the first Family Compact, he had helped to prevent Spanish dependence upon France as a result of that
treaty. Patiño's successors were men of a different caliber.
By their very weakness they eliminated the danger to
England (and to Gibraltar) of an aggressive Spanish
policy.

The long dispute over British trade with Spanish America finally led to war in 1739, despite the sincere efforts of
the ministers of both powers to avoid it. Spain had ample
proof of British trade violations and aggressions in the
Indies,[5] but she did not want to defend her position by
force of arms. In England, Robert Walpole was equally

3. Armstrong, *Elisabeth Farnese,* pp. 309–312.
4. Sabine to Newcastle, Apr. 28/May 9, 1735, C.O. 91:10.
5. Vera Lee Brown, "The South Sea Company and Contraband
Trade," in *American Historical Review,* XXXI (July 1926), pp. 662–678.

anxious to avoid hostilities. He had to face a hostile and increasingly numerous war party, however, which, as in 1729, demanded a war with Spain in defense of England's Indies trade, regardless of its legality. Walpole succeeded in preventing a war in 1738; and Keene at Madrid negotiated a settlement of the trade disputes, embodied in the Convention of the Pardo, signed January 14, 1739. Parliament approved this convention in March. The British refusal to withdraw their fleet from Gibraltar, as agreed to in the convention, led to a deadlock with the Spanish court. Both nations prepared for war, which Great Britain finally declared in October 1739.[6]

The threat of war with England led Spain, in the summer of 1738, to seek a reaffirmation of the Family Compact with France. The Spanish hoped that if they were drawn into war with England, the French would at least support their efforts to reconquer Gibraltar and Minorca. In June 1738, the Spanish minister at Paris received instructions to sound the French court on the question of a new secret treaty, under which, if war were declared, a joint effort should be made to capture Gibraltar, Minorca, and Georgia. France, though willing to reaffirm her general intention to support Spain defensively, was not prepared to commit herself by a new treaty of alliance, at least not until Spain should consent to enter into a new and satisfactory treaty of commerce. The French sent a new ambassador, the Count de la Marck, to Madrid in September 1738 to pursue the negotiation of these two treaties. La Marck was cautioned, however, not to accept any Spanish proposal for an attack on Gibraltar or Minorca without referring it back to Paris; for it was feared that such a proposal, if known, might upset the peace of Europe.[7]

6. Coxe, *Kings of Spain*, III, 297–316. P. Vaucher, *Robert Walpole et la politique de Fleury, 1731–1742* (Paris, 1924), pp. 253–289. Wilson, *French Foreign Policy, 1726–1743*, pp. 283–289.

7. Baudrillart, *Philippe V et la cour de France*, IV, 467–470. *Recueil des instructions*, vol. XIIbis, *Espagne, 1722–1795*, p. 202.

The Spanish submitted their project for an alliance to the French minister Amelot at Paris late in October 1738. Article Five of this project provided for a joint attack on Gibraltar. In response, Amelot informed the Spanish minister that no treaty of alliance would be entered into without the signature, at the same time, of a treaty of commerce—a serious check, since Spain was loath to grant the commercial privileges demanded by France. To his minister at Madrid, Amelot wrote on December 8 that Article Five relative to Gibraltar must be omitted from the projected treaty. "That will be," he wrote, "the point on which you will have the most trouble to defend yourself; but it is not necessary to believe that France should ever oblige herself to make war for that." French objections to the Spanish treaty project, together with the signature of the Pardo Convention between England and Spain, led the Spanish monarchs to postpone further negotiations for the double treaty.[8]

Despite the outbreak of hostilities between Spain and England in 1739, France and Spain made little progress toward a settlement of their differences over the terms of the projected treaties, though relations were improved by a new marriage alliance between the Bourbon courts. Of course France stood ready to aid Spain if things went too badly. But Cardinal Fleury did not want a war with England, and he staved off the solicitations of Spain for a new compact that might have drawn France into the conflict.

Although France and Spain failed in their effort to negotiate a new treaty of alliance, reports to the contrary helped to fan the belligerency of England. From the beginning of 1739, the English suspected that a negotiation was in progress for a new offensive and defensive treaty of alliance between France and Spain.[9] By April they believed that the new Bourbon treaty had been virtually concluded, and that it had the recovery of Gibraltar

8. Baudrillart, *Philippe V et la cour de France*, IV, 473–479.
9. Keene to Newcastle, Jan. 14, 1739, S.P. 94:133.

as one of its paramount objectives.[10] A copy of the treaty project was obtained in Paris, and the Duke of Newcastle instructed the British ministers at Paris and Madrid to report the progress of the negotiation; in his instructions, Newcastle noted that "the article about Gibraltar was stronger, and more offensive, in the former treaty [1733], than in this."[11] Keene had already secured information about the terms of the project before the receipt of Newcastle's letter. He had been privately informed that the new Family Compact and the Treaty of Commerce had already been signed, and he observed that the new treaty was an ample proof of the "constant ill-humor, by which this Court is incessantly animated against us."[12]

Keene soon learned that, contrary to his previous information, the Franco-Spanish treaties had not yet been signed. The principal obstacle to their conclusion, he reported, was Spain's desire to secure "a greater Handle upon France, with regard to His Majesty's Possessions in the Mediterranean."[13] In mid-July he reported that few Spaniards, aside from their Catholic Majesties, had any real confidence in the intention of the French to support them in the approaching conflict. Without French assistance, Spain could hope to do nothing but fight a defensive war. While Spain was in an excellent position to defend her European area against British attack, Keene felt certain that the Spanish could not by themselves undertake an offensive war "without some miracles wrought in favour of their Finances, and the Capacitys of the Persons by whom this Country is governed at present."[14]

The reports of the British minister at Madrid confirm

10. Horatio Walpole to Robert Trevor, Apr. 17/28, 1739, *H.M.C., Buckinghamshire MSS.,* p. 28.

11. Newcastle to Keene, May 8/19, 1739, Add. MSS. 35,884, fols. 110–118. Newcastle to Waldegrave, May 8/19, 1739, *British Diplomatic Instructions,* VI, *France, 1727–1744,* pp. 219–220.

12. Keene to Newcastle, June 9, 1739, Add. MSS. 35,884, fols. 121–123.

13. Keene to Newcastle, June 29, 1739, S.P. 94:133.

14. Keene to Newcastle, July 14, 1739, S.P. 94:133.

the evidence of Spanish reluctance to begin a war with England until sure of French support. On the other hand, the knowledge that France and Spain were negotiating a new Family Compact, with the conquest of Gibraltar and Minorca among its principal objectives, undoubtedly strengthened the hand of those British ministers who, in opposition to Walpole's efforts to preserve peace, favored a war with Spain. The English did not really fear a Spanish attack on Gibraltar and Minorca. Spain could not undertake such an attack without French aid; and Cardinal Fleury, by his hesitancy toward the projected alliance with Spain, manifested his disinclination to embroil France in a general war with England by supporting an attack on Britain's Mediterranean possessions.

The Spanish presented a new draft for a treaty of alliance to France in February 1740. This draft virtually reproduced the terms of the Escurial treaty. The response of the French minister Amelot was not enthusiastic. Above all, he insisted that the Spanish must not expect that, if France joined in the war against Britain, the French would agree not to make peace before the conquest of Gibraltar.[15] Despite the objections of some of his ministers, Louis XV approved the projected treaty of alliance in June 1740, including the article relative to Gibraltar. The French king insisted, however, that the treaty be kept secret. The guiding hand of Cardinal Fleury had yet to be reckoned with. Fleury secretly objected to the treaty; and the obstinacy of the Spanish with regard to the terms of the commercial treaty, coupled with the news of the death of the Prussian king, which threatened complications in Central Europe, furnished the cardinal with a pretext to secure an indefinite postponement of the negotiations. The Spanish were so informed in September 1740.

15. Baudrillart, *Philippe V et la cour de France,* IV, 550–551. One of the most influential advisors of the French foreign office, du Theil, in a memorandum dated March 20, 1740, argued that the terms which might offend the English ought to be eliminated; in particular, he added: "Ought not the two courts be ashamed of renewing so often between themselves the article relative to Gibraltar?" *Ibid.,* IV, 551, footnote.

The astute cardinal managed to placate to a degree the chagrin of the Spanish monarchs by sending two fleets, totaling thirty vessels, to assist the Spanish in repelling England in the West Indies.[16]

After Fleury's death in January 1743, the Spanish immediately resumed their effort to negotiate a new Family Compact. The new French ambassador at Madrid, Vaureal, reported that King Philip was now firmly resolved never to make peace with England without having at least secured the return of Gibraltar.[17] Freed from the determination of the cardinal to prevent a general war between France and Great Britain (war had not been officially declared between those nations), the alliance project moved forward rapidly. A new offensive alliance between England, Austria, and Sardinia, concluded in September 1743, provided the final impetus. Lacking the restraining hand of Fleury, France surrendered completely to the demands of Spain. The Bourbon powers signed the Treaty of Fontainebleau on October 25, 1743. Under the terms of this treaty, France obligated herself to join Spain in the war against Great Britain, and not to make peace until Gibraltar and Minorca had been secured for Spain.[18]

Despite the earnest desires of Spain and the obligations of France under the Treaty of Fontainebleau, the English possession of Gibraltar does not seem to have been threatened seriously during the long general War of the Austrian Succession, which developed out of the trade war between Spain and England. Indeed, Spanish threats and feints against Gibraltar were far fewer and less real than during the decade after the siege of 1727. In June 1740 the governor of the fortress expressed no particular concern over a limited concentration of Spanish troops before Gibraltar. In sharp contrast to its earlier history, the defenses of the Rock were in good condition and the garrison

16. Baudrillart, *Philippe V et la cour de France*, IV, 557–562.

17. *Ibid.*, V, 134.

18. Armstrong, *Elisabeth Farnese*, pp. 367–369. Baudrillart, *Philippe V et la cour de France*, V, 164–165. Cantillo, *Tratados de paz y de comercio*, pp. 367–371.

well supplied during the war.[19] Spanish hopes for the recovery of the fortress depended on a favorable outcome of
the conflict in the Indies, in Italy, and in Germany. If
Britain met with general defeat, the Spanish anticipated
that she might be forced by French pressure to restore
Gibraltar and Minorca in the peace. An even greater hindrance to the recovery of Gibraltar was the continued ori-
entation of Spanish policy in favor of the queen's ambitions in Italy. Until Philip's death in 1746, Queen Elizabeth continued to dominate the direction of affairs; and
her heart was set on carving out a kingdom in northern
Italy for her younger son, Don Philip.

The death of Philip V paved the way for peace, at least
between England and Spain. His successor, Ferdinand
VI, a son of Philip's first wife, could be counted on not
only to oppose the ambitions of his step-mother, but also,
because of his known inclination for an independent Spanish policy, to neutralize French influence under the Family Compact. The new king wanted peace, and England

19. Reports in C.O. 91:8 and 10. The size of the garrison does not seem
to have been greatly augmented after the outbreak of hostilities. In
May 1743 it consisted of five regiments and an artillery company, num-
bering about 3800 officers and men.

An interesting truce in naval activities in the Straits is described in
the following extract from Governor Hargrave's letter to Lord Carteret
of Oct. 30/Nov. 10, 1743 (C.O. 91:2):

"My Lord—

"Since I had the honour of writing to your Lordship last, the General
of the Spanish camp finding great inconveniency in supplying Ceuta
with Provisions, since the Plague has been there, writ to His Catholic
Majesty to desire an Order might be sent that all the Privateers that
lay at Algazira, and Tarrif might be sent out of the Gut to lye near
Cadiz, and that they should not take any English Vessels between Cape
Spartel and Ceuta; provided that I agreed that our Cruizers should not
molest any of their Boats carrying Provisions to Ceuta, and returning
from thence to their Ports; This he communicated to me in a letter,
which I shewed to the Captain that Commands the Ships on this Sta-
tion, who agreed to it; being very Adventagious to the Trade of His
Majesty's Subjects."

This arrangement is somewhat revealing as to the utility of Gibraltar
in protecting English commerce during the war. Despite the mutual ad-
vantageousness of this agreement, the Spanish annulled it as soon as the
plague had abated at Ceuta. Hargrave to Newcastle, March 24/Apr. 4,
1744, C.O. 91:10.

proceeded to open secret negotiations with Spain on two fronts. Benjamin Keene, who had been sent to Lisbon as minister in 1746, was authorized to treat with Spain through Portuguese channels; and the young Earl of Sandwich, a protégé and colleague of the Duke of Bedford on the Admiralty Board, was chosen to conduct negotiations with both France and Spain at Breda, in Holland.

The prime objective of England's efforts to negotiate a separate peace with Spain during 1747 and 1748 was to break the hold of France upon her Bourbon ally. The Duke of Newcastle had, by the beginning of 1747, secured almost supreme control over the direction of British policy. His principal aim was to secure a peace which would not arouse popular clamor and threaten his political position. For this reason he opposed the cession of Gibraltar, even though Cape Breton and its fortress of Louisbourg had to be sacrificed in its place. A contrary view was held by Lord Chesterfield, the secretary for the Northern Department; by his successor, the Duke of Bedford; and by other English statesmen. Yet those who favored the cession did so only on the supposition that the union of France and Spain could be broken by that act.[20]

The first Spanish demand for Gibraltar in the secret negotiations for a separate peace with England was made by Macanaz, an elderly Spaniard who went to Holland early in 1747 and initiated a secret negotiation at The Hague with the Earl of Sandwich. Though Spain was already carrying on a negotiation with the English at Lisbon through the mediation of the Portuguese court, Macanaz presented a new and different set of proposals to Sandwich. The authority of Macanaz and the sincerity of his proposals are open to some doubt; but there can be no doubt that Spain longed for peace and that, if favorable terms could be made, the Spanish were entirely willing to settle apart from the French.

20. The most recent and complete treatise on the peace negotiations of 1747 and 1748 is that of Sir Richard Lodge, *Studies in Eighteenth Century Diplomacy, 1740–1748* (London, 1930).

The demand for the restitution of Gibraltar and Minorca headed the list of the terms submitted by Macanaz to Sandwich and transmitted by the latter to London on February 7, 1747.[21] The other notable demand of the Spaniard concerned an establishment in Italy for Don Philip. Sandwich informed Macanaz that his demands, especially those concerning the restitution of Gibraltar and Minorca, would certainly encounter objections at London. The Spaniard responded that he recognized England's need for a suitable port in the Mediterranean, and he suggested Porto Longone, on the island of Elba, as an equivalent.[22] In answering the Spanish proposals, Lord Chesterfield officially stated that there was no possibility of securing the British king's approval to the cession of Gibraltar under any circumstances. He instructed Sandwich to inform Macanaz "in the most polite manner . . . that the King will never, upon any Account, recede from This His Determination."[23] In a private letter, Chesterfield revealed his personal views on Gibraltar in the following extract:

Were nobody here wiser than I, I confess I should be *tractable* upon the affair of Gibraltar, rather than let the negotiation with Spain break off and throw the new King into the arms of France, from which I am convinced he is sincerely disposed to disengage himself. Nay, I am persuaded that, if we could, by the price of Gibraltar, purchase advantageous and unequivocal conditions for our commerce to America, the measure would be approved by all reasoning people. But this is by no means the opinion of *others* here, and we are not of a *tournure* to stand the least degree of popular clamour.[24]

21. Sandwich to Chesterfield, Feb. 7, 1747, Add. MSS. 32,807, fol. 59.

22. Sandwich to Chesterfield, Feb. 10, 1747, Add. MSS. 32,807, fols. 47–48.

23. Chesterfield to Sandwich, Feb. 3/14 and Feb. 6/17, 1747, Add. MSS. 32,807, fols. 51–52, 68.

24. Chesterfield to Sandwich, Feb. 6/17, 1747, in Lodge, *Studies in Eighteenth Century Diplomacy*, pp. 229–230.

Sandwich next attempted to persuade the Duke of Newcastle of the wisdom of securing a separate peace with Spain at the price of Gibraltar. If by surrendering that fortress England could assure the retention of Cape Breton and could obtain a favorable commercial settlement with Spain, Sandwich felt that the maritime and trading interests of the country would be properly sensible of the bargain. Fortunately for Britain, he asserted, Spain was far more interested in the restitution of Gibraltar than of Minorca, and would be willing to pay well for it. Gibraltar, Sandwich insisted, was "at best but a negative advantage . . . by no means adequate to the expense of its maintenance," and of much less real value to England than Minorca. To Sandwich's argument Newcastle responded that a separate peace which would insure a permanent disruption of the Bourbon alliance would be worth purchasing, but "even That might be dearly bought, by the Cession of Gibraltar." As to the question of Cape Breton *vs.* Gibraltar, he observed that there was no promise that France would surrender Cape Breton, even if Gibraltar were granted to Spain; and there was some disagreement in England at this time as to the real value of Cape Breton to England, unless it was backed up by further conquests in Canada.[25]

Meanwhile, Sandwich had informed Macanaz on March 1 that the Spanish proposals had been rejected at London, but that the British ministry hoped the negotiation would be continued in an effort to reach some settlement satisfactory to both nations. Sandwich plainly stated that the points of Gibraltar and Minorca were entirely inadmissible. Macanaz answered that he feared the negotiation would come to naught if that were the case, for the Spanish king laid his chief stress upon those points. But Macanaz was also anxious for the negotiation to continue.[26]

25. Sandwich to Newcastle, Feb. 24, 1747, Add. MSS. 32,807, fols. 99–102. Newcastle to Sandwich, March 6/17, 1747, Add. MSS. 32,807, fols. 176–180.

26. Sandwich to Chesterfield, March 2, 1747, Add. MSS. 32,807, fols. 129–130.

After a week of argument, the Spaniard agreed to withdraw every point in his demands except that of Gibraltar, which he insisted was the *sine qua non* upon which Spain would treat. Sandwich transmitted this new project to London, but with some hesitancy, insisting that he did so only to keep open the secret channel of negotiation with Spain and to prevent Spain from throwing herself into the arms of France. In response, Lord Chesterfield stated that it was no more acceptable to England than the former proposals, but that the British ministry was still willing and even anxious to enter into negotiations on a "reasonable" basis.[27]

At the request of Macanaz, Sandwich handed him a written statement of the English position on the point of Gibraltar. In return, Macanaz delivered to the English minister a statement of the Spanish position, in which he based the Spanish demand primarily on the letter of George I in 1721, and stated categorically that no permanent peace could ever be made between Spain and England without the restitution.[28] Lord Chesterfield's insistence that nothing but an absolute and peremptory refusal could be returned to Macanaz' proposal seemingly ended all hope of a settlement. Sandwich discontinued his conferences with the Spaniard and proceeded to Breda, where the main negotiation was in progress.[29]

At Breda, Macanaz pursued the issue with Sandwich. At length he agreed to dispatch a courier to Madrid requesting instructions to proceed without the necessity of insisting upon Gibraltar. His conciliatory attitude revived Sandwich's hopes.[30] Within a few days, and before he could possibly have received new instructions from Ma-

27. Sandwich to Chesterfield, private and public letters of March 10, 1747, Add. MSS. 32,807, fols. 150, 159. Chesterfield to Sandwich, March 6/17, 1747, Add. MSS. 32,807, fols. 170–174.

28. Add. MSS. 32,807, fol. 229.

29. Chesterfield to Sandwich, March 20/31, 1747, Add. MSS. 32,807, fol. 248. Sandwich to Chesterfield, April 4, 1747, Add. MSS. 32,807, fol. 255.

30. Sandwich to Chesterfield, Apr. 11 and 17, 1747, Add. MSS. 32,807, fols. 269–276, and 32,808, fol. 15.

drid, Macanaz submitted a new plan for negotiations. In his new proposals, Gibraltar was not to be mentioned in the public articles; but a secret article was appended which provided that, although his Catholic Majesty would not insist on the restitution of Gibraltar in the treaty of peace, after peace had been established the kings of England and Spain should endeavor to find some expedient to solve the difficulties with regard to the restitution.[31] Sandwich was reluctant to forward this new proposition to London; but since he considered that such a future negotiation could be founded only upon an equivalent, he thought it better to accept the article rather than to break off the negotiation once more.[32]

Before this new Spanish proposal reached London, the British ministry had drawn up and transmitted to Sandwich a new set of proposals, from which all mention of Gibraltar had been deleted. No official response to the project of Macanaz was given, therefore, until he made known his reaction to the English proposals. Lord Chesterfield did advise Sandwich privately that the suggested secret article could not be accepted by England. Sandwich presented Macanaz with the British project, and for the moment had strong hopes that the Spaniard, having retreated so far, would finally consent to terms which made no mention whatsoever of Gibraltar.[33]

The personal ambitions of both Sandwich and Macanaz were doomed to disappointment. The French finally succeeded in obtaining the transmission of orders from Madrid directing Macanaz to break off the secret negotiation with England and to concert his future efforts with those of the French representatives at Breda.[34] The collapse of

31. Sandwich to Chesterfield, Apr. 21, 1747, enclosing a copy of the new Spanish project, Add. MSS. 32,808, fol. 38.

32. Sandwich to Chesterfield, Apr. 24, 1747, Add. MSS. 32,808, fols. 66–67.

33. Chesterfield to Sandwich, Apr. 14/25, 1747; and Sandwich to Chesterfield, Apr. 25, 1747; Add. MSS. 32,808, fols. 71, 73–74.

34. Chesterfield to Sandwich, May 5/16, 1747, Add. MSS. 32,808, fol. 179. Wm. Bentinck to Sandwich, May 22, 1747, Add. MSS. 32,808, fol. 197.

this negotiation can be credited chiefly to the point of Gibraltar, but the final suggestion of Macanaz bore some fruit, as we shall see in reviewing the conferences of the Spanish representative Wall in London at the end of the year.[35]

The subject of Gibraltar was not mentioned to Keene at Lisbon until August 1747. For some months previous Keene had conducted his negotiation under the mediation of the Portuguese Cardinal de Motta. Keene felt that the French had too strong a hold on the cardinal for any satisfactory settlement to come through his efforts, and accordingly took advantage of an opportunity to establish direct contact with the Spanish at Madrid. The Spanish minister Carvajal appeared willing to make a separate peace, but insisted that no real peace could be made without Gibraltar, although he did not demand it as a *sine qua non*. Keene in reporting this overture to Newcastle remarked: "The Article of Gibraltar is couched rather as a matter of Conveniency than a Demand founded upon any pretended Right. I have however rejected it."[36] In a subsequent report of his correspondence with Madrid, Keene observed that the two principal demands of the Spaniards were those for a satisfactory establishment for Don Philip and for the restitution of Gibraltar; and he felt that the latter point was chiefly mentioned to induce the British to consent more readily to the former.[37]

Keene's correspondence with Madrid elicited a response from the Duke of Newcastle on November 3, 1747, enclosing a memorandum which the British minister was instructed to forward to the Spanish. Newcastle noted that the sole points standing in the way of a reconciliation between Spain and England were those of Gibraltar and an establishment for Don Philip. The Duke agreed to the latter; as for Gibraltar, Newcastle's memorandum read:

35. See below, p. 152.
36. Keene to Newcastle, July 31 and Aug. 21, 1747, Add. MSS. 32,809, fols. 85–86, 162–163.
37. Keene to Newcastle, Sept. 18, 1747, Add. MSS. 32,809, fols. 329–330.

As to the first point; that it was only the renewal of a demand which had so often been made; and to which the king had not consented, and can not now consent; that furthermore, if ever in the future the two nations should find it to their mutual advantage to take notice of it in some new adjustment, that ought without question to be the effect and result of a good and perfect understanding, established at the same time, with an entire union of interests and sentiments; and it can not, and ought not, ever to be treated or considered as an object or basis for the reëstablishment of peace.[38]

This statement, be it noted, did not preclude consideration of the restitution of Gibraltar *after* the establishment of peace; it might even be construed as an indication that England would be willing to consider the restitution. Perhaps it had no other object than to entice the Spaniards into a separate peace, and thereby to break the connection between the Bourbon courts; on the other hand, Newcastle made the same or a similar proposition to the Spanish representative Wall in London a few weeks later.

Newcastle's memorandum was forwarded to Carvajal at Madrid, and the Spanish minister responded on December 22. The Spaniard repeated his demand for Gibraltar in the peace settlement, and also objected to the terms of the establishment proposed for Don Philip. Privately, Keene wrote that he despaired of any prospect for peace through these exchanges. "Such is the Weakness and Irresolution of that [the Spanish] Court," he wrote, "that though the Reigning King and Queen, as They certainly are, and both their Ministers should be, desirous and earnest to put an End to the present Troubles, Yet the Dread They have of the French, who sometimes cajole and sometimes menace Them, And who have their Army and their Infanta in their Power, will deter Them from coming to any separate Conclusion with the Allies."[39]

38. Newcastle to Keene, Oct. 23/Nov. 3, 1747, Add. MSS. 32,810, fols. 199–203. See below, p. 154.
39. Keene to Newcastle, Dec. 28, 1747, Add. MSS. 32,810, fol. 368.

A third effort of Spain to negotiate a separate peace with England opened with the arrival in London in September 1747 of Major General Wall, an Irishman in high standing with their Catholic Majesties, and subsequently for some years the foreign minister of Spain. Wall had authority to carry on a secret negotiation to be founded upon the cession of Gibraltar and Minorca and a suitable establishment for Don Philip. Through the medium of the Marquis de Tabuerniga, a Spanish friend and confidential agent of the Duke of Newcastle, he met the British ministers. Wall's first overtures met with no success, though Newcastle did not at once reject his demands.[40]

Since it appeared that the problem of Gibraltar was the only point of real difficulty—Wall almost immediately gave up his demand for Minorca—Tabuerniga proposed that a solution might be found by securing from England the promise to consider the restitution of Gibraltar at some future date.[41] Specifically, Tabuerniga proposed to Newcastle that England submit terms for peace to Wall in writing, these to include a statement that the British king would promise to present the question of Gibraltar to Parliament at a suitable future date, on the basis of restitution for an equivalent in money. Even in the case that Parliament refused to effect the restitution, Spain would agree to carry out all the other articles in the treaty of peace.[42]

On various pretexts, the English ministry delayed a formal answer to Wall's overtures for some weeks. The Spanish envoy grew restive and threatened to leave London, for he felt that there was no hope of obtaining Gibraltar, nor did he believe that any satisfactory peace could be concluded through his efforts. Finally, after a

40. Tabuerniga to Newcastle, Sept. 14/25, 1747, Add. MSS. 32,810, fol. 20. Newcastle to Sandwich, Sept. 25/Oct. 6, 1747, Add. MSS. 32,810, fol. 76.

41. Mémoire of conferences between Tabuerniga and Wall, Sept. 14–15/25–26, 1747, Add. MSS. 32,810, fols. 30–34.

42. Tabuerniga to Newcastle, Oct. 8/19, 1747, Add. MSS. 32,810, fol. 132.

conference with Newcastle and Chesterfield, it was agreed to transmit certain propositions to Madrid and these were sent during November.[43]

Pending a response to the above propositions, Wall had further conversations with the British ministers. Just what passed on the subject of Gibraltar is not clear; but by the end of December Wall's objections were centered not on that subject, but on the question of a suitable establishment for Don Philip. Newcastle for the moment evinced enthusiasm for a settlement with Wall, as shown when he wrote to the Earl of Sandwich: "We had last Night a meeting about our final Answer to Wall. We are all for this Project for separating Spain from France. The only Point will be whether, in order to accomplish it, We shall engage to do it with, or without the Consent of our Allies."[44]

The Spanish minister Carvajal responded on December 22 to the English proposals by way of Keene at Madrid; in fact, Carvajal's letter served as an answer both to the overtures of Keene and to the propositions from London. The Spanish reply reached London on January 19, and further conferences with Wall followed. But the English ministers were evasive, the Duke of Newcastle deciding to wait for a more favorable turn in the military situation.[45] Wall became disgusted with the treatment accorded to him, and prepared to leave London. To Tabuerniga he wrote: "It is true however that, with the apparent design of separating Spain from France, they [the English] have made vague offers to me, but, as if they feared that they might be accepted, the conditions which they have added to them have always been as little fixed as

43. Tabuerniga to Newcastle, Nov. 3/14, 1747 and Nov. 15/26, 1747, Add. MSS. 32,810, fols. 247, 335.

44. Newcastle to Sandwich, Dec. 22/Jan. 2, 1747/1748, Add. MSS. 32,810, fol. 388.

45. Newcastle to Sandwich, Jan. 12/23, 1748, Add. MSS. 32,811, fols. 44–46. Tabuerniga to Newcastle, Jan. 26/Feb. 6, 1748, Add. MSS. 32,811, fols. 117–122.

just."[46] During March the Spanish envoy abandoned his negotiation, and went to Paris.

Tabuerniga, still hopeful that a separate peace could be arranged, continued to press Newcastle, and the duke finally granted an audience to him. As a result of this conference, Newcastle authorized the Spaniard to draw up a new response to Carvajal's letter of December 22. Tabuerniga did so, and submitted a draft of the letter to the Duke for approval. It contained the following passage:

As to the Article of Gibraltar, his Grace said; that it was plain, and to be believed, that my Court [the Spanish] must be sensible itself, that the Restitution of that Place could not be proposed in the present Circumstances; (but that the Settling of this Point would depend upon Spain itself, if when She was at Peace, and sincerely united with England, She showed in a manner not to be doubted that She had shaken off the mischievous Influence of France; that then This nation would be as tractable upon that Head, as She would be inflexible now, if Endeavours should be used to induce Her to part with the Key of the Streights at so ticklish a time, as would give Her room for Fears and Apprehensions that the Passage of that Streight would shortly be blocked up, which was so necessary for Her Levant Trade.) and referr'd to what was said upon that Head in the answer to Major General Wall.[47]

This passage reveals the answer previously made to Wall on the point of Gibraltar—an answer similar to that already made by way of Keene on the previous November 3. Tabuerniga forwarded his letter to Madrid early in April, but that ended the matter, for the unexpected news of the signature of the preliminaries at Aix reached London early in May. The significance of this negotiation lies in

46. Wall to Tabuerniga, Feb. 10 (N.S.), 1748, Add. MSS. 32,811, fol. 133.

47. Add. MSS. 32,811, fols. 415–416. This draft is in the handwriting of Newcastle's secretary. Newcastle himself crossed out the section enclosed in parentheses, and in its place added the concluding clause; and the letter was probably sent to Spain in the latter form.

the evident willingness of the Duke of Newcastle to agree to a *future* consideration of the cession of Gibraltar if and when the Bourbon alliance was effectively broken up and the old Anglo-Spanish friendship reëstablished.

While the futile negotiations with Wall were being carried on in London, the Earl of Sandwich continued his efforts in Holland. After a brief sojourn in London, Sandwich returned to Holland in August 1747. He carried no new instructions, and his former instructions precluded the mention of Gibraltar in any manner in the treaty of peace. In September, Chesterfield again stated that the restitution of Gibraltar would not be considered under any circumstances. Indeed, he suggested that the French court indirectly had pressed the Spanish to demand the fortress in the secret negotiations already described, with the real view of subjecting the King of Spain "to unavoidable Refusals, in order to keep Him by means thereof, under the most absolute, and tyrannical Dependence."[48]

British reverses on the Continent so increased the desire for peace at the opening of the new year that the Duke of Newcastle found himself virtually alone in his desire to postpone further negotiations until a more favorable turn in the military situation. The Duke of Bedford, who had succeeded Chesterfield as secretary for the Northern Department, was the chief advocate of an immediate peace, and he frankly told Newcastle that every member of the Cabinet was against him.[49] Newcastle, as usual master of the political situation, succeeded in stemming the near-panic for peace that gripped his colleagues. However Newcastle's attributes as a leader and diplomatist may be viewed, his tenacity in refusing to make peace until satisfactory terms could be obtained and all mention of Gibraltar dropped, saved the situation for England at this time. From the standpoint of value or strategic position, New-

48. Chesterfield to Sandwich, Sept. 22/Oct. 3, 1747, Add. MSS. 32,810, fol. 60.

49. Newcastle to Sandwich, Jan. 19/30, 1748, Add. MSS. 32,811, fols. 87–88.

castle showed no great interest in either Gibraltar or
Louisbourg. But it is obvious that as political questions
there was a vast difference between them in his mind. The
restitution of Gibraltar would have rocked England, because of the long struggle over it and the violent outbursts
over the question in the past. On the other hand, Louisbourg could be restored with but scant repercussion on
political thought in England; it had no past associations
and, unlike Gibraltar, was not an idol in the public mind.

During February 1748, Governor Hargrave at Gibraltar secured secret information that the Spaniards were
planning a surprise attack on the fortress.[50] He begged
for reinforcements, but nothing came of this scheme; and
it is probable that Hargrave was misinformed, for the desire for peace at the Spanish court seems to have been very
real at this time, judging by its diplomatic efforts. Possibly, however, as in 1720 and 1728, Spain thought to ex-
pedite her diplomacy by a threat against Gibraltar.

The Duke of Bedford, unable directly to dissuade Newcastle from a continuance of the war, resorted to indirect
pressure through the Earl of Sandwich. Early in March,
he wrote a private letter to Sandwich arguing the necessity of peace, if it could be obtained "on admissible
terms." He urged the wisdom of a separate peace with
Spain, at the price of Gibraltar, in return for trade concessions in the West Indies. "I must own that place seems
to be of very little or no utility to this country," he wrote,
"and that the cession of it to Spain would not be near so
dangerous as that of Louisbourg to the French." Sandwich repeated Bedford's arguments to Newcastle, and
added: "You know how much my sentiments agree with
the latter part of this extract. I heartily wish you would
follow his advice about Gibraltar."[51] But Newcastle was
adamant in his response, stating: "I own I don't at all
taste the Notion about Gibraltar. These Times (as I have

50. Hargrave to Newcastle, Feb. 7/18, 1748, C.O. 91:8.
51. Sandwich to Newcastle, March 16, 1748, Add. MSS. 32,811, fols.
341–342.

before observed to you), will not bear such Strokes as Those."[52]

In the midst of the English apprehensions for the outcome of the peace negotiations, news arrived of the signature of the preliminaries with France and Spain. The unexpected ease with which peace was obtained is shown by the fact that new instructions were sent to Sandwich on the very day the preliminaries were signed, and the tone of these instructions was by no means hopeful with regard to resistance to Spanish demands.[53] The French had reasserted their domination over the Spanish court, and had made peace in their own favor, with scant regard to the promises made in the Treaty of Fontainebleau. The King of Spain acceded to the preliminaries on May 28, and nothing more was said about Gibraltar in the final negotiations.

Thus in the peace negotiations of 1747 and 1748, Gibraltar was again preserved for the English Crown, despite the willingness of several influential ministers to surrender it. Against the almost united opposition of his Cabinet, Newcastle had persevered and secured a relatively advantageous peace. As shown in the secret negotiations with Spain, he does not seem to have been opposed, in the event that Spain had been willing to make a separate peace with England on otherwise advantageous terms, to a promise to consider the restitution of Gibraltar subsequent to, and apart from, the peace negotiation. Save on the sea, Britain and her allies were in no condition to continue the war; and so strong was the English peace party by March 1748, that if France and Spain had forced the issue, England might have been persuaded to part with both Louisbourg and Gibraltar.

In truth, neither France nor Spain pressed the question of Gibraltar to the limit in the peace negotiation. Despite

52. Newcastle to Sandwich, March 11/22, 1748, Add. MSS. 32,811, fol. 371.
53. Newcastle to Sandwich, Apr. 19/30, 1748, Add. MSS. 32,812, fols. 86–87.

the recent military successes of France, both France and Spain were exhausted by the war, and desired a quick peace. Spain, in each of her three separate channels of negotiation with England, had at first insisted upon the immediate cession of Gibraltar, and then had backed down to the point of requesting merely that England promise to consider the restitution at some future date. Thus Spain evinced no unalterable resolution to insist upon Gibraltar. The Spanish court, as in previous years, was more vitally interested in a satisfactory Italian settlement for the sons of Elizabeth Farnese. Furthermore, as the negotiations progressed, Spain fell more and more under French influence, and the Spanish envoy at Aix, Sotomayor (whom Sandwich described as a "weak" man), was completely dominated by his French colleagues. The French themselves made no efforts to secure Gibraltar for Spain. Why? Fundamentally, the French saw that the restoration of Gibraltar would remove the greatest seed of discord in Anglo-Spanish relations, and thus weaken the Family Compact. More immediately, the French probably feared that Gibraltar could be secured only at the price of Louisbourg; and, as in the subsequent negotiations at Paris in 1782, they secretly objected to the surrender of any French advantage for the benefit of Spain. Finally, the French were piqued at the efforts of Spain to conclude a separate peace with England; consequently they slighted Spanish claims and interests in the public negotiation at Aix. The failure of France and Spain to insist upon the cession, and not the refusal of England to consider the restitution of Gibraltar on any terms, determined the fate of the fortress in the peace negotiations of 1748.

VII

GIBRALTAR IN PEACE AND WAR
1748–1763

FOR more than a decade after the peace of Aix-la-Chapelle, Anglo-Spanish relations were marked by a harmony unequaled in any other extended period of the eighteenth century. Ferdinand VI ardently desired peace, and he tried to maintain a position of neutrality and independence in opposition to the rival efforts of England and France to win Spanish support. The Family Compact was dead in spirit if not in form. On the other hand, disputes over commerce and other matters prevented a solid reconciliation between England and Spain. Above all, the old thorn of Gibraltar remained a basic hindrance to true friendship. Despite such obstacles, the ability and diplomatic ingenuity of Benjamin Keene enabled England to maintain a diplomatic equilibrium with France at the Spanish court.[1]

The resumption of friendly relations between England and Spain was reflected in the improvement in the local situation at Gibraltar. In the decade after 1748, England seems to have had no fears whatsoever of any Spanish attack on the fortress, and even reduced the numbers of the garrison. In return for the coöperation of the governor of Gibraltar in aiding the suppression of tobacco smuggling, the Spanish removed the absolute restriction on communication between Gibraltar and the Spanish coast. Free communication by sea between the fortress and Spanish ports was authorized, making it possible once more to send let-

1. Keene to Abraham Castres, Aug. 23, 1750, in Sir Richard Lodge, *The Private Correspondence of Sir Benjamin Keene* (Cambridge, 1933), p. 247. For a recent appreciation of Keene, see Lodge's presidential address, "Sir Benjamin Keene, K. B.: A Study in Anglo-Spanish Relations," in *Transactions of the Royal Historical Society,* Fourth Series, XV (London, 1932), 1–43.

ters overland to England. Keene might have obtained permission for the provisioning of Gibraltar by land, but Governor Humphrey Bland advised that such communication was no longer necessary nor indeed desirable, the supply from Barbary being satisfactory.[2]

Despite freer communication with Spain, the amount of trade at Gibraltar was negligible in 1750. Prior to 1749, the volume of trade cannot be ascertained, for there had been no accounting of revenues. Theoretically, Gibraltar had been a free port, though actually the governors had collected numerous exactions, many of which they pocketed. A new accounting system was installed in 1749, but at the end of the first fiscal year the revenue amounted to only £5500, far less than had been anticipated. Governor Bland attributed this to "the Deadness of Trade in this Place, and the Troops being much soberer than they were."[3]

The possession of Gibraltar was a powerful lever in British negotiations with the Barbary states during this period. The governor of Gibraltar was charged with the conduct of diplomatic negotiations with Barbary, and much of his attention and that of his agents was directed to the maintenance of a virtual English monopoly of the Barbary trade. Through much of the eighteenth century, Great Britain was the only European power at peace with Barbary, and accordingly the British could carry on their commerce without danger of piracy, not only to Barbary but to the whole Mediterranean area. Of course, the argument of Gibraltar was strengthened on the one hand by copious bribery and on the other by the constant command of the shores of the Mediterranean by the English fleet. England permitted the Jews and Moors to remain at Gibraltar, in violation of the Treaty of Utrecht, in order to prevent friction with Barbary. England also used her ar-

2. C.O. 91:11, especially Governor Bland to Captain Richardson, April 6/17, 1750.
3. Governor Bland to the Duke of Bedford, July 5/16, 1750, C.O. 91: 11.

guments of Gibraltar and naval strength with success to dissuade the Emperor of Morocco from entering into treaties of peace with other powers, especially the Dutch.[4]

England did not maintain a regular naval force at Gibraltar at this time, nor indeed until some years later. During 1755 a French cruiser seized a vessel flying the British flag and conveying provisions for the garrison from Tetuan. After protest, the vessel was finally released, though the cargo in the meantime had spoiled. The governor felt that he could do nothing but protest, for, he wrote, "We have no Naval Force here, except one Sloop; and if we had I know not how far the Commanders might think themselves authorized to redress us without particular Orders."[5]

The outbreak of the Seven Years' War with France found England ill prepared for any attack on her Mediterranean possessions of Gibraltar and Minorca. Though Spanish neutrality in the contest seemed assured, France threatened to attack those fortresses from her Mediterranean naval bases. The inexcusable negligence of the British ministry, despite the earnest warnings of Keene and the governor at Port Mahón, resulted in the delay of a projected relief for Minorca and a speedy capture of that island by France. Keene believed that the French would not attempt "to break their heads" against Gibraltar, but this feeling was not shared by the officers of the garrison. Even before the fall of Minorca, apprehensions were felt for the safety of Gibraltar, if France should gain naval superiority in the Mediterranean.[6]

4. C.O. 91:8, especially the letter of Wm. Pettigrew (an English emissary in Morocco) to the Emperor of Morocco, New Fez, Feb. 25, 1751.

5. Governor Thomas Fowke to Sir Thomas Robertson, July 25, 1755, C.O. 91:11.

6. Keene to Castres, Feb. 16, 1756, in Lodge, *Correspondence of Sir B. Keene,* p. 454. Minorca was attacked in the spring of 1756, and orders were sent to Gibraltar to detach some of its garrison for the relief of Minorca. But a council of war held on May 15, 1756, presided over by Governor Fowke, decided that no force that could be sent from Gibraltar would be sufficient to save Minorca, even if it could be landed, which was dubious; and that such a detachment would so weaken Gibraltar

Despite English fears, the French did not attempt, or even seriously contemplate, an attack on Gibraltar after their capture of Minorca. That they did not can be attributed to several factors. England's possession of Minorca had menaced both the French fleet and naval bases, and French trade in the Mediterranean, while the more distant fortress at the Straits was no real threat to either. The French realized that England's possession of Gibraltar was a valuable aid in forestalling a genuine reconciliation between England and Spain, and a surety for the continuance of the Family Compact. Furthermore, the French could not hope to capture the citadel of the Straits unless they could first establish naval superiority in the western Mediterranean. The English, after the bitter lesson of Minorca, strengthened the garrison at Gibraltar and (after the summer of 1756) maintained a naval force in the Mediterranean superior to that of the French. Thus when William Pitt warned the governor in the fall of 1758 that reports of renewed activity in the French naval bases of Toulon and Marseilles should put the garrison on its guard, he expressed no particular apprehension that any French attack could be successful.[7] The most serious threat to Gibraltar during the war came not from the Bourbon powers but from an abortive insurrection within the garrison itself![8]

Gibraltar played a significant rôle in the Seven Years' War. Using Gibraltar as a base, England checked French naval power and protected her Mediterranean trade. In a series of maneuvers during the winter of 1757–1758, the French Mediterranean fleet failed in an effort to break through the British naval cordon and join the Atlantic squadrons of France.[9] Likewise, Britain's superiority in

that it might itself fall a prey to the French. The ill-fated Admiral Byng did not participate in this council, but subsequently approved its decision. C.O. 91:12. See Brian Tunstall, *Admiral Byng and the Loss of Minorca* (London, 1928).

7. Pitt to the Earl of Home, Oct. 20, 1758, C.O. 91:12.

8. Earl of Bristol to Pitt, Madrid, Oct. 20, 1760, S.P. 94:162.

9. A running account of these naval maneuvers is to be found in C.O. 91:12.

sea power explains the fact that her Mediterranean trade continued on an undiminished scale throughout the war. Having lost Minorca, England needed Gibraltar as a base from which this naval supremacy in the Mediterranean could be maintained. As a naval base Gibraltar had many disadvantages—bad weather during the naval maneuvers mentioned above drove the English fleet from the open roadstead on several occasions, once for more than a week —but it is doubtful whether any other point could have been so easily and surely defended, and thus retained under all circumstances.

Not Gibraltar alone, but Gibraltar combined with superior naval power, enabled Britain to defend her position in the Mediterranean in the Seven Years' War. This can be shown most clearly by a comparison with the situation in the succeeding conflict of 1778–1782. Then England managed to defend Gibraltar against the onslaught of French and Spanish land and naval forces, but she lost her naval control in the western Mediterranean for three years. As a result, the French and Spanish fleets moved at will through the Straits. As for trade, comparative statistics of Britain's commerce with Italy and the Levant tell the story. In the three-year period from 1757 to 1759, the value of Britain's trade with Italy, Venice, and Turkey actually exceeded that of the years of peace, 1750– 1752. In the succeeding war, the value of that trade fell to less than one-fourth of its pre-war level; the meager trade that continued had to be handled almost exclusively in neutral bottoms.[10] In the eighteenth century, as today,

10. According to customs figures of both dutiable and free goods, the average annual value of Britain's trade with Italy, Venice, and Turkey for the years 1750–1752 was approximately £1,091,000; for 1757–1759, £1,109,000; for 1770–1772, £2,003,000; for 1779–1781, £466,000. Normally, vessels of British registry virtually monopolized this trade. In the years of peace, 1774 and 1786, 98.5 per cent and 96.5 per cent, respectively, of the vessels engaged in this trade were British. In 1781, only *one* of the 151 vessels recorded as participating in it was of British registry. These statistics have been compiled from a copy of Charles Whitworth's *State of the Trade of Great Britain in its Exports and Imports, Progressively from the Year 1697* . . . (London, 1776). This copy, in the Manuscripts

superior naval power was the fundamental in Britain's defense of her position in the Mediterranean.

The most momentous event in the diplomacy of Gibraltar during the Seven Years' War was the proposal made by William Pitt to Spain in 1757, offering to restore the fortress in return for Spanish aid in the recovery of Minorca and in a general descent upon France. Spain had not lost her desire for the recovery of Gibraltar after the peace of 1748. Indeed, Richard Wall, while acting as Spanish ambassador at the English court from 1749 to 1752, had made efforts to re-open the question, but to no avail. Ferdinand VI did not inherit his father's earnest yearning for the restitution of Gibraltar, and he did not press his minister's efforts to obtain the fortress. After his return to Madrid and his elevation to the post of chief minister, Wall showed himself to be most friendly to England and particularly to Benjamin Keene, who had a hand in Wall's advancement. The war between Britain and France created a difficult situation for Wall, and he tried to maintain as neutral a position as possible between the contestants. His position was made doubly difficult by English attacks on Spanish and French vessels within Spanish territorial waters and by the application of England's famous Rule of the War of 1756. Such incidents spurred on the hopes of the pro-French party in Spain, and largely undid the brilliant diplomacy of Keene in weaning Spain away from the French connection. Although the Spanish king and his minister Wall were sincerely anxious to prevent a rupture with England, it seems clear that there was no possibility that Spain would have been willing to join England in an attack on France for any consideration whatsoever.[11] Such was the setting for Pitt's proposal.

Division of the Library of Congress, belonged to George Chalmers, who added corrections and additional information to Whitworth's figures and continued them in manuscript to 1804.

11. Keene said practically as much in a cypher letter to Pitt, April 21, 1757, S.P. 94:155. For general surveys of Anglo-Spanish relations, 1748–1757, see Coxe, *Kings of Spain*, vol. IV; and Sir Richard Lodge's presi-

The idea of exchanging Gibraltar for Spanish aid in the recapture of Minorca did not originate with Pitt. Early in July 1756, less than a fortnight after the news of Minorca's fall reached London, Henry Fox, secretary of state in the government then dominated by Newcastle, proposed the exchange to the Cabinet. Although rebuffed by Newcastle, Fox pursued his idea in conversations with the Sardinian, and probably with the Spanish, ministers at London. His efforts were to no avail, for Newcastle silenced the proposal. Public opinion had already been outraged by the administration's negligence in failing to protect Minorca, and Newcastle did not dare to risk his political position by sponsoring a measure that might arouse even greater opposition.[12]

By the summer of 1757, the military position of England had become desperate. The success of French arms threatened the German possessions of George II; and he pressed his ministry, now a coalition dominated by William Pitt, to find some means of mending the situation. The proposal to exchange Gibraltar for the armed support of Spain was accordingly revived. A month before Pitt's formal proposal to Spain, the project was the subject of "London Coffee house Conjectures."[13]

On August 9, Newcastle discussed the matter with Pitt, and reported his conversation to the Earl of Hardwicke as follows:

Mr. Pitt, very rightly, entered into General Politicks; and said Since we could do nothing in the North, We must see what could be done in the South. That, for that Reason, We should endeavour to get Spain, not only by putting an End to all Our Maritime and Commercial Disputes, but also by doing Something Solid for Spain; And Then proposed, the Offering Gibraltar to Spain; If they would help us to Port

dential address on Keene, *Royal Hist. Society Trans.*, 4th Series, XV, 1–43.

12. T. W. Riker, *Henry Fox* (Oxford, 1911), I, 433–435.

13. Rev. Stephen Sleech (Provost of Eton College) to Edward Weston, July 25, 1757, *H.M.C., Tenth Report*, pp. 313–314.

Mahon. For without Port Mahon, Nobody would *venture* to make Peace. That in return for Gibraltar we might have *Oran*, or some port on the Barbary Coast.—Your Lordship knows, That this Exchange for Gibraltar is not a new Thought. Munchhausen [the Hanoverian minister] mentioned it some Time ago to The King; I also had some Discourse with His Majesty upon it.—I own I always liked it, and Therefore I gave much into it.—I believe Pitt has been talking with Count Viry [the Sardinian minister] upon it.— Mr. Pitt desired, That it might be seriously considered by the King's Servants.—That, If this did not do, He was ready *To do any Thing;*—By which I thought, He meant to make such Peace as We could get.[14]

This letter shows the agitation of the king and ministry over English misfortunes in the war, and reveals the most evident preference for the recovery of Minorca to the retention of Gibraltar. Even Newcastle now professed his enthusiasm for such a scheme. Hardwicke, in his response to this letter, was not so certain of the wisdom of giving up Gibraltar:

Is He [Pitt] sure that as much popular Clamour will not arise upon giving up Gibraltar, as from letting those Possessions remain where the Fortune of the War has cast them? But I admit that Clamour must not govern Measures in this great and dangerous Crisis; and, if the one or the other becomes necessary, the different importance of the two Places to Great Britain must be the Rule to go by.[15]

The proposed exchange was finally considered at a meeting of the Cabinet on the evening of August 17. The ministry approved the project, and authorized Pitt to submit the terms to Spain through Keene at Madrid. Certainly the English ministry failed to realize the true feeling at

14. Newcastle to Hardwicke, Aug. 9, 1757, Add. MSS. 32,872, fol. 493. See also Philip C. Yorke, *The Life and Correspondence of Philip Yorke, Earl of Hardwicke* . . . (Cambridge, 1913), III, 165–168.
15. Hardwicke to Newcastle, Aug. 11, 1757, Add. MSS. 32,873, fols. 24–25.

the Spanish court, as previously reported by Keene, in placing any hope upon the acceptance of the project by Spain, regardless of the bait of Gibraltar. "Are they mad on the other side of the water," exclaimed Keene on receiving Pitt's letter. "What can they mean! It is now too late! But I must fulfill my orders, whatever may be the consequence."[16]

Briefly stated, Pitt's letter of August 23 proposed that Spain, by joining in an armed alliance with England against France, should aid in the recapture of Minorca and the prosecution of the war in the Mediterranean area. In return, Britain would restore Gibraltar to Spain and also evacuate all establishments of British subjects on the Mosquito Shore and in the Bay of Honduras, made since the Peace of Aix-la-Chapelle. Gibraltar was not to be handed over to Spain until the island of Minorca, with all its harbors and fortifications, had been "actually and effectually" restored to the Crown of England. In announcing these proposals to the Spanish court, Keene was to exercise the "utmost precaution and circumspection," lest thereafter Spain might construe this offer as a conditional promise to restore Gibraltar on any other terms than those proposed.[17] The Spanish answer was awaited in London with the greatest anxiety. On September 16, Pitt wrote: "In the present gloomy and almost overwhelming Conjuncture, His Majesty's Expectation is fixed, with Royal Solicitude, on the Return of the Messenger, Evans, . . . with my Dispatch of the 23rd Past."[18]

Although he had no hope of success, Keene presented Pitt's propositions to the Spanish minister Wall as best he could, and with proper caution on the point of Gibraltar.

16. Coxe, *Kings of Spain,* IV, 197, footnote. Keene's expression that the ministry was "mad" referred, of course, to the impossibility of any hope that Spain would accept the British proposal and join England in the war, and not to any abhorrence toward the idea of ceding Gibraltar.

17. William Pitt to Keene (most secret and confidential), Aug. 23, 1757, S.P. 94:155. Copies of this famous dispatch are to be found in several collections; it has been reprinted in full in Coxe, *Kings of Spain,* IV, 187–196.

18. Pitt to Keene, Sept. 16, 1757, S.P. 94:156.

Wall's only response was an absolute negative, though
tinged with some regret that a similar proposition had not
been made at an earlier date, when some hope of its acceptance might have been entertained. Wall even refused
to report the overture to the Spanish king or to the other
ministers at Madrid, and Keene advised that it was hopeless to pursue the project through any other channel. In
a word, Keene's response left no hope that the appeal for
Spanish aid could possibly succeed.[19] Keene's letter reached
London on October 10, and it was accepted as the conclusion of a hopeless overture.[20] Keene was instructed to do
nothing further with the proposal.[21] Fortunately, the German situation soon improved through a decisive and unexpected victory of Prussia, which lessened the desirability
of Spanish support in the war.

Spain did not disclose the English overture to France.
Nevertheless, the French suspected that England had proposed an alliance with Spain, Sardinia, and Naples for
joint action against the empress in Italy. The Marquis
d'Aubeterre, the French ambassador at Madrid, was instructed to sound Wall on the subject; but he had no success. Wall failed to make any direct answer to his questions, merely pointing out the absurdity of such a proposition. In his report to Paris, Aubeterre insisted that Spain
was in no condition to attack anyone, and that the most
manifest desire of the Spanish court was to remain neutral. Accordingly, he deprecated the possibility of England's seducing Spain by any offers whatsoever.[22] During
the following year the French solicited a new treaty of alliance at the Spanish court that would draw Spain into

19. Keene to Pitt, Sept. 26, 1757, Add. MSS. 34,412, fols. 36–44. Also
printed in Coxe, *Kings of Spain,* IV, 197–208.

This was the last important matter handled by Keene at the Spanish
court. His health failing, he had solicited permission to return to England, but that permission came too late. He died on December 15, 1757.

20. Pitt to Newcastle, Oct. 11, 1757, referring only to "the unhappy
contents of Sir B. Keene's dispatch," Add. MSS. 32,875, fol. 40.

21. Pitt to Keene, Oct. 21, 1757, S.P. 94:156.

22. Cor. Pol., Espagne, vol. 522, especially Aubeterre to Bernis (the
French foreign minister), Nov. 16, 1757, fols. 418–420.

the war on the side of France. France promised to restore Minorca to Spain and to aid in a descent on Gibraltar, but the French met with no greater success than had Britain in the previous year.[23] Ferdinand VI and his minister Wall were determined to maintain Spanish neutrality.

In retrospect, it may be said that the initiative for this conditional offer of Gibraltar apparently came not from Pitt or the ministry, but from the king, who feared for the safety of his German dominions. Frederick of Prussia had been defeated, and it appeared that the French and Austrian armies were about to overwhelm him. In this extremity, Spanish aid seemed the only solution for England; Gibraltar and the logwood settlements were considered a proper sacrifice for a Spanish alliance and the return of Minorca. Spain refused to be drawn into the conflict, but the terms set forth by Pitt established a new basis for a future consideration of the restitution of Gibraltar. This basis, already implied in the secret negotiations of 1747 and 1748, was the definite abrogation of the Family Compact and a close friendship if not an open alliance with England.

The neutral and peace-loving Ferdinand VI died in August 1759; he was succeeded by his half-brother Charles, the son of Elizabeth Farnese who had been established on the throne of Naples. Under the wise direction of Charles III, Spain underwent a material and spiritual rehabilitation that restored a measure of her former greatness. Unlike his predecessor, Charles III had acquired the strong anti-English feeling of his father and mother. Almost immediately he indicated his preference for a revival of the Family Compact with France.

Yet the accession of Charles III did not at once interrupt the system of Spanish neutrality and the tolerably good relations existing between Spain and England. During 1759 and 1760, Spain showed no disposition to join France in the war, despite French pressure. The chief and

23. *Recueil des instructions* . . ., XIIbis, *Espagne, 1722–1793*, p. 323. Cantillo, *Tratados de paz y de comercio*, pp. 473–482.

immediate concern of the new Spanish king was internal
reform—to repair the lamentable state into which Spanish
finances and armaments had fallen under the listless Ferdinand—and externally his most apparent interest was
the security of Spain's Italian appendages against Austria. During 1760 the Spanish court was much less concerned over the continued success of the English against
France than over the plight of Prussia, which seemed
again on the verge of capitulating to the forces of the empress and France. Spain wholeheartedly hoped for a
Prussian victory, in order that Austria might be held in
check by a strong power on the north.

The fact that Charles III retained as his foreign secretary Richard Wall showed plainly that no sudden change
in Spanish policy was intended. Wall's alleged sympathies
for England made him a target for the French party at
Madrid. He apparently did exert what influence he could
to prevent Spain from joining with France in the war.
His relations with the new British ambassador at Madrid,
the Earl of Bristol, were most cordial. Certain matters
were in dispute between the two countries—the logwood
settlements, the Newfoundland fishery, and spoliation
cases—but they had been in controversy for years past.
When, in May 1760, a new Spanish commander of the
forces before Gibraltar closed the existing communication
with the garrison, orders were at once sent from Madrid
countermanding his action.[24] When rumors of an impending surprise attack by Spain on Gibraltar were current

24. S.P. 94:161, 162. Under a friendly understanding between the governor of Gibraltar and the local Spanish commander, the officers of the
British garrison had been permitted to ride out through the Spanish
lines into the surrounding country at their pleasure. In return, the governor did all he could to aid in the prevention of smuggling. "I have allowed the Spanish Tobacco Guards," he wrote, "to search the Town, and
the Vessels in the Mole, and on finding Tobacco or Smugglers have delivered them up to the Spanish General. I have permitted them, to keep
persons of their own appointing at the Wharfe to watch the Smugglers.
I have built a Guard House, and mounted an additional Guard, on purpose to prevent this Smuggling Trade." Governor Home to Bristol, May
30, 1760, S.P. 94:161. Such coöperation at Gibraltar would have been un-
thinkable under Philip V.

early in 1761, Wall categorically denied that his Catholic Majesty would entertain such an idea; he even assured Bristol that "upon hearing of the Disturbances at Gibraltar, his Catholic Majesty bid him [General Wall] suspend the sending of fresh Troops to Algeciras, where they were to embark [for Ceuta], least any sinister Constructions should be put upon that Measure happening to be so timed."[25]

The military situation of England and her allies rapidly improved during the winter and spring of 1761. Prussia turned back the armies of France and Austria, and British arms registered a steady succession of victories and conquests over France in all parts of the world. Spain was worried above all over the progress of British arms in America. Until the summer of 1761, however, although relations with England were becoming strained, Spain did not want to enter the war, but rather desired a quick and equitable peace between Britain and France. Even after the renewal of the Family Compact in August 1761, Spain seems to have dreaded being drawn into the war. England, on the other hand, having by now thoroughly trounced France, had no fear of Spain's entry into the contest, and did little or nothing to avert such an eventuality.[26]

France renewed her efforts to negotiate an alliance with Spain during January 1761. The Spanish king gave some encouragement to the French overtures; and his pro-French minister at Paris, Grimaldi, went so far as to propose an offensive alliance against England between the two nations. Before agreeing to the French proposals, Charles III tried unsuccessfully to mediate between France and Britain. Later, during July, he authorized the French to include Spanish demands in the terms for peace

25. Bristol to Wm. Pitt, March 16, 1761, S.P. 94:163. The "Disturbances" referred to the near-mutiny in October 1760, mentioned on p. 162.

26. Correspondence in S.P. 94:163. The correspondence dealing with the rupture between England and Spain has been published in *Papers Relative to the Rupture with Spain . . . Published by Authority* (London, 1762).

submitted to England, but the British indignantly refused
to include in the negotiation with France any matters then
in controversy with Spain. Finally, the Spanish king felt
impelled to desert his neutrality and ally himself with
France. The new Family Compact was signed at Paris on
August 15, 1761. At the same time, Spain and France also
signed a secret convention under which the Catholic King
bound himself to declare war against England by May 1,
1762, if peace had not been made between France and
England by that time; in return for Spanish participation in the war, Louis XV promised to cede Minorca to
Spain.[27]

Gibraltar was not mentioned in the new Family Compact, nor did Spain raise the issue in the negotiations with
Great Britain leading up to the rupture. When war had
threatened or occurred in previous decades, Spain had
been wont to urge the restitution of Gibraltar as the price
of keeping the peace. But in 1761 Spain herself wanted
peace, and England was pressing for war; consequently,
Gibraltar could not be mentioned. Nor does Spain seem to
have had any plan whatsoever for attacking Gibraltar
after the outbreak of war. Judging from the contemporary correspondence, it appears that both England and
Spain felt that Gibraltar was too strong to be taken by a
sudden assault, or by any siege which the condition of
Spain's military and financial circumstances would have
permitted. It is indeed surprising that Spain did not extract from France a renewal of the promise previously
made of aid for the recovery of Gibraltar. France had offered as much at the beginning of the war. But Charles
III in the summer of 1761 had no thought for Gibraltar;
he feared above all that England would impose too igno-
minious a peace on France and extend her American interests, possessions, and trade in such a way as to threaten
gravely the Spanish Indies.

27. Cantillo, *Tratados de paz y de comercio,* pp. 468–482. Louis Blart,
*Les rapports de la France et de l'Espagne après le Pacte de Famille
jusqu'à la fin du ministère du Duc de Choiseul* (Paris, 1915), pp. 1–16.

England finally forced a rupture with Spain in December 1761. Spain had postponed the evil day as long as possible, hoping for a pacific settlement. The Indies flota arriving in September 1761 brought only £330,000 on the king's account, a most disappointing total, entirely insufficient to permit the financing of an offensive war.[28] The signature of the new Family Compact had cast the die, however. When news of it reached London, the British ambassador at Madrid was instructed either to secure a disavowal of the new treaty or to ask for his passports. No disavowal was forthcoming, and diplomatic relations were broken off.

Spain's participation in the war brought only disaster to herself, and no aid to France. The Family Compact was supplemented by a convention for coördinating the military activity of the Bourbon powers, signed on February 4, 1762, but without mention of Gibraltar.[29] A succession of British victories during the year only accentuated the necessity for peace, and Spanish entry into the war did not interrupt the negotiations already in progress between England and France. Preliminaries were signed on November 3, 1762, and the final peace on February 10, 1763. Gibraltar did not enter into the negotiation of the Treaty of Paris. The Spanish did raise objections to the article renewing all prior treaties, since that article renewed their treaties guaranteeing England's possession of Gibraltar. Such objections were to no avail. In 1762 England was virtually dictating, not negotiating peace; any consideration of Gibraltar was out of the question.[30]

28. Bristol to Pitt, Sept. 21, 1761, S.P. 94: 164.
29. Cantillo, *Tratados de paz y de comercio,* pp. 482–485.
30. *Ibid.,* pp. 486–497. Blart, *Les rapports de la France et l'Espagne,* pp. 26–42. I have examined the correspondence in the Shelburne Papers in the Clements Library, vols. 9–12 and 38, which contain a very complete record of the secret and public negotiations leading up to the Treaty of Paris. They contain no mention of Gibraltar.

VIII

THE REVIVAL OF SPAIN, AND THE QUESTION OF GIBRALTAR DURING THE WAR FOR AMERICAN INDEPENDENCE, 1763–1782

AFTER the conclusion of the Seven Years' War, Spain, under the invigorating guidance of Charles III, gradually recuperated from her decadence and lethargy of the previous decades. No longer did Italian interests and ambitions sap the strength of the Spanish Empire. The Spanish king concentrated upon the improvement of the administration at home and in the Indies. The keynote of his foreign policy was the maintenance of the Family Compact on the basis of equality. The old rancor against England had been revived by her overwhelming victory and by her encroachments on Spanish America, in Florida, and in the logwood settlements. Gibraltar continued to be a seed of discord; but Spain, by her renewal of the Bourbon alliance, had closed the door to any peaceful negotiation for its restitution.

British fears for the safety of Gibraltar revived with the internal and external rehabilitation of Spain. Gibraltar was generally considered to be invulnerable to any siege by land; but it was apprehended that a sudden and concentrated assault, supported by a superior naval force, might be successful. In the event of a siege, the garrison would have had to rely on relief from England—a relief that would have taken from two to four months to reach the fortress.[1] No naval vessels were regularly stationed at

1. A report of Major Hugh Debbing, made in 1768, stated that Gibraltar could not be reduced by siege as long as the garrison could be relieved by sea. A siege, he asserted, was *"the only method by which it never will be reduced."* British Museum, King's MSS. 41, fols. 32–34. Another officer expressed a similar opinion in 1751; see Add. MSS. 30,196, fol. 16.

Governor Cornwallis summed up his opinion of Gibraltar's vulnerability

Gibraltar until 1766. In the previous year, Governor Irwin had petitioned that *one* naval vessel be kept permanently at Gibraltar so that he might send for aid if the garrison were beleaguered; but his request was refused.[2] After the threat to Gibraltar following a disastrous storm that swept the Rock early in 1766, Irwin renewed his request; and it was now granted.[3]

In the midst of a dispute over the Falkland Islands that almost led to hostilities between Spain and England, Gibraltar was struck, early in February 1766, by a storm of terrific intensity, which seriously damaged the fortifications and left the garrison in such a weakened condition that the Spaniards might have taken it if they had acted promptly. The Marquis de Crillon, commander of the Spanish troops before the fortress, sent an express to Madrid recommending that Gibraltar be attacked at once. The Spanish court decided against the proposal, but instituted measures to harass the garrison. Communication between Gibraltar and the mainland—open by informal

in the following extract from his letter to the Earl of Shelburne, dated September 18, 1768: "As your Lordship has desired my Opinion I am willing to say that Gibraltar has its faults, but, with them, as tenable in my opinion as any place in Europe; where it is vulnerable, is to the Sea— And I think the strictest Attention should be paid to that; I mean on no account to suffer a Fleet of the Enemy to get the start of ours upon an approach of War, for tho' it has often been said, that Gibraltar was impregnable, which no place is according to my notions, it was always understood, 'while you command the Sea'; The Bay is extensive, our Garrison small. If they by the contiguousness of their Ports should be able to bring a large Fleet of the Line before you do, it would puzle much, they would of course make a feint by Land to the Northward, those works must be maintained, in which Situation you would not have A Relief. How long men constantly on Duty could hold out is difficult to say, but I should hope, while there was a man left; I lay some stress upon this, for I really think that it is almost the only Danger we have to apprehend." Cornwallis agreed with his predecessor, General Irwin, that no plan for a surprise attack by land on Gibraltar had much chance of success. He discounted, as did the other governors, rumors of plots against the fortress. The only real danger to Gibraltar, as he stated above, was in an enemy's gaining command of Gibraltar from the sea with a superior force. C.O. 91:16.

2. C.O. 91:14.

3. Conway to Irwin, April 29, 1766, C.O. 91:15.

agreement for most of the time since 1748—was entirely cut off, and the duty on all articles shipped to Gibraltar from Spanish ports was doubled. Governor Irwin cared little about the stoppage of communications, but he was concerned over the signs of ill will which the Spanish were again beginning to show toward the garrison.[4]

Even before this threat, Governor Irwin had sent a number of officers to spy out the military and naval preparations then under way throughout southern Spain. These officers reported that the Spanish were not yet ready to begin hostilities, and that they would not be ready for at least two or three years. Irwin believed that the chief reason that the Spanish did not attack Gibraltar after the recommendation of Crillon was that neither the army and navy nor the finances of Spain were in a condition to sustain a war against England.[5] As a result of these reports, Irwin expressed but slight concern over subsequent rumors of secret Spanish plots for an assault on Gibraltar.[6] Probably the Spanish realized that as long as England remained mistress of the seas any such assault would have led to reprisals in the Spanish Indies and on Spanish trade that would have been far too high a price to pay for Gibraltar, no matter how badly Spain wanted it.

Animosity between Spain and England grew apace in the years preceding the American Revolution. Spain continued her program of rearmament and administrative reorganization, in preparation for a seemingly inevitable conflict in defense of her possessions and pretensions in America. The increased tension over local issues at Gibraltar[7] and the renewed English fears for the safety of their

4. Irwin to Conway, Feb. 10 and 28, 1766, C.O. 91:15.

This was the same Crillon who later led the great siege of Gibraltar, 1779–1783; M. Danvila y Collado states that Crillon "en 1766 se brindó a tomar la plaza de Gibraltar." *Reinado de Carlos III* (Madrid, 1893–1896), V, 4.

5. Irwin to Conway, April 6, 1766, C.O. 91:15.

6. Irwin to Shelburne, Feb. 8, 1767, C.O. 91:15.

7. One of the minor problems that recurred at this time concerned Catholic jurisdiction at Gibraltar. The Treaty of Utrecht guaranteed the maintenance of the Catholic religion, and after the occupation of the

Mediterranean fortress were portents of the growing hostility that animated Charles III and his ministers. The principal minister of the Spanish king was Grimaldi, an able Italian who, as Spanish ambassador at Paris in 1761, had championed the renewal of the Family Compact. The Conde de Aranda, leader of the Spanish party that demanded war with England, became the Spanish emissary to France in 1773, and left no stone unturned in his efforts to promote hostilities. With the appointment of the Comte de Vergennes to the Ministry of Foreign Affairs in 1774, French policy also became more aggressive, and by 1776 the Bourbon powers were united in their determination to make war on England as soon as their armaments should permit and the opportune moment should arrive.

The conflict between Spain and Portugal over the demarcation between their South American possessions threatened to initiate the anticipated conflict. These two powers had arranged a settlement of their boundary disputes by treaty in 1750, but colonial opposition prevented its execution. After 1770 the friction between the opposing forces, especially over the possession of the Banda Oriental (Uruguay), became critical. Additional to the conflict in America was the revival of agitation in Spain for the conquest of Portugal itself. In view of the close alliance between Great Britain and Portugal, Anglo-Span-

Rock by England the Bishop of Cádiz had continued to exercise his jurisdiction over the Catholic church in the town. The bishop himself visited Gibraltar in 1717, and his representative was permitted to enter on a subsequent occasion. After 1727, however, the English refused to countenance any supervision by the Spanish hierarchy over the Catholic population of Gibraltar. In 1768, application was made for a visitation by the vicar of San Roque. Governor Cornwallis denied this request, and was upheld by Lord Shelburne. The Spanish again raised the issue in 1773. The local prelate having died, Governor Cornwallis proceeded to appoint his successor. The Spanish protested, contending that the Bishop of Cádiz should at least be permitted to nominate several persons, of whom the governor could choose the one he wanted. England refused to listen to the Spanish plea. Lord Grantham, the British minister at Madrid, informed the Spanish minister Grimaldi "that the Bishop of Cadiz could not have the least Pretence whatever to interfere with that Business." C.O. 91:16, and Add. MSS. 24,174 (Grantham Papers).

ish hostilities seemed imminent. Aranda, upon his arrival in Paris, openly advocated aggressive action against both Portugal and England; and his urgings added to the growing sentiment in Spain in favor of the conquest of Portugal. England's hands already were tied by the incipient revolt of her American colonies. Escarano, the Spanish chargé at London, reported to Grimaldi on August 30, 1774, that, in view of the crisis in her colonies, England would go to almost any length—even to the abandonment of Portugal—to prevent a war with Spain.[8] Such an assurance fanned the Spanish spirit for war. Open hostilities broke out in 1774 with a Spanish invasion of the Banda Oriental. Early in the following year a project was formulated by Aranda, and approved by both the Spanish and French courts, for a general attack on England, including her Mediterranean possessions of Gibraltar and Minorca.[9]

Despite the increasing evidence of Spanish bellicosity, the dispatches of the British ambassador at Madrid, Lord Grantham, expressed no particular concern over the military preparations of Spain. When the Spanish fitted out an expedition at Cádiz in 1775, ostensibly for a campaign against the Moors, Grantham denied that it was designed for an attack either on Portugal or on Gibraltar; his only concern was over the possible Spanish occupation of Tangier, which might interfere with the provisioning of Gibraltar. A new concentration of forces at Cádiz in the summer of 1776 aroused the suspicions of the British consul, who thought that an attack on Gibraltar was in the offing; but Grantham again assured the London ministry that no such hostile attack was anticipated, and that the troops were destined for Buenos Aires. Throughout the Portuguese conflict, Grantham maintained his belief that Spain would make no attack on the *European* territory of Portugal, and that Aranda's overtures at Paris for a gen-

8. Juan F. Yela Utrilla, *España ante la independencia de los Estados Unidos* (Lérida, 1925), I, 42.

9. Danvila y Collado, *Reinado de Carlos III,* IV, 409–411.

eral offensive against Portugal were unauthorized and did not reflect the true intentions of Spain.[10]

Whatever the reality of Spanish designs on Portugal, France, not England, blocked them. In October 1775, Spain proposed a joint Franco-Spanish invasion of Portugal, France to be recompensed by Brazil. Vergennes evaded this overture and attempted to restrain Spain's efforts to precipitate war. The French, intent on keeping control of the situation themselves, shrank from any project that would involve Spanish leadership. They were equally indisposed, at heart, to the Spanish conquest of Portugal, an objective contrary to the well-established policy of France to prevent the union of the Iberian kingdoms.[11] Faced with French intransigence on the subject of Portugal, the Spanish suspended their plans for a general war, and confined hostilities to South America. A settlement between Spain and Portugal resolved itself out of several fortuitous developments in the Lusitanian kingdom by February 1777, and Portugal ceased to be the paramount objective in Spanish policy. Thereafter, the reacquisition of Gibraltar, not Portugal, became the goal of Spain.

France took the initiative in the direction of Bourbon policy against England by granting first secret, then open, aid to the American Revolution. By such aid France sought to weaken Great Britain and recover her diplomatic prestige in Europe. Spain also welcomed the American revolt, which promised to weaken both England and the fast-growing settlements in America, and consequently to ease British pressure on the Spanish Indies. Spain did not dare openly to aid the American Revolution; not only did she fear the establishment of a vigorous and independent English state in America, but also the example of aid to a colonial rebellion, which might prove disastrous to her own colonial empire. Accordingly, Spain furnished secret aid to the Americans at various intervals from the sum-

10. Add. MSS. 24,175.
11. Yela Utrilla, *España ante la independencia,* I, 56–61.

mer of 1776 on, but consistently refused to ally herself with them or even to recognize the new American nation until after the conclusion of hostilities.

The settlement of the Portuguese conflict coincided with the elevation to power of a new minister in Spain, Moniño, the Conde de Floridablanca, who took over the direction of Spanish policy from the Italian Grimaldi. Floridablanca proved to be one of the greatest of Spanish ministers. In general, he followed the policies of his predecessor; but the frustration by France of Spanish designs on Portugal had cooled the ardor of the Spanish for war. When France finally entered into an open alliance with the United States, in February 1778 (which soon led to war with England), she did so without the approval of Spain. The Spanish, irked by the failure of France to consult them before embarking upon such a momentous step, refused to follow her example. Instead, Spain sought through mediation to end the war and to prevent the achievement of that perfect American independence which France had bound herself to secure. As a price for her mediation, Spain asked for the restitution of Gibraltar. When England rebuffed her efforts to secure Gibraltar by pacific means, Spain entered the war with the dual objectives of regaining the Mediterranean fortress and of protecting and strengthening her colonial empire in America against England.[12]

Before considering the relevant aspects of Spain's attempted mediation in the War for American Independence, we should note two obstacles that helped to frustrate that attempt. First, a strong faction at the Spanish court advocated a more forceful intervention in the struggle.

12. In this general discussion of the embroilment of Spain and France in the War for American Independence, I have depended principally upon the following works: Samuel Flagg Bemis, *The Diplomacy of the American Revolution* (New York, 1935); Henri Doniol, *Histoire de la participation de la France à l'établissement des Etats-Unis d'Amérique* (Paris, 1886–1899); Richard Konetzke, *Die Politik des Grafen Aranda* (Berlin, 1929); Valentín Urtasún, *Historia diplomática de América* (Pamplona, 1920–1924); and the previously cited works of Yela Utrilla and Danvila y Collado.

Lord Grantham's reports during 1777 indicated a growing uneasiness over the attitude of Spain toward the
American conflict. Though Floridablanca maintained in
his conversations with Grantham a civility and moderation
which augured well for the continuance of Spanish neutrality, the British ambassador reported, on November 19,
1777, that "he has certainly used more confident Language than I have heard employed by this Court since my
residence here." Further, in this same dispatch, he remarked:

If I were to admit, that there was no real hostile Intention in
this Court, I would not however engage for the permanency
of such a System. The Temptation of a growing Commerce
in France, the many Cases that may and must arise from it,
the backwardness of this Court to act against the Americans,
are all Circumstances which will certainly leave the most delicate and dangerous openings for the worst Consequences as
long as the present unhappy Rebellion shall last.[13]

Secondly, after the signing of the American alliance,
France exerted all her influence to draw Spain into the
war. Spanish attempts at mediation consequently were
handicapped from the beginning both by French efforts
to detach Spain from her neutrality and by the warlike
attitude of a strong party at Madrid, abetted by the efforts of Aranda at Paris.

Following the announcement of the formal alliance between France and the American States, Floridablanca informed the British that Spain had no intention of following the French example. To Lord Grantham he expressed
his sincere desire for a continuance of friendly relations
with England; and the British ambassador advised his superior that there was no doubt that "the Sudden Decision
and Violence of the French Measures, has occasioned great
surprize at this Court, and in this Nation, and the want
of confidence on the part of France has given high Offense,

13. Grantham to Weymouth, Nov. 19, 1777, Add. MSS. 24,176, fols.
36–37.

and the Rashness of blindly adopting such dangerous Designs is seen in its true Light."[14] Escarano, the Spanish chargé at London, informed the British ministry that Spain "neither wished for war nor would she make it." In reply, Lord Weymouth, the British secretary of state, expressed his earnest desire for friendship with Spain; indirectly he suggested that Spain interpose her good offices to bring an end to the conflict. Acting upon this suggestion, Floridablanca instructed Escarano on April 19 to find out whether England would accept a Spanish proposal for mediation, it being understood that such a mediation would include a settlement between England and the American colonies.[15]

In accordance with his instructions, Escarano held a series of conferences with Lord Weymouth and other English ministers, beginning on April 30. Although the Spanish chargé assured the British that he was uninstructed as to the "adjustments" in her relations with England which Spain herself hoped to secure in connection with her offer of mediation, he hinted that Gibraltar was the most considerable difficulty between the two nations. The suggestion of Gibraltar seems at once to have cooled the English desire for Spanish mediation. Lord Mansfield told Escarano "that Gibraltar was of great importance for this country [Great Britain], and that in addition it would be very difficult, if not impossible to compose things after they have reached such an extreme."[16] A few days later Lord North sought out Escarano during an audience at the Palace, and assured him that England would be under

14. Grantham to Weymouth, March 31, 1778, Add. MSS. 24,176, fol. 60.
15. Yela Utrilla, *España ante la independencia,* I, 344–348. Grantham to Weymouth, April 19, 1778, Add. MSS. 24,176, fols. 73–74. The most complete account of this Spanish mediation is that of Danvila y Collado in *Reinado de Carlos III,* V, 3–74.
16. Escarano to Floridablanca, May 11, 1778, Spain, Archivo Nacional, Papeles de Estado, Legajo 4199, Apartado 4. (Hereafter cited as A.N., Est.) Photocopy in the Manuscripts Division of the Library of Congress. Subsequent citations to Spanish, French, and English documentary material that I have obtained from the photocopy and transcript collections of the Library of Congress will be suffixed by (L.C.).

a great obligation to his Catholic Majesty if by his mediation a solution to the conflict might be found. But, though Escarano noted that North expressed a stronger desire than Weymouth to avoid hostilities with Spain, North made no offer to compensate Spain for her proposed mediation, nor did he indicate that England was willing to make the least sacrifice in return for peace. Escarano concluded his report of this conversation with the following significant observation: "It seems to me that we will not be able to draw the least advantage from them; that we ought to be sure that far from desiring to attack us, they look on us with indifference; and that if France is not the first to make propositions they will not do it from here."[17] From the beginning, it appears that the proffered Spanish mediation was doomed to frustration, and that the Spanish insinuations on the subject of Gibraltar fell on deaf ears.

Perceiving the obvious reluctance of the British ministry to accept Spanish mediation, Floridablanca informed the British that the Catholic king would not accept the rôle of mediator until both parties specifically requested him to do so.[18] He instructed Escarano to discontinue his conversations with the British ministers about the terms of Spanish mediation, pending the arrival of the newly chosen ambassador to Great Britain, the Marquis de Almodóvar. At the same time, Escarano was told that King Charles wished him to listen attentively to anything that might be dropped about Gibraltar, but not to discuss the matter.[19]

France at once accepted the Spanish offer of mediation, but English replies were evasive. At London, Escarano was told that before mediation could be accepted France must annul her alliance with the Americans.[20] In Spain,

17. Escarano to Floridablanca, May 20, 1778, A.N., Est., Leg. 4199, Apar. 4 (L.C.).
18. Yela Utrilla, *España ante la independencia*, I, 351.
19. Floridablanca to Escarano, June 1, 1778, A.N., Est., Leg. 4199, Apar. 4 (L.C.).
20. Danvila y Collado, *Reinado de Carlos III*, V, 9.

Lord Grantham informed Floridablanca on June 2 that England would be "willing to listen" to whatever terms the Spanish king might draw up as the basis for mediation.[21] Meanwhile, further steps were suspended until Almodóvar reached London early in July. Following his first interviews with Lord Weymouth, Almodóvar expressed the opinion that England had no sincere desire for Spanish mediation, but sought only to divide the Bourbon allies and postpone Spanish entry into the war. After the outbreak of actual hostilities between England and France in the same month, Vergennes redoubled his efforts to get Spain into the war. But Floridablanca and his royal master were not yet willing to enter the conflict. They still hoped to mediate advantageously, that is, to secure Gibraltar (and possibly Minorca) as the price of Spanish good offices. So Floridablanca advised the French on August 11.[22]

Though still hopeful of achieving her objectives by mediation, Spain continued her military preparations, especially in the south. Grantham as early as August 7 indicated his belief that Spain would surely enter the contest if the war with France continued.[23] Ominously, the Spanish were most active in their concentration of military materials—including a large number of battering cannon at Málaga—in the vicinity of Gibraltar. "These measures," reported the British ambassador, "argue an Intention in this Court, to be prepared at least, and seem to point out the object against which they will be employed if ever called forth to action. In which case I clearly think that an Attempt on Gibraltar will be attempted [sic]."[24]

After further conferences with the English ministers during September, Almodóvar arranged a tentative course for the Spanish mediation. He was now more hopeful of its success, and for the realization of Spain's own objective—

21. Yela Utrilla, *España ante la independencia*, I, 353.
22. Doniol, *Histoire de la participation de la France*, III, 536–544.
23. Grantham to Weymouth, Aug. 7, 1778, Add. MSS. 24,176, fol. 97.
24. Grantham to Weymouth, Aug. 28, 1778, Add. MSS. 24,176, fol. 100.

the restitution of Gibraltar. Lord Barrington, the English
secretary of war, assured Almodóvar "that he had no
doubt but that his court would give up Gibraltar, and
even Minorca," in return for a Spanish settlement of the
war on terms satisfactory to England. Led on by such
statements, Almodóvar suggested that France and England submit their demands through their ambassadors at
Madrid to Floridablanca; these propositions would serve
as a basis for a peace settlement to be concluded at Madrid, and at the same time an adjustment of the differences between Britain and Spain would be concluded and
signed. To this arrangement the British seemingly agreed.
Floridablanca, on receiving his ambassador's letter of September 18 communicating the above proposals, still suspected the sincerity of the British and thought they sought
only to gain time. Nevertheless, he decided to go ahead;
and on September 28 he formally notified Grantham and
Montmorin, the French ambassador at Madrid, that if
England and France would submit their terms as proposed, Spain would now assume the mediatory rôle between them. The French promptly accepted this overture,
and on October 17 Montmorin submitted the terms of
France to Floridablanca. They included the recognition
of American independence and a goodly number of compensations for France herself. At London, the Spanish
proposal of September 28 was viewed as too forceful; and
the ministry hesitated to accept it, especially in view of
the Spanish insinuation that her good offices were to be
had only in return for Gibraltar. Yet the British still insisted that they desired to pursue the mediation, and
Grantham was finally authorized to present the British
terms. This he did on November 10. The substance of the
British position was that they would be ready to discuss
peace with France just as soon as the French withdrew all
support from America. To the solicitations of Spain herself, the English returned a sufficiently ambiguous response: "As to the mutual interests of Great Britain and
Spain, his Britannic Majesty was desirous to enter into

that discussion, with the greatest inclination of adjusting them, in a manner that should produce a useful and advantageous union between the two nations."[25]

Despite apparent progress toward an understanding, the attitude of distrust and hostility between Spain and England had so ripened by October 1778 that the subsequent course of the mediation seems largely a matter of form and of the postponement of the inevitable. On October 6, the Spanish king, in a personal note to Floridablanca written after a perusal of Almodóvar's dispatches, expressed his gratification, not at the seeming receptiveness of the British to Spanish mediation, but at the British "determination not to trust us," and concluded: "We will continue to arm ourselves."[26] Lord Weymouth, in transmitting the British response to Floridablanca's proposal of September 28, confidentially wrote: "It seems to me difficult to believe that the Court of Spain is really determined to use its efforts to reëstablish peace and prevent the independency of America from being established. . . . It seems impossible not to apprehend that Spain has hostile Views and that the part she now takes is at the instigation of France, and the menace at the end can only be interpreted as hostile to this Country."[27]

Floridablanca, though "distrustful" of the wide differences between the terms submitted by France and England, decided to continue the mediation. On November 20 he communicated the demands of the belligerents to each other, by joint notes to Vergennes and to Almodóvar. The French responded on December 24. The substance of their reply was that there seemed to be no possibility of an understanding with England on the question of the Americans; the French were willing to agree to a solution that would have left the new nation with something short of perfect independence, but they could not completely dis-

25. Danvila y Collado, *Reinado de Carlos III,* V, 23–30.

26. Charles III to Floridablanca, San Lorenzo, Oct. 6, 1778, A.N., Est., Leg. 4199bis, Apar. 7 (L.C.).

27. Weymouth to Grantham, Oct. 27, 1778, Add. MSS. 24,165, fol. 282.

avow their American alliance as a preliminary to negotiation with Great Britain. With the answer to the mediation proposals, Vergennes enclosed a new plan of war for the Bourbon allies against England! The English ministry submitted its response to Almodóvar on December 29, and completely rejected the demands of France. Confronted by the unconciliatory response of England, Almodóvar proceeded to press Lord Weymouth on the points of Gibraltar and Minorca, without touching on the matter of equivalents. Weymouth answered that their restitution could be considered only when the friendship between Britain and Spain had been reëstablished on "very solid terms."[28] The English minister followed up his interview with Almodóvar by a confidential letter of the same date to Grantham, urging him to use every effort to discover the *secret* intention of Spain behind her mediation proposals.[29]

The Spanish minister now abandoned his interlocutory rôle, and on January 20 instructed Almodóvar to deliver to the British ministry a new set of proposals for an accommodation, practically in the form of an ultimatum. The Spanish demanded that a truce be arranged between Great Britain, France, and the Americans; and that a settlement between Britain and her colonies be arranged at Madrid under Spanish auspices. In addition, Floridablanca repeated his insinuation that the services and friendship of Spain were to be had only if England would give up Gibraltar. He asserted that Spain was prepared to grant a handsome equivalent. The English did not reply to this overture until March 16, when they brusquely rejected the terms submitted by Floridablanca as bases for a negotiation. Before then, Almodóvar had reported that a majority in Parliament favored war with Spain. The English response of March 16 ended the pretense of Spanish mediation and neutrality. True, Spain transmitted a

28. Doniol, *Histoire de la participation de la France,* III, chap. X. Danvila y Collado, *Reinado de Carlos III,* V, 30–33.
29. Weymouth to Grantham, Dec. 29, 1778, Add. MSS. 24,165, fol. 332.

final ultimatum to England on April 3.[30] But without ex-
pecting or awaiting a favorable reply, Floridablanca
signed the Convention of Aranjuez with France on April
12, and thereby committed Spain to the course of war.

Although Spain's effort to end the war met with failure,
the delay served to strengthen both her military and her
diplomatic position. Hostilities were postponed until the
arrival of the spring flota from the Indies, and Spain was
able to build up her navy and accumulate military supplies for an assault on Gibraltar. France, eager for Spanish assistance, became increasingly amenable to the terms
which Spain demanded as the price of her aid. The Convention of Aranjuez must be considered a diplomatic triumph for Spain. Not only did she enter the conflict without committing herself in any way to support the cause
of American independence, but also she obligated France
not to make peace until Gibraltar had been recovered. Article Nine of the "private treaty" of Aranjuez read as
follows:

Their Catholic and Very Christian Majesties promise to
make every effort to procure and acquire for themselves all
the advantages specified above, and to continue these efforts
until they have obtained the end which they have proposed
to themselves, mutually offering not to lay down their arms
and not to make any treaty of peace, truce, or suspension of
hostilities, without having at least obtained and having respectively assured themselves of the restitution of Gibraltar,

30. Danvila y Collado, *Reinado de Carlos III*, V, 37–49. The ultimatum
of April 3 is given in full on pp. 48–49. It proposed: an indefinite suspension of hostilities between England and France, with general disarmament in the various theatres of war at the earliest possible date;
an Anglo-French peace conference at Madrid; a similar armistice and
disarmament between England and "the American colonies," with an
uti possidetis arrangement during the interim; that British and American
commissioners negotiate separately at Madrid under Spanish mediation,
and in this negotiation the "colonies" be treated as "independent in
fact"; that the King of Spain guarantee the proper conduct of the preliminary arrangements provided that the "belligerent powers guarantee
to Spain the treaties or adjustments that should be made" on her behalf
(*i.e.* Gibraltar, etc.).

and of the abolition of the treaties relative to the fortifications of Dunkirk, or, in default of this article, anything else that his Very Christian Majesty may desire.[31]

The conflicting obligations of the Convention of Aranjuez and of the Franco-American Alliance placed France in a delicate position. On the one hand, France had promised not to make peace until American independence had been secured; and on the other, she bound herself to continue the war until Spain had obtained Gibraltar. We shall presently see how Vergennes, that master of eighteenth-century diplomacy, rescued France from this dilemma in the peace negotiations of 1782.

After the conclusion of the Convention of Aranjuez, Spain rapidly prepared for war. Floridablanca informed Grantham on June 20, 1779, that the Spanish ambassador at London had asked for his passports; and Grantham prepared to leave Madrid. On the same day, Spain drew up regulations to govern the blockade of Gibraltar, for the capture of that fortress was her immediate goal in the war. The Spanish also proceeded to join their fleet to the French, in preparation for a descent upon England. They hoped to finish the war in one campaign, for they did not feel that their resources would permit a longer struggle.[32]

A miscarriage in the naval maneuvers of the Bourbon fleet frustrated the intended invasion of England in the summer of 1779, and the English succeeded in relieving Gibraltar by the end of that year. Spanish hopes for a quick and victorious conclusion of the war faded. The growing weakness of their military and financial position quickly revived the desire of the Spanish for peace—a separate peace if need be—if favorable terms could be obtained. The Spanish were determined that the cession of

31. Doniol, *Histoire de la participation de la France*, III, 809, appendix. Gibraltar headed the list of the "advantages specified above"; the others included Minorca and the ejection of the English from Honduras and the shores of the Gulf of Mexico.

32. Grantham to Weymouth, June 20, 1779, Add. MSS. 24,176, fols. 194–195.

Gibraltar should be a *sine qua non* in any negotiation that might be undertaken. They also hoped to secure Minorca, to oust the British from the vicinity of the Gulf of Mexico, and to find some solution that would satisfy the American engagements of France and yet leave the Americans bound in some manner to Great Britain.

Floridablanca found a medium for initiating a secret negotiation with England in the person of Thomas Hussey, an Irish priest who actually was a secret agent of Spain, and known as such to the English. Hussey in some manner established a contact with Richard Cumberland, the secretary of the Board of Trade and a protégé of Lord George Germain, the secretary of state.[33] The Spanish agent insinuated to Cumberland, and afterward to Germain himself, that, if England would give up Gibraltar, Spain might negotiate a separate peace with England and grant a suitable equivalent for the surrender of the Rock. On the latter score he mentioned Orán and "a strong footing on the Mosquito Shore," and a sum of money as well. Hussey suggested that he would be willing to make a secret journey to Madrid and sound the Spanish court on its disposition for peace, if one of the English ministers would give him a letter that would lend credit to his undertaking. The English ministers (North and Hillsborough were also privy to the approaches of Hussey), though not wholly averse to the thought of ceding Gibraltar, had no intention of authorizing Hussey to inform the Spanish court of their disposition. On the other hand, they felt that Hussey's mission would do no harm, and might at least sow a seed of discord in Franco-Spanish relations. Germain finally gave Hussey a letter of credence (November 29, 1779), and the Irishman hustled off to Madrid.

A secret and complex negotiation followed. The story

33. It is not clear whether Hussey acted on any specific authority from the Spanish minister in his conversations with Cumberland and others. The date when those conversations began is also uncertain. The correspondence in the Sackville (Germain) MSS. in the Clements Library seems to indicate that Hussey was in contact with Cumberland before the beginning of November 1779.

has already been told by Bemis,[34] and need not be repeated in all its intricate detail. Both England and Spain wanted peace, if it could be obtained on advantageous terms. Despite the common desire to put an end to the conflict, certain fundamental obstacles prevented this negotiation from having any real chance of success. Spain was adamant on the subject of Gibraltar, though her chief minister was not unwilling to exclude the question of the Rock from the treaty of peace, if England would agree to make a separate treaty arranging the cession. Nor would Spain agree to desert France. The British ministry, although divided on the question of Gibraltar, absolutely refused to submit to Spanish mediation in the struggle with the colonies, even though Spain sought to found her intervention on a compromise that would have limited American independence.

Floridablanca suspected the sincerity of England in this negotiation from the beginning, believing that any English overture for a secret peace had as its true objective the hope of dividing France and Spain. Finally, after Hussey had assured the Spanish minister that there was at least some sentiment in the English Cabinet in favor of the cession of Gibraltar, Floridablanca permitted the priest to return to London with the message that Spain would welcome a negotiation, provided that England would give up Gibraltar. He was prompted to do so not only by the overtures of Hussey, but also by some representations of Commodore George Johnstone, the commander of a British fleet stationed off the Portuguese coast, that England was pre-

34. S. F. Bemis, *The Hussey-Cumberland Mission and American Independence* (Princeton, 1931). I have supplemented Bemis' volume with three accounts composed by Cumberland: a memorandum covering the background of the secret negotiation, December–February, 1779–1780, printed in Coxe, *Kings of Spain*, V, 69–80; and two manuscript narratives, the first entitled "Particulars of the Secret Negotiation between Great Britain and Spain, Carried on at Madrid in the Years 1780 and 1781," dated June 4, 1781 (three days after Cumberland's return to London from his mission), in the Shelburne Papers, vol. 168, fols. 408–415 (Clements Library); and the second, "Narrative of a Secret Negotiation in Spain," dated May 20, 1782, Add. MSS. 28,851.

pared to cede Gibraltar in return for a resumption of
Spanish neutrality in the war.[35]

Following Hussey's return to London at the end of January 1780, the British Cabinet considered the question of
a separate peace with Spain in four successive meetings.
The ministers were divided on the question of Gibraltar.
Nevertheless, a project was drawn up setting forth the
conditions upon which England would consider the cession. It specified that Gibraltar might be ceded in return
for the following: the cession of Puerto Rico; the cession
of the "fortress Omoa [in the Bay of Honduras], and its
territory"; the cession of Orán; payment by Spain not
only for the stores and artillery at Gibraltar, but also of
an additional sum of £2,000,000; a separate peace on the
basis of the Treaty of Paris, and the renunciation by
Spain of all engagements to France that might involve her
in a future war with Great Britain; the promise by Spain
"in the clearest and most solemn manner not to assist the
British colonies in America, nor to receive any minister or
agent from them, nor to suffer their ships to enter any
ports in the Spanish dominions"—in return, England
would make a similar engagement on behalf of Spain's
American colonies; "a cessation of arms to be agreed upon
as soon as the above articles are signed and ratified; but
the cession of Gibraltar on our part, and that of Porto
Rico on the part of Spain not to take place till the American rebellion is ended."[36]

These terms were not communicated to Hussey officially;
instead, it was resolved "that the secretaries of state
should, in person, jointly communicate to Mr. Hussey the

35. Johnstone, like Cumberland, was a protégé of Germain. Without
doubt, his overture reflected his patron's opinion, but it was made without any shadow of authority. He was promptly disavowed officially, but
not reprimanded, even though he continued his overtures for some
months.

36. Coxe, *Kings of Spain,* V, 72–74, quoting a memorandum of Cumberland then in the possession of Porten, the secretary to the British
Cabinet. In a footnote, Coxe dryly adds: "It must be confessed, that if
it could be deemed policy to relinquish Gibraltar, the framer of these
conditions was not deficient in his demand for an equivalent."

result of these deliberations, and the mind of the British ministry towards the proposed accommodation with Spain." Lords Stormont and Hillsborough, the secretaries, jointly advised Hussey that England sincerely desired peace; but they completely disavowed the overtures of Johnstone, and left no hope that England would cede Gibraltar under any circumstances. Hussey, knowing that Floridablanca would not consider a negotiation on any other basis, decided to abandon his efforts.[37]

After a private conversation with Richard Cumberland, Hussey was persuaded to reconsider his decision. Cumberland told the Irishman that the Cabinet could not very well impart its true intentions on Gibraltar, for fear that Hussey's report to Floridablanca might raise false hopes in the minds of the Spaniards. With the assistance of Cumberland, Hussey composed a letter to Floridablanca, stating that although "the tender of Gibraltar, as a previous and indispensable article of the treaty [of peace], is what the cabinet could not be brought to grant . . . they offer to treat upon the basis of the treaty of Paris; and then Spain may start the subject under the title of Change of Territory." Hussey added: "I really believe that they will cede Gibraltar upon terms; but for this I have no authority from the british cabinet, neither written nor verbal." This letter was not officially communicated to the British ministry, but Cumberland privately showed it to Germain and Hillsborough.[38]

Did the British Cabinet, in February 1780, have any intention of ceding Gibraltar in a separate treaty, subsequent to the conclusion of the treaty of peace? That is a moot question.[39] At any rate, the above letter of Hussey

37. Coxe, Kings of Spain, V, 74–78.

38. Coxe, Kings of Spain, V, 78–80. The draft quoted by Cumberland (in Coxe) was dated February 13, and Cumberland stated that it was dispatched to Madrid on February 14. Bemis, Hussey-Cumberland Mission, pp. 32–33, quotes the same letter from the Spanish archives, with the date of February 16.

39. Hussey wrote to Floridablanca, on March 8, 1780: "Lord North and Lord Germain are more disposed than the rest [of the British

convinced Floridablanca that they did have such an intention. But the instructions for Richard Cumberland, the envoy chosen for a secret mission to negotiate a separate peace, prohibited him from discussing anything about Gibraltar or even from entering Spain until Floridablanca had given his word that the subject of Gibraltar would not be introduced into the negotiation.

Cumberland, accompanied by Hussey, set out for Spain in April 1780, going first to Lisbon, where he was to wait until assurance had been received that the Spanish would not bring up the question of Gibraltar if he proceeded to Madrid. Hussey hurried on to the Spanish court, and sent back an ambiguous message which Cumberland construed as an assurance that Floridablanca would not project the subject of Gibraltar into his conferences with the English envoy. Cumberland then continued on into Spain, arriving at Aranjuez in mid-June.

In his conferences with Floridablanca, Cumberland soon discovered that the Spanish minister intended to found the negotiation upon the bases outlined in his earlier memoranda to Hussey: Spain would be willing to enter into a separate peace, but only if England would agree to cede Gibraltar in a separate and secret article or treaty, to be arranged coincidentally with the treaty of peace. The English envoy also found that recent events had cooled the ardor of Floridablanca for any negotiation. The news from England of growing parliamentary opposition and of the Gordon riots (news of which reached Madrid on the eve of Cumberland's first formal conference) stiffened the Spanish toward any compromise. The military position of Spain had also improved; the blockade of Gibraltar had been resumed with renewed vigor; and the Spanish, recuperating from their late naval disaster at the hands of Rodney, had accumulated a large fleet at Cádiz for of-

ministers] to give up Gibraltar. The others say, that while they might agree to cede Gibraltar, it will not be done as long as Spain is allied with France against England." Danvila y Collado, *Reinado de Carlos III*, V, 155.

fensive action. Early in August a joint Franco-Spanish fleet dealt the British a devastating blow by capturing the combined East and West Indian merchant flotilla off Cape St. Vincent. The French, fully aware of the dangers that lurked in Cumberland's mission, endeavored to frustrate it by every possible means. Under such circumstances, the desire of Spain for a separate peace, so evident at the beginning of the year, seemed about to vanish, unless England were willing immediately to give up Gibraltar.

The barrenness of his initial conferences led Cumberland to request further instructions from his superiors at London. Lord Hillsborough responded on August 3, 1780, in a letter couched in general terms, asking that Spain state her proposals for peace. Floridablanca appeared irked at Hillsborough's response and suspicious of English sincerity, for he insisted that Spain had already submitted her proposals through Hussey earlier in the year. Cumberland answered that those proposals had been founded upon the unauthorized overtures of Commodore Johnstone, which he had been expressly instructed to disavow; and that they had also included as a necessary basis for a settlement the cession of Gibraltar, which he was forbidden to discuss. After some parrying, Floridablanca agreed that Gibraltar could not be introduced into the negotiation with Cumberland, but insisted that Spain would never make peace unless Gibraltar were secured. At length it was agreed that Hussey should be sent to London to inform the English ministers of the Spanish position. Practically, Hussey's instructions, both written and verbal, were in the form of an ultimatum: Gibraltar must be restored, if necessary by a separate and secret treaty; if England agreed to surrender the fortress, Spain would arrange a peace on the basis of a "middle term" that would restrict American independence and at the same time provide a formula for extricating France from her American engagements.

Hussey reached London in the middle of October, and presented Floridablanca's demands to the British ministry. At a Cabinet meeting held a few days thereafter, there was some division on the wisdom of ceding Gibraltar, but the ministers deemed it politically inexpedient, in view of the approaching elections, to give any answer to Hussey for the time being. Above all, the king and ministry were adamant toward the projected mediation of Spain in the American conflict; throughout this negotiation, the British never wavered on that point. Despite the refusal to give any answer to Spain, the ministry wished to keep the negotiation open, in order to prevent Spanish recognition of the Americans and to disrupt the harmony of the Bourbon courts. At length, Hussey received a vague and unsatisfactory reply to Floridablanca's "ultimatum." He set out with it for Madrid, but his account of the English response transmitted from Lisbon (December 28, 1780) was so unsatisfactory to Floridablanca that Hussey was not permitted to proceed to the Spanish capital.[40] Instead, the Spanish minister sent him back to London with a message that effectively put an end to the negotiation.[41]

40. Shelburne MSS., vol. 168. In his letter of Dec. 28, 1780, to Floridablanca, Hussey remarked: "After dictating to me this reply, Lord Hillsborough entered into further conversation on the point of Gibraltar, saying that so far as he was concerned it would please him if it were ceded to Spain, but that he would not dare to advise it to the King, for if the Nation should revolt this advice might cost him his head." Bemis, *Hussey-Cumberland Mission*, p. 95, footnote.

41. Floridablanca's response summarized the Spanish position on the point of Gibraltar in this negotiation in the following passage: "Fully comprehending the answer which Ld. Hillsborough directed you to give me relative to the Negotiation of peace intended to be established: I see that that Minister, and his Court have formed the Idea that Gibraltar was Not to be mentioned, nor the Colonies, in case of Mr. Cumberland's coming to Madrid. In this point there is a great equivocation, because on our side, it was only agreed upon that nothing should be mentioned about Gibraltar in the *Preliminaries:* but it was proposed that by a secret convention or separate Treaty, the Cession or exchange of that Fortress might be regulated, and concluded at the same time with the Preliminaries of Peace. This was uniformly my language, to which I always added that without such cession or exchange it would be impossible that the peace should be lasting, nor that the amity between the two nations should be true or solid. The negative therefore put, in such *absolute* terms, by the Court of London on this matter, is to us an undeceiving proof that G. Britain does not desire to be the friend of Spain, nor indeed never can whils't this apple of discord subsists between both

Shortly after Hussey delivered Floridablanca's reply to the British ministry, Cumberland was recalled from Spain.[42]

The departure of Cumberland ended the attempt of Spain to make a secret peace with England for the price of Gibraltar. That effort failed principally because King George and the North ministry refused to consider any compromise with regard to America. The principal result of Cumberland's mission (as he himself emphasized when he returned) was temporarily to disrupt the coöperation of the Bourbon courts in their prosecution of the war.

The Spanish, undaunted by the failure of their efforts to secure Gibraltar by direct negotiation with England, turned to the proffered mediation of Austria and Russia as the means to secure their favorite objective. Both the empress and the tsarina had sounded the belligerent powers on the subject of mediation in the summer of 1779. The failure of the Spanish to achieve any success in their secret negotiations with England gradually made them more receptive to mediation from a neutral power. Finally, on January 28, 1781, Kaunitz, the Austrian minister of Foreign Affairs, officially offered the joint mediation of the Empire and Russia to the court of Madrid. Acting upon this offer, Floridablanca sent the Marquis de la Torre to St. Petersburg with instructions (dated March 1, 1781) to make known the terms upon which Spain would

Nations." Floridablanca to Hussey, Jan. 20, 1781, Sackville MSS., Cumberland Papers (Clements Library).

42. "Particulars of a Secret Negotiation . . ." (Cumberland's report of June 4, 1781), Shelburne MSS., vol. 168. Bemis, *Hussey-Cumberland Mission*, p. 96. Cumberland's recall was dated at London, Feb. 14, 1781; he left Madrid on March 24 and arrived in London on June 1. Hussey stayed in London for some months in the capacity of a Spanish secret agent. In June 1781, Hillsborough suggested to Hussey that England might exchange Gibraltar for Puerto Rico, if Spain would resume her efforts to arrange a settlement of the conflict. Hussey refused to reopen the negotiation, though he reported Hillsborough's remark to Floridablanca. Cumberland subsequently offered to renew his efforts through the channel of Floridablanca's assistant, Bernardo del Campo, but Hillsborough would not permit him to do so. Bemis, *Hussey-Cumberland Mission*, p. 95, footnote. Add. MSS. 28,851, fol. 47.

make peace; among them, the cession of Gibraltar was insisted upon, either outright or in exchange for a sum of
money or Orán. The competition between Austria and
Russia for the lead in the mediation, as well as the apparent disinclination of Britain to accept any mediation that
would be satisfactory to the Bourbon allies, delayed the
negotiation. The British insisted that the Spanish demand
for Gibraltar must be removed from the terms of the mediation, and that they would not accept any mediation
whatsoever for a settlement between England and the
Americans. Austria and Russia then proposed a compromise, by joint notes of May 21, 1781, under which the
peace should be arranged at a joint congress at Vienna.
Again the Spanish insisted that they would not accept any
terms that would not admit the negotiation of the restitution of Gibraltar; the only concession that Spain would
make would be to grant an equivalent for the Rock, if
necessary.[43]

The projected Austro-Russian mediation failed to make
any progress against the obstinate determination of
George III to reject any outside attempt to intercede in
the American conflict. An anecdote related by Floridablanca epitomized the feeling of the English king and
Tory ministry: Lord Stormont, one of the secretaries of
state, had exclaimed to the Austrian ambassador, "that
the King of England would recognize the independence
of the colonies when the French were masters of the Tower
of London, and that with respect to Gibraltar, only Madrid would be recognized as an equivalent for that place."[44]
But the argument of Yorktown, coupled with the loss of
Minorca, finally undermined the already tottering North
ministry and forced George III to accept the inevitable.
Peace was not to come through mediation, however, but
through direct negotiations begun by the new Whig administration in England.

43. Danvila y Collado, *Reinado de Carlos III*, V, 345–355.
44. *Ibid.*, p. 358.

IX

GIBRALTAR IN THE PEACE NEGOTIATIONS OF 1782

THE fall of the North ministry in England laid the foundation for the peace negotiations of 1782. The new ministry, nominally under the leadership of Lord Rockingham, took office with the understanding that the independence of the United States should be recognized in the forthcoming peace negotiations, provided that France and Spain should agree to make peace on the basis of the Treaty of Paris of 1763 with such rectifications as might be necessary. In the new Cabinet, Lord Shelburne, a confidant of the king, and Charles James Fox, brilliant opposition leader and *persona non grata* alike to the king and to his colleague, held the home and foreign secretaryships, respectively.

Fox, in his brief tenure of office (March–July 1782), embarked on an ambitious program to rescue England from her unpleasant diplomatic position. He first aimed to detach America from France by a favorable peace; then, if the Bourbon powers would not negotiate on reasonable terms, he hoped to secure an alliance with the northern powers—Russia and Prussia—that would force them to do so. In mid-April Fox approached Count Lusi, the Prussian minister at London, and suggested that the Prussian king intervene to put an end to the war. According to Lusi, Fox stated that he was willing to grant American independence, to arrange with France a mutual restoration of their possessions in the two Indies, and to cede either Minorca or Florida, or both, to Spain; Gibraltar would be given up only as a last resort.[1] Three days later, Fox announced to Lusi that he contemplated the opening of a di-

1. Lusi to Frederick, April 23, 1782, Clements Library, Shelburne MSS., vol. 35 (interceptions).

rect negotiation with France and Spain, but that he was dubious of its results, for Gibraltar would probably prove a stumbling-block to success. Fox also said that if the Bourbon powers were obstinate on the point of Gibraltar, he hoped that Prussia would stand by Great Britain, and that the Prussian king would prevail on the northern maritime powers, especially Russia, to join with England and Prussia to prevent the surrender of Gibraltar to Spain.[2] King Frederick rejected the overtures made by Fox. He stated that Prussia was in no position to back the British demands by force, and he was doubtful whether Russia would do so.[3] Fox nevertheless persisted in his project. He sent Thomas Grenville to Paris in May 1782 to open negotiations with France, Spain, and the American commissioners; but he continued until his downfall in July 1782 to solicit the aid of the northern powers.[4]

The appearance of Thomas Grenville in Paris marked the opening of the preliminary negotiations for peace between England and the Bourbon allies. Floridablanca authorized Aranda to treat with England, and on May 24 sent the Spanish envoy a memorandum to serve as a guide in his negotiations. Its cardinal points were: freeing the Mexican basin from all foreign domination up to the mouth of the Bahama channel; elimination of the English logwood colonies in Campeche, Yucatán, and Honduras; and, in Europe, restitution of Gibraltar and Minorca. Floridablanca stated further that if Jamaica should be captured from Great Britain, it would serve as more than an adequate exchange for the Mediterranean fortress; if necessary, Spain might be willing to cede for Gibraltar some of the Spanish possessions on the Guinea coast, and one or more of the North African presidios, except Ceuta.

2. Lusi to Frederick, April 26, 1782, Shelburne MSS., vol. 35.

3. Frederick to Lusi, June 11 and 27, 1782, Shelburne MSS., vol. 35.

4. The Holland House Photostats (3 vols., 1781–1783) at the Clements Library contain much material on Fox's efforts to secure the aid of the northern powers, but nothing specifically on the Gibraltar question. It may be noted that when Fox resumed office in 1783 he took up the same scheme again.

As Spanish plans for a grand attack on Gibraltar ma-
tured, the desire for any hasty negotiation with England
faded; every effort was made to postpone discussions until
after that attack should occur. In a conference on June 1,
Aranda and Vergennes definitely decided on this policy of
delay.[5]

Lord Shelburne in the meantime had sent over his own
representative, Richard Oswald, to discuss peace with the
American commissioners. Benjamin Franklin lured Oswald into a discussion of the terms of the European peace.
Oswald mentioned Spanish obstinacy on Gibraltar as the
principal obstacle to peace; whereupon Franklin inti-
mated that the problem might be solved by the granting of
an equivalent. Pressed by Oswald as to what that equivalent should be, Franklin suggested trade privileges in the
Spanish Indies. Oswald observed that England had already had sufficient difficulties with arrangements of that
sort since the Treaty of Utrecht. Franklin's suggestion,
which undoubtedly was merely a lead, had its effect, for
Oswald indignantly stated that only an equivalent in territory, such as Puerto Rico, would ever satisfy the English nation in return for Gibraltar. Significantly, in reporting this conversation to Shelburne, Oswald added: "I
have a strong notion that the Doctor had it in view to
throw out this proposal, by way of Trial, in commission
from this [French] Court, who very possibly are not fond
of granting all that is expected of them for the reduction
of that Place."[6] If Franklin made this overture at the request of Vergennes, he accomplished his purpose most clev-
erly. By suggesting an impossible equivalent for Gibraltar, he led Oswald into proposing what England really
wanted in exchange, if Gibraltar had to be given up in the
negotiation: the island of Puerto Rico. Franklin's success
in extracting an English proposal for an equivalent

5. Danvila y Collado, *Reinado de Carlos III*, V, 360–364. Aranda,
nevertheless, conferred with Grenville during June on several occasions.
At one meeting (June 23), the Englishman inquired whether Ceuta
would be exchanged for Gibraltar. Aranda replied in the negative.
6. Oswald to Shelburne, June 12, 1782, Shelburne MSS., vol. 71 (L.C.).

brought a warning to Oswald to eschew any further conversations with the "Doctor" on any points of the peace
that did not distinctly concern America.[7]

Following the death of Rockingham on July 1, 1782,
Shelburne became prime minister, and henceforth the
peace negotiations proceeded under his direction. Fox re-
signed, and Lord Grantham became foreign secretary.
Grantham took over the conduct of the peace negotiations
with France and Spain, although Shelburne exercised a
guiding and decisive influence over the whole negotiation.
Grenville, Fox's envoy at Paris, was replaced by Alleyne
Fitzherbert.

Fitzherbert reached Paris early in August. His instructions anticipated a Spanish refusal to acknowledge that
the grant of American independence was any concession to
Spain. He was therefore to inform Aranda "that the
Questions said by Her [Spain] to be in Dispute shall have
the fullest and fairest Discussion, and that as the Prin-
ciple of adopting the Treaty of Paris as a Basis of Negotiation does not preclude any subsequent Restitutions and
Compensations, you are ready to receive any Proposals
which the Court of Spain may think fit to make."[8] Fitzherbert, in his first conference with Aranda and Vergennes, found them little disposed to press the negotiation.
Not only was the issue at Gibraltar awaited, but also there
was much talk of continuing the war for another year.
Since the apparent eagerness of the French and Spanish
for a continuance of hostilities rested on the continued
participation of America in the conflict, Fitzherbert urged
that the sooner an accommodation with the Americans
could be arranged, the better would be the prospects for a
general peace.[9] Actually, the agitation for continuing the

7. Shelburne to the king, June 17, 1782, in Sir John Fortescue (ed.),
The Correspondence of King George the Third (London, 1928), VI, 60–
61. Oswald to Shelburne, July 11, 1782, Public Record Office, Foreign
Office 27:2 (L.C.). (Hereafter cited as F.O.)

8. Instructions for Alleyne Fitzherbert, July 27, 1782, F.O. 27:3.

9. Fitzherbert to Shelburne, Aug. 17, 1782, Shelburne MSS., vol. 71
(L.C.).

war came principally from the Spanish;[10] Vergennes gladly seized upon a new set of proposals, brought over from London by Admiral De Grasse, as a means of hastening the conclusion of a satisfactory peace.

Admiral De Grasse, who had been held prisoner in England since his defeat and capture by Rodney, had a long conversation with Lord Shelburne prior to his release and return to Paris. De Grasse, anxious to be the instrument for laying the foundation of the peace, made some proposals to Shelburne, who reported them rather meagerly to the king. According to Shelburne, De Grasse said that "the French Ministry look upon the Independence of America, and the retention of Santa Lucia and Dominique as the Essential points to be insisted upon, and everything else as very negotiable."[11] After reaching Paris, De Grasse submitted to Vergennes a memorandum of his recollections of what he and Shelburne had agreed upon as bases for a peace. Vergennes believed that the admiral's report reflected a sincere desire for peace on the part of England, though he was not certain that De Grasse had represented the English position correctly. He therefore decided to send an emissary to London to verify the suggested terms of peace as reported by De Grasse. If Shelburne acknowledged them, this French agent would announce the necessary modifications and extensions, and urge that the English plenipotentiary at Paris be immediately instructed, so that peace could be concluded with the least possible delay.[12]

10. Spain was unwilling, of course, to enter into any serious discussion of the terms of peace until the fate of Gibraltar had been decided. Before any terms had been discussed with Spain, Fitzherbert anticipated that the Spanish demands would include the cession of both Gibraltar and Minorca, and the renunciation of the logwood settlements, irrespective of the fate of Gibraltar in the projected grand assault. Fitzherbert to Grantham, Aug. 17, 1782, F.O. 27:3.

11. Shelburne to the king, Aug. 11, 1782, in *Correspondence of George III*, VI, 99–100.

12. Vergennes to Montmorin, Aug. 18, 1782, Cor. Pol., Espagne, vol. 608 (L.C.).

The De Grasse proposals as submitted to Vergennes contained the following terms on behalf of Spain:

For Spain . . . . Cession or a definitive regulation of their [English] conquests in the Gulf of Mexico. Mahón or Gibraltar at their [Spanish] choice; England to have in return for it a port in the Mediterranean for her commerce to the Levant.[13]

Vergennes reported these terms to Madrid; and the Spanish government promptly sent full powers to Aranda to carry through the negotiation. In his accompanying letter of instruction, Floridablanca stressed the following conditions:

The three points which can be looked upon as conditions *sine qua non* are: the clearing of the Gulfs of Honduras and Campeche, freeing those establishments for the cutting of logwood [from England], or reducing them to a status of supervised permission; the exclusion from the Gulf of Mexico of all foreigners as far as the exit of the Bahama channel at Cape Carnaveral; the cession of Gibraltar and Minorca, although Orán and Mazalquivir may be given for them if Gibraltar has not been conquered [at the time of the negotiation. If Gibraltar is conquered] the king does not wish those places exchanged, and will only give the English the use of the free port of Mahón for their commerce, without jurisdiction or authority.[14]

These terms are substantially the same as those outlined by Floridablanca in his memorandum of May 24. Spain did not modify her terms until November, despite the failure of the grand assault on Gibraltar in September.[15]

13. Cor. Pol., Angleterre, vol. 538 (L.C.).
14. Floridablanca to Aranda, Aug. 29, 1782, A.N., Est., Leg. 4203, Apar. 3 (L.C.).
15. Before receiving his new instructions, Aranda on Sept. 4 submitted to Vergennes a reply to the De Grasse proposals. In addition to the basic demands of Spain (as outlined by Floridablanca on Aug. 29),

Vergennes selected for the mission to London his first secretary, T. M. Gerard de Rayneval, who had already been actively participating in the negotiation. Rayneval's instructions authorized him, in the event that Lord Shelburne disavowed the De Grasse proposals, to declare that his commission was ended and to leave England without further explanation. Although Vergennes communicated the Spanish demands to Rayneval, he told his envoy not to enter into any explanation regarding the disposition and views of Spain, but to confine himself to saying that his Catholic Majesty desired peace as sincerely as the French king and that Spain was ready to consider just and reasonable terms.[16] During Rayneval's absence Aranda made no attempt to continue the negotiation in Paris, although he presented his full powers to the British plenipotentiary.[17]

Rayneval reached London on September 12, and, finding that Shelburne was at his country residence of Bowood Park, hastened there to see him. Shelburne promptly disavowed some of the most important of the De Grasse terms —notably, the cession of either Gibraltar or Minorca. Nevertheless the French envoy, convinced that the English minister sincerely desired peace, felt justified in not following the letter of his instructions by immediately breaking off his conversations.

In touching upon the point of Gibraltar, Rayneval was cautious; he constantly and truthfully professed his lack of powers to discuss Spanish terms. He did insist that he believed no peace would be possible without the cession of Gibraltar. He stated that the King of Spain was determined to acquire it, either by conquest or by negotiation, and that its cession had therefore to be considered a *sine qua non* of the peace. Shelburne answered that the cession

Aranda asked for participation in the Newfoundland fisheries, the cession of New Providence in the Bahamas, and new commercial regulations. A.N., Est., Leg. 4203, Apar. 1 (L.C.).

16. Vergennes to Rayneval, Sept. 6, 1782, Cor. Pol., Angleterre, vol. 538 (L.C.).

17. Fitzherbert to Grantham, Sept. 11, 1782, F.O. 27:3 (L.C.).

seemed impossible to England. He also observed that it was really in the interest of France for England to keep Gibraltar, and suggested that France ought therefore to exercise her influence at Madrid to dissuade the Spanish court from its demand. Rayneval granted that reports to the effect that France opposed the cession were current in Spain, but protested that any representations of France at Madrid to force Spain to give up Gibraltar must be avoided at all costs, as an appearance of bad faith. After much parrying, Rayneval suggested that Spain might cede Orán in exchange. Shelburne countered with the proposal that either Majorca or some West Indian territory might satisfy the English demand for an equivalent.[18]

In reporting to the king his conversations with Rayneval relating to Gibraltar, Shelburne remarked: "I upheld the impossibility of ever ceding it so strongly, that I could form no guess about their disposition regarding Porto Rico." The king answered: "That Oran is a good port is quite new to me, and I certainly doubt it, as it is offered as an equivalent for Gibraltar; Porto Rico is the object which we must get for that fortress." In response, Shelburne stated: "I have held the point of Gibraltar so high that the alternative of Porto Rico may be catched at, I flatter myself, whenever the time comes for it to be hinted by way of compensation or exchange on the part of Your Majesty." The king again expressed approval of Shelburne's caution: "The holding of Gibraltar very high is judicious and if not taken I hope Porto Rico may be got for it."[19] These exchanges certainly indicate British willingness to part with Gibraltar, and the equivalent they aimed to get for it: Puerto Rico.

At each of the subsequent interviews with Rayneval, the subject of Gibraltar was raised. The Frenchman expressed the opinion that, assuming England's primary desire was

18. Rayneval to Vergennes, Sept. 15, 1782, and Rayneval's "Précis de mes entretiens avec les ministres anglais concernant l'Espagne. 12–20 Septembre, 1782," Cor. Pol., Angleterre, vol. 538 (L.C.). Shelburne to the king, Sept. 13, 1782, in *Correspondence of George III*, VI, 123–125.

19. *Correspondence of George III*, VI, 123–129.

to have a point of support for her commerce with the Levant, he was persuaded that if the King of Spain should in some manner acquire Gibraltar, he would be disposed to assure to Great Britain such a point of support. On September 16, Rayneval suggested the possibility of ceding West Florida and New Orleans for Gibraltar. Shelburne mentioned Puerto Rico; but Rayneval opposed this idea, for Puerto Rico was to the windward of the Spanish (and French) possessions. He insisted that Spain wished to obtain exclusive control of the Gulf of Mexico, and that would make any American cession a difficult matter. At the final interview of September 20, the British ministers stated that no further discussion could take place until propositions had been submitted by Spain, but Rayneval thought it evident that the British were anxious to receive such propositions.[20] To Vergennes, Rayneval wrote that he foresaw "great difficulties regarding Spain; I anticipate that if they give way regarding Gibraltar, they will make pretensions to West Florida, or to Puerto Rico; they know only too well the bad naval and financial state of Spain, and that knowledge is calculated on highly."[21]

As a result of the conversations with Rayneval, Lord Grantham instructed Fitzherbert that if anything concerning the cession of Gibraltar should come to him in any indirect manner, he was to take no notice of it, nor to give the least encouragement to any supposition but that of keeping Gibraltar. But if the Spanish ambassador submitted a definite proposal on the subject, Fitzherbert should accept it *ad referendum* and "remitt notice of it immediately, not failing to communicate in the most particular manner everything which may be suggested or proposed by him concerning it."[22] Fitzherbert's response is an

20. Rayneval, "Précis de mes entretiens . . . 12–20 Septembre 1782." Also his "Note confidencielle remis aux ministres anglais le 16 7bre 1782." Cor. Pol., Angleterre, vol. 538 (L.C.).

21. Rayneval to Vergennes, Sept. 18, 1782, Cor. Pol., Angleterre, vol. 538 (L.C.).

22. Grantham to Fitzherbert, London, Sept. 23, 1782, in *British Diplomatic Instructions*, VII, *France, 1745–1789*, p. 190.

interesting reflection of his opinion of Vergennes' disposition, and of the influence of the Rayneval mission on the French court; he wrote:

M. de Rayneval talks to me in raptures of Your Lordship's reception of him. . . . I could wish for my own sake, that since he seems to have a just sense of the inestimable value of these qualities he would contrive to instill a portion of them into the mind of his principal at this Court, however I apprehend that his labours would be entirely fruitless, both on account of the natural bent of that minister's disposition and because the success of the crooked and insidious line of conduct which he followed with regard to America . . . will probably rivet him forever in the same system of politics. . . . The report which M. de Rayneval has made to him of the dispositions of Your Lordship and the rest of the King's ministers has operated an almost miraculous change for the better on his conduct with regard to forwarding the negotiations, insomuch that . . . I really begin to hope that he will be brought to consent to such an accomodation as (America apart) England will be no loser by.[23]

Meanwhile, the projected attack on Gibraltar had taken place, resulting on September 13 in disaster to the Spanish floating batteries and complete failure. Admiral Howe had been sent to provision the garrison, which he subsequently did without having to engage the Franco-Spanish fleet in a decisive action.[24] Before news of the failure reached him, John Adams, the American envoy at The

23. Fitzherbert to Shelburne (private), Oct. 3, 1782, Shelburne MSS., vol. 71 (L.C.).

24. C. F. Duro, *Armada española* . . . (Madrid, 1901), VII, gives a brief and standard Spanish account of the siege. One of the most extensive contemporary English accounts is that of John Drinkwater, *A History of the Late Siege of Gibraltar* . . . (London, 1783).

The failure of the grand assault can be credited in part to the lack of coördination between the Spanish and French forces, and to the fact that the French failed to make more than half-hearted efforts to capture the Rock. Benjamin Vaughn, a confidential agent of Lord Shelburne, had forecast as much in the following excerpt from his letter from Paris of August 7: "Perhaps I am informing your lordship of nothing new, when

Hague, had written with remarkable foresight: "I have no expectation at all in my own mind that the combined fleet will meet Howe, that there will be any naval engagement, or that Gibraltar will surrender. They will make a horrid noise with their artillery against the place; but this noise will not terrify Elliot [the commander], and Gibraltar will remain to the English another year, and Lord Howe return to England, and all Europe will laugh."[25]

The failure of the great assault on Gibraltar in September left the Spanish dejected, but still firm in their determination to acquire the fortress either by diplomacy or by force. Despite her acute financial distress,[26] Spain continued the siege until the following February, though half-heartedly and without any result that influenced the

I mention that the French troops so little exposed themselves at Minorca, as to give great jealousies to Spain. The consequences having been almost serious respecting the good understanding of the courts. The French troops are supposed to take a more active part before Gibraltar than at Minorca, unless the presence of the French princes should be held a sufficient token of the sincerity of France. *This, with many other circumstances, induces me to think that at a peace it will not be very important to lose what France so much wishes we would keep."* (Italics mine.) Clements Library, Vaughn MSS., vol. I (photocopy of typescript).

That the blockade and siege of Gibraltar had been anything but effective is illustrated in the following anecdote. After the disaster to the floating batteries, many Spanish and French prisoners were taken. General Elliot, the commander of Gibraltar, treated the captured officers to a sumptuous banquet of forty "very delicate" courses, including many of the fruits of Spain itself, which had been smuggled in from the adjoining coasts. As a final courtesy, Elliot presented the officers with the latest Gazette from Madrid, which they had been unable to procure in their own camp for some weeks past! Elliot then returned the officers to their camp on parole, where they "exhausted themselves in praises of the attention and affability of the said General." Secret intelligence from Madrid, Sept. 30, 1782, F.O. 27:4.

25. Adams to Livingston, Sept. 23, 1782, in Francis Wharton (ed.), *Revolutionary Diplomatic Correspondence of the United States* (Washington, 1889), V, 750–752.

26. On the financial straits of Spain at this time, see Carmichael to Livingston, Sept. 29, 1782, in *Revolutionary Diplomatic Correspondence,* V, 783–785; and a memorandum entitled "Copy of Intelligence from a Person of Credit upon the present State of Finance in Spain, 1782," in Shelburne MSS., vol. 168.

course of the peace negotiation.[27] The Spanish also wished to embark upon another naval campaign in the West Indies, with the hope of capturing Jamaica, which in turn could be exchanged for Gibraltar. The continuation of the war, however, depended on French coöperation. France presently withdrew her contingent of troops from before Gibraltar;[28] and the French had no intention of prolonging the war by participating in a new attack on Britain's West Indies. After September, the Spanish quest for Gibraltar was in reality confined to diplomatic channels.

Spain opened direct negotiations with England on October 6, when Aranda submitted a statement of the Spanish terms for peace to Fitzherbert, terms that were identical with those proposed before the disaster at Gibraltar. In explaining the Spanish proposals, Aranda did not insist very strongly on the fisheries and the cession of the Bahamas, but stated that the cession of Gibraltar, Minorca, and West Florida, and the elimination of English logwood settlements on the Spanish mainland, could be considered as the Spanish ultimatum. As compensation for Gibraltar, Spain offered Orán; in conversation, Aranda hinted to Fitzherbert that, if England would not accept Orán, something else might be offered.[29]

The ministers at London termed the Spanish proposals extravagant and unreasonable, as indeed they were under the circumstances. Grantham stated that Orán would never be accepted as an equivalent for Gibraltar; that nothing but pride had prevented the Spaniards from previously abandoning the place; and that even if Gibraltar had been captured, Britain would never have agreed to such an uneven exchange.[30] To the other demands of Spain, the Brit-

27. Spain's determination to continue the siege is reflected in a secret report from Madrid, Oct. 3, 1782, F.O. 27:4.

28. Fitzherbert to Grantham, Nov. 5, 1782, F.O. 27:3.

29. Propositions of Spain to England communicated by Aranda to Fitzherbert, Oct. 6, 1782, Cor. Pol., Angleterre, vol. 538 (L.C.). Fitzherbert to Grantham, Oct. 7, 1782, Add. MSS. 28,068, fols. 22–25.

30. Grantham to Fitzherbert, Oct. 21, 1782, in *British Diplomatic Instructions*, VII, 193–195. Shelburne to Fitzherbert, Oct. 21, 1782, Shelburne MSS., vol. 71 (L.C.). In a letter to Vergennes, Montmorin com-

ish made no formal reply save a sweeping condemnation of their unreasonableness. Fitzherbert was authorized to offer West Florida and an abandonment of the logwood settlements on the Mosquito coast (providing the opportunity for cutting logwood was assured), if Spain would return Minorca, restore its fortifications, and desist from the demand for Gibraltar. If Spain continued to insist on the cession of the Rock, England would make peace only on the basis of an adequate exchange, and the restoration by Spain of all conquests made by her during the war. The British insisted that it was up to Spain to make a fair proposal for an exchange; and Puerto Rico was still the goal of Britain.[31]

The wide discrepancy between the English and Spanish proposals for peace, especially the English refusal to entertain the idea of exchanging Gibraltar for Orán, led Aranda to seek new instructions from his court. On October 4, two days before he submitted the Spanish proposals to Fitzherbert, the Spanish envoy suggested to Floridablanca that it would probably be necessary to find a suitable equivalent for Gibraltar in Spanish America. He feared any increase in British territory in the region of the West Indies and Gulf of Mexico. He thought that under no circumstances should Spain part with either Cuba or Puerto Rico, the "Pearls of the Indies"; but that either West Florida or Spanish Santo Domingo might serve, and the sacrifice of either of those possessions would be the least harmful to Spanish interests.[32] Responding to this suggestion, Floridablanca on October 20 authorized Aranda to offer Spanish Santo Domingo to the English in

mented that Floridablanca had for a long time looked upon Orán as a charge upon Spain, and that he had previously proposed that Spain rid herself of it by presenting it to Russia or even to Algiers. No wonder that the Spanish urged so strongly that England accept it in exchange for Gibraltar! Sept. 26, 1782, Cor. Pol., Espagne, vol. 608 (L.C.).

31. "Réponse aux propositions de l'Espagne, 9 Nov. 1782," Cor. Pol., Angleterre, vol. 538 (L.C.). Grantham to Fitzherbert, Nov. 9, 1782, in *British Diplomatic Instructions,* VII, 195–199. Shelburne to Rayneval (secret), Nov. 13, 1782, Shelburne MSS., vol. 71 (L.C.).

32. Konetzke, *Die Politik des Grafen Aranda,* pp. 163–164.

exchange for Gibraltar, providing that all the other demands of Spain were met.[33] Instead of making a direct
proposal to that effect, Aranda merely informed Fitzherbert that Spain would be willing to cede as an exchange
any of her American colonies except Cuba, Puerto Rico,
and the mainland from Mexico south. In accordance with
his instructions not to respond to any but a specific proposal, Fitzherbert received this suggestion without comment.[34] Even this hesitant offer left the British and Spanish proposals almost as far apart as ever.

Probably aware that France would oppose any suggestion of joint occupancy of Santo Domingo with the English, Floridablanca instructed Aranda on October 30 to
offer the Spanish portion of the island to France. The
French in turn should cede to England either Corsica or
some of their West Indian possessions, and England would
cede Gibraltar to Spain. Aranda submitted this proposal
for a three-cornered exchange to Vergennes on November
7, attaching to it two conditions: that France persuade
Britain to accept all of the other Spanish demands; and
that the terms of peace be concluded within one month.[35]
Vergennes expressed no enthusiasm for the proposed
French acquisition of Spanish Santo Domingo, and he absolutely refused to consider the cession of Corsica to England.[36] But this Spanish offer provided Vergennes with the
opportunity to intervene and resolve the deadlock in the
Anglo-Spanish peace negotiation.

For more than a month prior to the transfer of the
Spanish negotiation into French hands, Vergennes tried
to influence the Spanish to modify their demands, particularly to impress them with the necessity of offering a satisfactory equivalent for Gibraltar. As a result of Rayne-

33. Danvila y Collado, *Reinado de Carlos III*, V, 375.
34. Fitzherbert to Grantham, Oct. 28, 1782, F.O. 27:3 (L.C.).
35. Danvila y Collado, *Reinado de Carlos III*, V, 375–376. Aranda to
Vergennes, Nov. 7, 1782, and Vergennes to Aranda, Nov. 7, 1782, A.N.,
Est., Leg. 4203, Apar. 1 (L.C.).
36. Vergennes to Montmorin, Nov. 12, 1782, Cor. Pol., Espagne, vol.
610, fols. 209–212.

val's conferences with the English ministers in September, Vergennes believed that the English were willing to cede Gibraltar, but not in exchange for Orán. Through Montmorin at Madrid, Vergennes suggested to the Spanish that they follow up a hint dropped by Shelburne, that England might accept as an equivalent the two Floridas, New Orleans and its environs, and "the vast areas which are situated between the Mississippi, the Lakes, and the western frontiers of the United States";[37] Shelburne had expressed the opinion that such a cession would satisfy the English nation and would not unduly expose his ministry to attack. Vergennes felt that since Minorca had been dismantled it would not satisfy the British as an exchange. In any event, Spain must raise her offer of an equivalent and work for a speedy conclusion of the peace.[38] Montmorin agreed that the British probably would not accept Minorca for Gibraltar, even though he thought the former of greater utility to Great Britain. He stated that France could not hope to make Spain accept any peace without Gibraltar; the Spanish king would rather continue the war alone than give up that demand.[39] Vergennes on October 19 confessed his belief that all the plans of attack against Gibraltar had been chimerical, and that the only way Spain would ever secure it would be by exchange. He announced that Count d'Estaing was leaving for Madrid

37. The implications of this suggestion illustrate the potential dangers that lurked in the diplomatic entanglements of the United States with France and her allies. Fortunately for the United States, Floridablanca mistrusted this overture and refused to consider it seriously. Montmorin to Vergennes, Oct. 24, 1782, Cor. Pol., Espagne, vol. 609 (L.C.).

38. Vergennes to Montmorin, Oct. 6, 1782 (No. 81 and No. 83), Cor. Pol., Espagne, vol. 609 (L.C.). Fitzherbert, in a letter of Oct. 3 to Grantham, stated that "Vergennes begins . . . to manifest an unequivocal Desire to putting an end to the war," that desire being founded upon "the declining state of their Navy . . ., the evident relaxation in their ties . . . [with] America . . ., and the miserable condition of the generality of the inhabitants of this Country, and their inability to pay even the present impositions of the Government, much less those which the exigencies of another Campaign may require." Add. MSS. 28,068, fols. 16–17.

39. Montmorin to Vergennes, Oct. 10, 1782, Cor. Pol., Espagne, vol. 609 (L.C.).

on October 21, ostensibly on his way to Cádiz to take
charge of the combined fleet being gathered for an attack
on the British West Indies, but he hinted that d'Estaing
had been instructed to attempt to influence the Spanish to
modify their demands.[40]

That Vergennes steadfastly supported the Spanish demand of Gibraltar during October and November seems
at first glance inconsistent with previous French policy
during the eighteenth century. England's possession of
the Rock had been one of the chief factors in the formation
and maintenance of the Family Compact.[41] There was a
strong pro-English party in Spain which might have been
able to promote a rapprochement with England if Spain
recovered those seeds of discord, Gibraltar and Minorca,
in the peace negotiation. Vergennes also realized that England would cede Gibraltar only for an equivalent that
would improve, rather than impair, her strategic position
and power; yet the whole policy of the French minister
had been directed toward the destruction of the power of
Britain. Why, then, did Vergennes remain steadfast in his
support of the Spanish claim to Gibraltar? Of course
France had obligated herself to continue the war until
Gibraltar should be secured for Spain. A weightier factor
seems to have been that until December Vergennes was
convinced that the Spanish king would never consent to a
peace without Gibraltar.

While apparently reconciled to the necessity of securing Gibraltar for Spain in the negotiation, Vergennes

40. Vergennes to Montmorin, Oct. 19, 1782, Cor. Pol., Espagne, vol.
609 (L.C.).

41. The connection between Gibraltar and the Family Compact has
been mentioned repeatedly in preceding chapters. The English fully realized the reluctance of France toward the restitution. Benjamin Vaughn's
statement (see p. 209, footnote), that "it will not be very important to
lose what France so much wishes we would keep," may be cited as an
example. An undated and unsigned memorandum in the Shelburne Papers (vol. 72, L.C.) states: "The Possession of Gibraltar by the English
is, perhaps, the Tye of all others, which France considers the most powerful to bind Spain to their Alliance; and if taken by the Spaniards may
more Easily bring Spain back to their connections with this Country."

wished to conclude the peace without delay. By early November, France had settled with Britain all disagreements
over her own terms, except the disposition of the British
island of Dominica captured by France during the war.
The American commissioners were publicly declaring in
Paris that they would think themselves authorized to sign
their treaty if France attempted to delay the peace negotiation on Spain's behalf.[42] Excepting Holland,[43] Spain
alone stood in the way of a final peace. In order to hasten
the Spanish phase of the negotiation Vergennes had resorted to several expedients. He had not scrupled to inform Fitzherbert that he believed Spain's demands were
exorbitant and far beyond what the Spanish court was
secretly resolved to accept.[44] Through Montmorin and
d'Estaing, Vergennes had brought direct pressure to bear
at Madrid in an effort to persuade the Spanish court to
modify its proposals. Toward Aranda, Vergennes maintained a cold reserve not calculated to encourage the Spaniard to sustain his extreme position.[45] The result of these
efforts to secure a modification of the Spanish terms had
been the offer of Spanish Santo Domingo to France. That
offer enabled Vergennes to assume control of the Spanish
peace negotiation.

Before Vergennes could act upon the Spanish offer of

42. Grantham to the king, Nov. 3, 1782, in *Correspondence of George
III*, VI, 150. The English were fully aware that a speedy conclusion of
the American peace would hasten the general negotiation. On Nov. 13,
1782, Grantham wrote to Fitzherbert: "I anxiously hope that the State
of the Treaty with America may be such, as, when known, it may quicken
the Desire of France to terminate the Negotiation, by employing her
best Offices with Spain for this purpose. Surely, M. de Vergennes will
see this in its true and strongest light." F.O. 27:3.

43. The Dutch were negotiating their peace separately, and with no
very enthusiastic support from the French, as the Dutch envoy Brantzen
informed John Adams. Brantzen excoriated the French for their duplicity, and expressed the opinion that France was secretly attempting to
play off her several allies against each other and against Great Britain
for her own benefit. See John Adams' "Journal of the Peace Negotiations," Dec. 3, 1782, in *Revolutionary Diplomatic Correspondence*, VI,
104–105.

44. Fitzherbert to Grantham, Oct. 24, 1782, F.O. 27:3 (L.C.).

45. Danvila y Collado, *Reinado de Carlos III*, V, 377.

Santo Domingo, he had to ascertain definitely whether or not the British would cede Gibraltar. To discover this, he decided to send his clever secretary, Rayneval, on a new mission to London. Rayneval's instructions directed him first to ask the British ministers if they had irrevocably decided to keep Gibraltar. If so, he should return to Paris immediately. If the English appeared willing to give up Gibraltar, Rayneval was instructed to request a definite statement of what England would require as an equivalent. Vergennes told his envoy not to discuss any equivalent that might be proposed, but to refer it to Paris for a decision and in the meantime await further instructions. Although instructed to concentrate on the point of Gibraltar, Rayneval was told not to minimize the other demands of Spain. Only the cession of Gibraltar, however, should be presented as a *sine qua non* of the Anglo-Spanish peace.[46]

Rayneval reached London on November 20, and spent the evening talking with Lord Shelburne. Shelburne first stressed the opposition in the Cabinet to the cession of Gibraltar. If it were ceded, he said, three ministers would immediately resign;[47] to acquire it, Spain must be prepared to make a great sacrifice. After a heated discussion, Shelburne finally stated that it was up to Spain to make a proposition, but that it could not be an offer of Florida or New Orleans, which England did not want.[48] Rayneval suggested Minorca, but (as he admitted to Vergennes) the destruction by Spain of the fortifications there had seriously impaired its value to England. Pressed by Rayneval for other suggestions, Shelburne finally mentioned the Antilles. He tentatively proposed that England would

46. Vergennes, "Instruction pour le Sr. Gerard de Rayneval," Nov. 15, 1782, Cor. Pol., Angleterre, vol. 538 (L.C.). Fitzherbert to Grantham, Nov. 15, 1782, F.O. 27:3 (L.C.).

47. Rayneval conjectured that these were Lord Keppel, of the Admiralty; the Duke of Richmond, master of the Ordnance; and Charles Townshend, home secretary.

48. For the very good reason that England had already agreed on the Mississippi River and the 31st parallel as the western and southern boundaries of the new American nation.

cede Gibraltar if Spain gave up all her other conquests; and if Puerto Rico, or Martinique and St. Lucia, or Guadeloupe and Dominica were given to England as an equivalent; it was understood in the latter two cases that France would be compensated by Spanish Santo Domingo. Rayneval promptly transmitted these three alternatives to Paris.[49] The king answered Shelburne's note reporting this conversation by acknowledging that he thought the exchange of Gibraltar for any one of the suggested alternatives would be highly advantageous to England; he indicated, however, that he would prefer St. Lucia and Martinique to Guadeloupe and Dominica.[50]

The negotiation now approached a crisis, for the English ministry felt that peace or war must be decided upon before the opening of Parliament. For this reason a direct proposal had been made to Rayneval, which Lord Shelburne termed "decidedly the real ultimatum of Great Britain." Realizing the necessity for action, Rayneval wrote Vergennes on November 23 that it would not suffice merely to acknowledge the British proposal and refer it to Spain for acceptance or rejection. The King of England must be able to announce at the opening of Parliament whether peace was to be made or the war continued. Rayneval recommended to Vergennes that France immediately assure Britain either that efforts would be made to influence Spain to give up her demand for Gibraltar or that France pledge herself to provide a suitable equivalent for the fortress. More concretely, he suggested an immediate offer to England of Guadeloupe and Dominica, with Minorca and the Bahamas; Gibraltar to be ceded to Spain; and the disposition of Florida and the logwood settlements to be left for settlement in the definitive treaty. In a separate letter, Rayneval emphasized the hostility in England to the cession of Gibraltar. Shelburne had remarked that

49. Rayneval to Vergennes, Nov. 21, 1782, Cor. Pol., Angleterre, vol. 539 (L.C.). Shelburne to the king, Nov. 20, 1782, in *Correspondence of George III*, VI, 157–158.

50. The king to Shelburne, Nov. 21 and 22, 1782, in *Correspondence of George III*, VI, 159–160.

if Spain would give up Gibraltar, "he would place the two
Floridas at the feet of that power, or he might offer to it
Minorca." Rayneval felt that use of this overture might
be made in Spain, but that it should not be permitted to
delay at least a conditional decision on the three alternatives proposed as equivalents.[51]

After receiving Rayneval's report, Vergennes immediately conferred with Aranda. The Spanish envoy consented to modify the demands of Spain to the extent of
abandoning claims to the fisheries and to the Bahamas,
but refused further concessions. He wrote Floridablanca
that Vergennes spoke most sarcastically of the proposed
cession to France of Spanish Santo Domingo; Vergennes
stated that that possession would require forty years to be
turned into a profitable colony. Spain, according to the
French minister, had in her possession many areas more
acceptable to France than Santo Domingo. Aranda had
replied with some heat that France should state frankly
whether or not the arrangement over Santo Domingo was
acceptable; if it were not, it would have been much better
if France had stated in the beginning that Santo Domingo
did not satisfy her. Aranda also reported that Vergennes
evinced great reluctance to support any further military
enterprise. The Spaniard's efforts to hasten the proposed
dispatch of ships from Brest to join the West Indian expedition had been unavailing.[52]

Rayneval, considering that a personal visit to Paris was
necessary, arrived in the French capital on the morning
of November 28. A hurried conference with Aranda and

51. Shelburne, "Notes Relative to the Negotiation, 22 November
1782," Shelburne MSS., vol. 71 (L.C.). Rayneval to Vergennes, Nov. 23,
1782 (two letters), Cor. Pol., Angleterre, vol. 539 (L.C.).

52. Vergennes to Rayneval, Nov. 25, 1782, Cor. Pol., Angleterre, vol.
539, fols. 36–40. Aranda to Floridablanca, Nov. 26, 1782, A.N., Est., Leg.
4215, Apar. 3 (L.C.). In a letter to Montmorin of Nov. 26, Vergennes
stated that the offer of Spanish Santo Domingo to France was far from
a satisfactory one, and that the suggestion of Corsica was out of the
question; that France would, however, be willing to give up Guadeloupe and Dominica for Gibraltar. Cor. Pol., Espagne, vol. 609, fols.
282–284.

Vergennes took place; and Rayneval left for London again in the evening of the same day, taking with him Vergennes' son as secretary, and a definite ultimatum of Spain. The ultimatum provided:

1. That Spain keep West Florida as far as Cape Carnaveral.[53]

2. That England cede Gibraltar, but keep all that belonged to it in arms, munitions, etc.

3. That Spain restore Minorca to Great Britain, but with the liberty of withdrawing all arms, munitions, etc.

4. That France, to indemnify Great Britain for Gibraltar, cede on behalf of Spain the islands of Guadeloupe and Dominica.

5. That all logwood establishments on the Bay of Honduras be abandoned, and never thereafter be reëstablished.

6. That England give up all authority over logwood establishments on the coast of Campeche, but that Spain guarantee to furnish a specific amount of wood annually at a stipulated price, the traffic to be handled in English vessels.[54]

Rayneval reached London again on December 1. The meeting of Parliament, meanwhile, had been postponed by the king for a ten-day period until December 5. The decision for peace had been made by Britain when Rayneval departed for Paris.[55] Rayneval saw Shelburne on December 2, and delivered the Spanish ultimatum. Shelburne made no direct answer, but insisted, in accordance with the king's expressed wish, that England would prefer Martinique and St. Lucia to Guadeloupe and Dominica. Shel-

53. After 1763, the English colony of West Florida extended only to the Apalachicola River; this Spanish construction of its boundary would have included a large portion of East Florida as well.

54. Ultimatum of Spain for guidance of Rayneval, in Aranda's hand, Nov. 28, 1782, A.N., Est., Leg. 4203, Apar. 1 (L.C.).

55. This postponement was arranged through an informal understanding between Rayneval and the English. Parliament had been scheduled to meet November 25, the day after Rayneval's departure for Paris. He had agreed to return before December 5, so that the king could definitely announce the prospect of peace when Parliament opened. See Doniol, *Histoire de la participation de la France,* V, 248.

burne's proposition was made as a strategic move, with the hope that Rayneval was authorized to change the Spanish terms without reference to Paris. The king wrote to Shelburne the same day (the 2nd) that it appeared to be a favorable portent that Vergennes' son had accompanied Rayneval, for he would never have been sent if the intention of the French had not been sincerely for peace. As to the terms, the king commented: "I therefore hope Mons. Rayneval has power to give St. Lucia and Martinique instead of Guadeloupe and Dominica, and that Spain will restore West Florida, but if he has not . . . I think peace so desireable, that so far as relates to Myself, I should not be for another Year's War." On the next day, he wrote to Grantham: "I trust he [Rayneval] has secret directions to give way rather than not have Peace . . . ; but should I be mistaken in my suggestion, after doing everything but letting them return to Paris to mend the Treaty, I think Peace so essential . . . that it would be madness not to conclude Peace on the best possible terms we can obtain."[56]

After a long meeting on December 3, the Cabinet approved the cession of Gibraltar. The Duke of Richmond and Lord Keppel were the only members opposed, especially to the exchange of Gibraltar for Guadeloupe. They protested to the king the following day, and Keppel hinted that he might resign if the exchange took place. In this meeting of December 3, the Cabinet decided that, in consideration of the retention of West Florida by Spain, the Spanish ought to grant an additional equivalent; the island of Trinidad was suggested.[57] The formal proposals drawn up by Grantham differed somewhat in expression. They provided for the restitution to England of Minorca

56. Shelburne to the king, Dec. 2, 1782. The king to Shelburne, Dec. 2. The king to Grantham, Dec. 3. *Correspondence of George III,* VI, 167–169. These letters show that the king was ready, if necessary, to accept the equivalent of Guadeloupe and Dominica for Gibraltar.

57. Cabinet minute, Dec. 3, 1782, in *Correspondence of George III,* VI, 170. Rayneval to Vergennes, Dec. 4, 1782 (private letter), Cor. Pol., Angleterre, vol. 539, fol. 145.

and the Bahamas; the renewal of commercial treaties; and
the retention of the right of cutting logwood, with proper
restrictions. The other provisions are quoted in full:

1. If Spain renounces the acquisition of Gibraltar, England
consents to the sacrifice of the two Floridas, and will negotiate equitably on the other conditions of the peace.
2. If the court of Madrid persists in the desire of acquiring
Gibraltar, the court of London demands, as an equivalent,
Puerto Rico, or else Guadeloupe, St. Lucia, and Dominica,
or Guadeloupe, Dominica and Trinidad.
3. If one of these alternatives is accepted, England agrees to
give up one of the two Floridas to Spain, at her choice.[58]

This offer approximates that made by Shelburne to Rayneval on November 21; St. Lucia or Trinidad was added
for England, one of the Floridas for Spain. It should be
noted that the Spanish propositions of November 28 demanded more than had been offered previously by Shelburne to Rayneval. The French envoy objected to what
he termed the additional equivalents now demanded by
England, but he lost no time in reporting the English
proposals to Paris.[59]

It has been alleged by Doniol[60] that the signature of the
American preliminaries stiffened the British toward the
Spanish demands and influenced the British Cabinet to increase its terms unduly. News of the signature of the
American peace reached London on December 3, and was
made known to the Cabinet; yet there is no evidence to
indicate that the news influenced the Cabinet's decision on
Gibraltar. While the Cabinet did not accept precisely the
terms demanded by Spain on November 28, it did not raise
the English demands above previous offers. Indeed, this
was the only occasion during the eighteenth century on

58. "Reponse aux propositions de l'Ambassadeur d'Espagne, datées
le 28 Nov. 1782," F.O. 27:2 (L.C.).
59. Rayneval to Vergennes, Dec. 4, 1782 (public letter), Cor. Pol.,
Angleterre, vol. 539 (L.C.).
60. Doniol, *Histoire de la participation de la France,* V, 202 ff.

which the English Cabinet formally approved the cession of Gibraltar on any terms. Nor did the Cabinet increase its demands after December 3. On the contrary, the English in their final decision on December 11 granted more liberal terms to Spain than they had proposed on December 3 or on any prior occasion.[61]

Parliament opened December 5; the king's address announced the prospect of peace, but was necessarily indefinite on terms. Fox answered the king, and opposed the cession of Gibraltar. He said: "The fortress of Gibraltar was to be ranked among the most important possessions of this country; it was that which gave us respect in the eyes of nations; it manifested our superiority, and gave us the means of obliging them by protection." But he did not express any unalterable opposition to the cession of the Rock. He remarked that if it should be determined to give up Gibraltar, it should be "rated as high as possible," and that the ministry should make the best bargain that it could, "either by getting the most money for it, or exchanging it for a valuable and adequate consideration."[62] Undoubtedly, if a cession had occurred, there would have been much partisan opposition, no matter what had been secured in exchange. But it is evident that the opposition of Fox, Richmond, and Keppel to the cession was largely partisan.

News of the latest proposals of England reached Paris on December 7. A conference between Vergennes and Aranda took place the same day. Vergennes (probably for effect) expressed great indignation over the new English demands before Aranda said anything. The Spaniard then asked what was expected from him. Vergennes inquired whether either Puerto Rico or Trinidad could be considered as exchanges; Aranda said they positively could not be so considered, nor was he authorized to deviate from his

61. Before December 11, the British had never agreed to cede more than the Floridas *or* Minorca, if Spain gave up her claim to Gibraltar. On that date they agreed to cede both Floridas *and* Minorca.

62. *The Speeches of the Right Honourable Charles James Fox in the House of Commons* (London, 1815), II, 96–107.

earlier proposal. While going over the Spanish ambassador's instructions, Vergennes' attention was drawn to a letter of Floridablanca of November 23, received in Paris on December 1, which contained the following paragraph:

It seems that the whole obstacle to the conclusion of peace is Gibraltar. I will not conceal from your Excellency that the king intends to sustain this desire with all his forces while he can. But nevertheless his Majesty would like to know what compensation or what considerable advantage Spain could draw from the treaty, if perchance he should make the sacrifice of giving up such a desire.[63]

In this Vergennes pretended to see some disposition on the part of the King of Spain to give up his claim to Gibraltar. Aranda stated that it was within his instructions to permit Rayneval to question the British on what might be given to Spain if Gibraltar were kept. He in no way authorized the acceptance, or even the hope of acceptance, of such a proposal; the British reply was to be referred back to Madrid for consideration.

Aranda himself was none too enthusiastic about granting England the extensive increase in West Indian possessions contemplated in the French and British proposals. He feared that England would be a constant threat to Spanish America, and that France would be left too weak to be of assistance. He wrote: "The case of Gibraltar is bad and grave, but it has not so many bad consequences as the placing of ourselves in such an unfortunate position in that part of the world." Aranda attributed the change in the British position (as described to him by Vergennes) to two factors: The conclusion of the preliminaries with America had freed Britain from fear of any further opposition on that score and thus strengthened her hand against France and Spain; also, the French minister had been too sanguine in his hopes based upon Shelburne's proposals. Vergennes, realizing the anxiety of the

63. Floridablanca to Aranda, Nov. 23, 1782, A.N., Est., Leg. 4203, Apar. 3 (L.C.).

British to conclude peace before the opening of Parliament, had hurriedly sent back Rayneval on November 28, hoping to rush the British into a favorable peace; but the result had been different, as Vergennes had discovered to his chagrin. It is open to question whether these ideas were Aranda's own or were suggested to him.[64]

Vergennes knew very well that Floridablanca's letter of November 23 had not been intended to authorize Aranda to desist from the demand of Gibraltar. The French ambassador Montmorin had written the same day that Floridablanca was threatening to make a direct offer to England either of Spanish Santo Domingo or of Puerto Rico for Gibraltar, in an effort to conclude the negotiation. Montmorin had endeavored to dissuade the Spanish secretary from making such a direct offer, and he clearly showed in his letters to Vergennes that he considered it would be disadvantageous for France to have either Santo Domingo or Puerto Rico pass into English hands.[65]

The French minister moved quickly to forestall any attempt by Spain to re-open direct negotiations with England. He informed Rayneval at once of the conference of December 7 with Aranda, and of the letter of Floridablanca of November 23. His communication is worth quoting in some detail:

M. Grantham . . . offers the two Floridas and arrangements on the other articles if Gibraltar were not ceded. In order not to leave my character of frankness, I confess that the two Floridas do not greatly interest Spain; she only at-

64. Aranda to Floridablanca, Dec. 9, 1782, A.N., Est., Leg. 4215, Apar. 3 (L.C.).

65. Montmorin to Vergennes, Nov. 23 and Dec. 1, 1782, Cor. Pol., Espagne, vol. 609, fols. 261–268, 332–334. On November 21, Floridablanca told Montmorin that, if France could not arrange a satisfactory settlement through the device of the cession of Spanish Santo Domingo to France, he intended to offer either that possession or (if absolutely necessary) Puerto Rico to England in exchange for Gibraltar. On this same day, Rayneval assured Lord Shelburne that Spain would *not* consent to a direct exchange of either Spanish Santo Domingo or Puerto Rico for Gibraltar. Rayneval to Vergennes, Nov. 21, 1782, Cor. Pol., Angleterre, vol. 539 (L.C.).

taches great weight to West Florida as far as Cape Carnaveral, but the conservation of Minorca is close to her heart,
and that island seems to lose its greatest attraction to the
English provided they keep Gibraltar which is the key to the
Mediterranean.

If the English ministers wish to authorize us to make such
a proposition, with satisfactions added regarding the other
objects contained in the note which M. le Cte. d'Aranda has
confided in you, . . . the French king will charge himself
voluntarily to transmit it to the King His Uncle and to rec-
ommend it with the most lively interest . . . [but Vergennes
of course could not guarantee that such propositions would
be accepted, and sufficient time must be left him to accomplish this mission].

His Majesty does not wish or seek to violate the resolution
of the King His Uncle, but His Majesty presses always forward with earnestness and fervor moved by his heart and the
interests of general goodwill.

If the King of Spain can be induced to give up Gibraltar,
how much easier it will be for the English ministry and for
ourselves. . . .[66]

Vergennes' letter reached London on the evening of December 10, and its contents were presented to the British
by Rayneval in a résumé dated December 11 (though perhaps communicated the evening before). The French note
ingeniously placed the proposition to desist from Gibraltar before the other alternatives. Three bases were proposed: 1. France, informed of the disinclination of England to cede Gibraltar, and having some grounds for ex-
pecting to be able to influence the Spanish king to desist
from his resolution of acquiring it, offered to make every
possible effort to secure the abandonment by Spain of her
demand; as a means to success, the French demanded that
the English frankly confide in them the terms upon which,
in such a case, they would be willing to make peace with

66. Vergennes to Rayneval, Dec. 7, 1782, Cor. Pol., Angleterre, vol.
539 (L.C.).

Spain. 2. If this proposal did not suit England, France renewed the offer of Guadeloupe and Dominica for Gibraltar, the balance of the terms to be arranged on the basis proposed on November 28. 3. Finally, if England persisted in her resolution to have St. Lucia, France would also have to give up Martinique, for that island would be left indefensible if the others were ceded; England in return must offer a satisfactory equivalent for Martinique in the West or East Indies.[67]

Both Shelburne and Grantham reported the new proposals to the king. The difficulty in finding any equivalent for Martinique in either of the Indies was manifest, and undoubtedly Vergennes clearly understood the improbability of England's acceding to such a proposition when he made it. Shelburne felt that England should return to the second of the alternatives only if the others failed. He therefore suggested that the wisest course would be to make a round offer to Spain of the Floridas and Minorca, and at the same time insist that Dominica be restored by France. If Spain would not agree, England would fall back, as honorably as possible, upon the basis of Guadeloupe and Dominica for Gibraltar, and the other bases outlined by France on November 28. Grantham acknowledged that the proposal of keeping Gibraltar was subject to some delay and risk, but he thought any proposal whereby Gibraltar might be kept was worthy of the most serious consideration.[68] The king in his responses showed unmistakably that he favored the cession of Gibraltar, but he acknowledged the difficulty of finding an equivalent for Martinique. To Grantham he said: "I am ready to avow that Peace is not complete unless Gibraltar be exchang'd with Spain." To Shelburne he wrote: "I would wish if possible to be rid of Gibraltar. . . . Minorca I should not willingly give up, because if Port Mahon was made a free

67. "Résumé des observations faites par Monsieur de Rayneval," London, Dec. 11, 1782, in *British Diplomatic Instructions*, VII, 202–203, footnote.

68. Shelburne to the king, Dec. 11, 1782. Grantham to the king, Dec. 11. In *Correspondence of George III*, VI, 180–181.

port, it might draw again into our hands the Mediterranean Trade." He concluded by again expressing his opinion that peace was absolutely necessary for England, and that no peace would be complete unless England got rid of Gibraltar; he also expressed surprise at the new and unexpected propositions made by France.[69]

At a meeting held on December 11, the Cabinet decided to offer the Floridas and Minorca to Spain, and to demand from Spain the restoration of the Bahamas and the preservation, under regulation, of the right of cutting logwood. In addition France should restore Dominica to England.[70] Grantham communicated these terms to Rayneval the same day; but in Grantham's note the demand for Dominica was placed in a separate paragraph, and not linked to the Spanish terms. He did this in accordance with the British contention that Dominica could not properly be considered an equivalent for Gibraltar. But since it was not mentioned specifically in the proposals concerning Spain, Vergennes later refused to give up Dominica unless England would grant an additional equivalent to France. Grantham at the same time informed Fitzherbert of the progress of the negotiations; twice he observed that this new offer of England would cause some delay, for, as he remarked, "a messenger must go and come from Madrid." He requested Fitzherbert to observe closely the reaction of the ministers at Paris to the English proposals.[71] It is evident that the English did not suspect that the offer of December 7 was initiated by Vergennes, and that they thought their offer could be accepted only after reference to Madrid.[72]

69. The king to Grantham, Dec. 11, 1782. The king to Shelburne, Dec. 11. In *Correspondence of George III*, VI, 182–184.

70. Minute of Cabinet, Dec. 11, 1782, in *Correspondence of George III*, VI, 182.

71. Grantham to Fitzherbert, Dec. 11 and 12, 1782, in *British Diplomatic Instructions*, VII, 201–205.

72. That Rayneval himself anticipated that the new propositions of England would have to be referred to Madrid for approval is shown by the following extract from his "Réflexion sur l'état actuel de négociation" (written on or about Dec. 12, 1782): "The Cabinet at London has

Rayneval transmitted the English proposal to Vergennes in his letter of December 12. He reported that the English had received the proposal of December 7 with surprise, and noted among other things that Grantham was much more anxious than Shelburne to avoid the cession of Gibraltar. Rayneval remarked on the widespread opposition to the cession, in the Cabinet, in Parliament, and in popular opinion. He also called Shelburne's position precarious, and suggested that, unless Spain were ready to sacrifice Gibraltar, Parliament might overthrow the Cabinet rather than permit the cession; if the ministry were overthrown, it would create a highly unfavorable situation for France. Rayneval also said that he had held out no hope to Grantham on the score of Dominica. In an accompanying *lettre particulière*, Rayneval confessed his own satisfaction with, and enthusiasm for, the offer made by England; he had not really expected that the English would offer such favorable terms.[73]

Rayneval saw Shelburne again two days later, and expressed the opinion that England's recent offer "lay the foundation of not only an honourable but a *fructueuse* negotiation." Rayneval's sentiments, as reported by Shelburne, are significant as reflecting the secret attitude of France. Shelburne wrote: "He is most earnest that the Intermediate Time should be employ'd in finding some equivalent or fresh arrangement, that might satisfye us, in case the Spanish Obstinacy regarding Gibraltar should still prove invincible, for he quoted so many passages from Monsr. de Vergennes' private letters and mention'd un-

attested its preference for this last proposition [that is, the French king 'to use his good offices at Madrid to determine His Catholic Majesty to desist from his desire of acquiring Gibraltar'], and in the supposition that his Catholic Majesty will desist from Gibraltar, has proposed as peace conditions the cession of Minorca; and the two Floridas. . . . *This proposition has been sent to Versailles to be examined, and sent to Madrid. Such is the present state of the negotiation.*" (Italics mine.) Cor. Pol., Angleterre, vol. 19 (Supplement), fols. 303–304.

73. Rayneval to Vergennes, no. 8 and *lettre particulière*, Dec. 12, 1782, Cor. Pol., Angleterre, vol. 539 (L.C.).

necessarily so many circumstances, that I have not myself the least Doubt that they are perfectly sincere in wishing Spain to close on any terms, and that the exchange of Guadeloupe for the Spanish part of St. Domingo is not an object of theirs, or at least a very secondary one."[74]

Vergennes seized upon the English proposals contained in Rayneval's dispatches of December 12 as a happy solution, for France, of this difficult negotiation. On the evening of December 15 he wrote to Aranda from Versailles: "The courier . . . whom I expected from London has arrived. . . . The article from the letter of M. de Floridablanca has had the *greatest* of success. If Your Excellency will be so good as to come here as early as possible tomorrow, I shall have the honor of communicating to you the terms, with which I hope you will be satisfied." With a masterly touch, Vergennes added: "It would be fortunate, if your instructions would permit you again to take charge of a negotiation, which will be better in your hands, than in my own."[75] Accordingly, Aranda went to Versailles on the morning of the 16th, and, after a brief conference, accepted *on his own responsibility* the English terms for peace without Gibraltar.[76] Vergennes was elated. "It is noon," he wrote to Rayneval on the same day, "he [Aranda] has just left, and that which will astonish you no less than it did me, Monsieur [is that] we do not have to await a reply from Spain. Count Aranda accepts the

74. Shelburne to the king, Dec. 14, 1782, in *Correspondence of George III*, VI, 185–186.

75. Vergennes to Aranda, Dec. 15, 1782, A.N., Est., Leg. 4215, Apar. 3 (L.C.).

76. Fitzherbert reported to Grantham on Dec. 18, 1782: "I understood yesterday, to my great satisfaction, from the Spanish Ambassador that he had ventured of himself to accept the propositions transmitted by Your Lordship on the 11th Instant to M. de Rayneval." F.O. 27:3 (L.C.).

On Jan. 2, 1783, Montmorin wrote to Vergennes: ". . . this minister [Floridablanca] has again repeated to me that M. d'Aranda has taken upon himself all of the steps which he has made in the recent situation. The King of Spain has confirmed the same thing to me and has added to it that he would write to the king his nephew so that his Majesty would know the truth." Cor. Pol., Espagne, vol. 610, fols. 7–8.

propositions which Lord Grantham has charged you to transmit to me."[77]

Aranda communicated his decision to accept the British terms to Floridablanca on December 18; but he did not pretend to assert that the Spanish court had at any time granted him authority to abandon the claim to Gibraltar. He attempted to justify his action on the ground that widespread opposition had developed in Paris to the cession of the French West Indies; the influence of those interested in Guadeloupe and Martinique, and the fear that French ownership of all Santo Domingo would produce excessive competition, created a dangerous situation.[78] Aranda also stated that the financial condition of France made peace imperative. Most important in Aranda's own mind was his disinclination to increase British strength in America. He wrote: "Convinced that our mainland possessions would be virtually enslaved from Trinidad to Mexico, if the English should possess the French islands in addition to their own, I confess that I was very far from persuading M. de Vergennes that I should insist on acquiring Gibraltar, and this spirit permeated the conversation which related to the ultimatum of Great Britain."[79]

The courier from Paris reached London on the morning of December 19. A Cabinet meeting immediately considered and accepted the terms as finally proposed. Grantham reported that Rayneval had informed him "that Count Aranda had received powers to relax on that head [Gibraltar] in consequence of the application made to His Catholic Majesty by the French King, who was convinced during every stage of the negotiation how great an obstacle the exchange of that fortress threw in the way of

77. Vergennes to Rayneval, Dec. 16, 1782, Cor. Pol., Angleterre, vol. 539, fol. 245.

78. One is tempted to wonder why the terms of secret negotiations became so well known that they aroused as much opposition as Aranda reported.

79. Aranda to Floridablanca, Dec. 18, 1782, A.N., Est., Leg. 4215, Apar. 3 (L.C.).

peace."[80] Rayneval, as we have seen, was in no way justified in making the first part of this statement, and the
second again reveals the disinclination of the French to
see Gibraltar go to Spain. The king agreed to the settlement, but still expressed his regret that Gibraltar had not
been given up; he wrote to Grantham:

I sincerely rejoice at Spain's acquiescing to our retaining
Gibraltar, as it now I hope makes Peace certain, which the
Want of Public Zeal and the deficiency of Army and Navy
makes me think indispensable. I should have liked Minorca,
the two Floridas and Guadeloupe better than this *proud fortress*, and in my opinion source of another War, or at least
of a constant lurking enmity. I trust that we have conde-
scended thus far that France is not to keep Dominique.[81]

The king's trust in regard to Dominica was not well
founded, although Lord Shelburne considered that the
restoration of that island had been made an integral part
of the terms offered to Spain on December 11. France had
no intention of giving up Dominica, except for an additional equivalent. Vergennes instructed Rayneval to insist upon this point, and suggested that Tobago would be
an acceptable exchange.[82] Rayneval assured Grantham on
December 27 that France had never thought of giving up
Dominica, except for an equivalent. This led to the following outburst from the king on December 28:

It is impossible to treat less above board than the French
Court does, and indeed at all times it has been famous for
losing nothing from too scrupulous a mode of Negotiating;
Dominica and Guadeloupe were offered for Gibraltar, which
we very absurdly refused, and in return offered the two Flor-

80. Grantham to Fitzherbert, Dec. 19, 1782, in *British Diplomatic Instructions*, VII, 209–212.
81. The king to Grantham, Dec. 19, 1782, in *Correspondence of George
III*, VI, 192.
82. Vergennes to Rayneval, Dec. 24, 1782, Cor. Pol., Angleterre, vol.
539 (L.C.).

idas and Minorca for Gibraltar, and specified that though in that case we would not claim Guadeloupe, we must have Dominica restored to Us.[83]

Despite the feeling that she had been tricked by France,[84] England agreed to surrender either Tobago, or an extension of territory around Pondicherry, as an equivalent for Dominica. France chose Tobago. Thus was settled the last question outstanding between the two nations.

Until news of the settlement of December 16 reached Madrid, the Spanish court had continued to insist that no peace would be accepted that did not include the cession of Gibraltar. Montmorin had written on December 10: "The King of Spain and the Prince of Asturias have done me the honor several times of telling me that if England does not accept the conditions of which M. de Rayneval was the bearer [on his journey to London, November 28] the war will be carried on with more vigor than ever and there will be no end to it until the belligerent powers become absolutely impotent to sustain the conflict."[85] Floridablanca, in response to Aranda's letter of December 9 informing him of the discussion of December 7, declared, "the king absolutely can not be pressed into the thought of giving up Gibraltar."[86]

Why, then, did Spain acquiesce in Aranda's unauthorized action of giving up the Spanish demand of Gibraltar? The most obvious reason is that Spain really had secured an advantageous peace, including the recovery of two of her most coveted objectives, Florida and Minorca. Significantly, Floridablanca had on one occasion told Montmorin that "they would rather consent to leave Gibraltar

83. The king to Grantham, Dec. 28, 1782, in *Correspondence of George III*, VI, 197.

84. Grantham to Fitzherbert, Jan. 1, 1783, F.O. 27:5.

85. Montmorin to Vergennes, Dec. 10, 1782, Cor. Pol., Espagne, vol. 609 (L.C.).

86. Floridablanca to Aranda, Dec. 18, 1782, A.N., Est., Leg. 4215, Apar. 3 (L.C.).

in the hands of England, than to surrender either of these two objects."[87] Further, the Spanish were in no condition to carry on the war alone; and France showed no disposition to continue hostilities. Vergennes and Aranda had presented the Spanish court with a *fait accompli*, and since America and France had already come to terms with England, the Spanish were forced to accept it. Another reason may be hazarded—that Floridablanca did not actually share his royal master's enthusiasm for the recovery of Gibraltar. This suggestion admittedly is based on insubstantial evidence; yet, subsequent to the peace negotiation, Floridablanca's efforts to effect the restitution, and his expressions in regard thereto, were not enthusiastic.[88] Spanish reluctance to accept the peace settlement arranged by Vergennes showed itself in expressions of bitterness and distrust from the Spanish ministers. Floridablanca remarked that "the French ministry was too precipitate in beginning the war, and was equally so in their endeavours to conclude it." The Spanish ministers suggested that there had been duplicity in the French handling of the negotiation, even insinuating that France had concerted with the Americans to force Spain to a quick peace. They even charged that Lord Shelburne had duped the French ministry in the negotiation![89]

Vergennes and Aranda attempted to justify their action in making peace without Gibraltar by alleging that the precipitate action of the American commissioners in concluding their preliminaries separately and (supposedly) secretly had stiffened the attitude of Britain and forced France to accept terms short of what might otherwise have been obtained. According to Benjamin Vaughn, the American peace met with a "good tempered" reception from both Vergennes and Aranda, the latter exclaiming

87. Montmorin to Vergennes, Dec. 1, 1782, Cor. Pol., Espagne, vol. 609, fol. 334.

88. See below, p. 243.

89. Carmichael to Livingston, Dec. 30, 1782, in *Revolutionary Diplomatic Correspondence*, VI, 184–185.

that he considered it to be "devilishly fine."[90] Vergennes
did not protest the action of the Americans until *after* he
had attained a sure basis for a peace without Gibraltar.[91]
On December 25, Rayneval introduced the idea that the
conduct of the Americans in signing their treaty so pre-
cipitously had strengthened the hand of Britain and made
the British ministry more obdurate in its negotiation with
France and Spain.[92] As already stated, the English did
not increase their demands in the Cabinet resolution of
December 3, adopted after news of the American peace
had arrived. If one may judge by the correspondence of
King George and Lord Shelburne, Britain would have
backed down from her demand for St. Lucia or Trinidad
if France had insisted, and would have accepted terms
identical with those proposed by France on November 28.[93]
In reality, the American peace strengthened the hand of
Vergennes, and served as an important factor in permitting the French minister to score his greatest diplomatic
victory of the peace negotiation—a Spanish peace without
Gibraltar.[94]

90. Vaughn to Shelburne, Dec. 7, 1782, Clements Library, Vaughn
MSS., vol. I.

91. Vergennes to Franklin, Dec. 15, 1782, *Revolutionary Diplomatic
Correspondence*, VI, 140. Confirmation that this note was not sent until
after the receipt of the last British proposal on the afternoon of Dec. 15
is given by Aranda's letter to Floridablanca, Dec. 18, 1782, A.N., Est.,
Leg. 4215, Apar. 3 (L.C.).

92. Rayneval to Vergennes, Dec. 25, 1782, Cor. Pol., Angleterre, vol.
539 (L.C.).

93. See above, pp. 220, 226.

94. Wm. Coxe, in his *Memoirs of the Kings of Spain*, V, 141–142, made
a fair assessment of Vergennes' conduct of the peace negotiation in the
following passage: "France even made a shew of tendering the restoration of Dominica, and all the conquered islands in the West Indies, with
the cession of her own possessions of Martinico and Guadaloupe; as a
compensation for which it was understood that she was to receive the
spanish part of St. Domingo. This proposal met with a favourable attention from lord Shelburne. But a specific arrangement was frustrated
by the insinuations and objections of the french minister himself, whose
conduct plainly evinced that he was in reality far from partaking the
eager desire felt by Spain for the recovery of Gibraltar; being well
aware that the removal of that chief and standing obstacle to a cordial
reconciliation between Spain and England, must materially diminish
the future influence of France over the spanish counsels."

The Spanish court, though acquiescing in the settlement arranged by Vergennes and Aranda, attempted to have inserted in the treaty of peace "a vague article . . . which would not engage the contracting parties to anything, but which would agree that they should occupy themselves with finding an equivalent for Gibraltar."[95] In accordance with his instructions, Aranda proposed to Fitzherbert that there should be inserted in the article of the preliminaries renewing the terms of the Treaty of Utrecht a promise to consider the exchange of Gibraltar at some future date. Fitzherbert refused even to report this proposal to London, and subsequently Vergennes convinced Aranda that the proposal had to be withdrawn in order to insure the safety of the peace negotiation.[96] Aranda also instructed his secretary, Ignacio de Heredia, who had been sent to London to arrange an adjustment of the dispute over the logwood settlements, to sound the British ministers on the matter of a secret article promising to consider the future exchange of Gibraltar. Heredia conferred with Shelburne and Grantham on the subject, and reiterated the old contention that no solid friendship could ever be established with England until Gibraltar had been restored to Spain. The English ministers refused to include any article or expression in the treaty that would leave an avenue open for the future consideration of an exchange; but Grantham vaguely hinted, in a conversation with Heredia on January 13, that the question of Gibraltar might be considered at a more appropriate time. Heredia had to content himself with this expression and

95. Montmorin to Vergennes, Jan. 2, 1783, Cor. Pol., Espagne, vol. 610, fols. 7–8.

96. Vergennes to Montmorin, Jan. 18, 1783, Cor. Pol., Espagne, vol. 610, fol. 35. Spain also attempted to engage France, by a new secret convention, to promise her mediation and good offices for the future recovery of Gibraltar, and, in case of a new rupture between Spain and England, to renew the pledge of the Convention of Aranjuez not to make peace until Gibraltar had been secured. (Aranda to Vergennes, Jan. 18, 1783, Cor. Pol., Espagne, vol. 610, fols. 28–29.) I have not found the response made by Vergennes to this formal application, but nothing came of it.

with the feeling that he had "sown the seed which may be cultivated by the ambassador who comes here."[97]

The signature of the preliminary articles of peace between Great Britain, France, and Spain, on January 20, 1783, concluded the most vigorous and most nearly successful attempt of Spain to recover Gibraltar in the eighteenth century. Why did that attempt fail? Great Britain had been willing to part with Gibraltar, in return for an adequate equivalent. King George was anxious to cede the Rock; his Cabinet approved the cession; and at least a portion of British opinion favored parting with the fortress.[98] The failure of Spain to secure Gibraltar in the peace negotiations of 1782 must be credited to the diplomacy of Vergennes. The French minister did not want to make the sacrifice of territory necessary to accomplish the exchange; nor did he wish to weaken the ties that bound the Bourbon powers by removing the greatest single obstacle to a reconciliation between Spain and England. The Spanish minister Aranda shared the opinions of Vergennes, and abetted his efforts, in defiance of the instructions of the Spanish court. In a masterly exhibition of eighteenth-century diplomacy,[99] Vergennes conducted this intricate negotiation to a conclusion that achieved his objectives. At the same time he managed to throw the burden of responsibility for the loss of Gibraltar on the English and Americans. A great diplomatic victory it was, yet a costly one; for the war so increased the financial burden of France that it inevitably led to the breakdown of the old régime, and to the eventual overthrow of that diplomatic hegemony of France that Vergennes had paid so dearly to retrieve.

97. Heredia to Aranda, Jan. 29, 1783, Spain, Archivo de Simancas, Estado, Legajo 2617, número 40 (L.C.).

98. During the course of the negotiation, Lord Shelburne requested the private opinion of several influential individuals as to the wisdom of retaining Gibraltar. None of the responses expressed any concern over the proposed cession of the Rock. For excerpts from these opinions (from Shelburne MSS., vol. 83), see text and footnotes of chap. XI.

99. For a brief appreciation of the methods of eighteenth-century diplomacy, see Bemis, *The Diplomacy of the American Revolution,* pp. 13–15.

X

THE PROBLEM OF GIBRALTAR IN THE
POST-WAR NEGOTIATIONS BETWEEN
SPAIN AND ENGLAND

THE peace secured by the preliminary articles of
January 20, 1783, failed to establish a firm basis
of friendship between England and Spain. Spain
had scored her greatest diplomatic and military victory of
the eighteenth century, but she had failed to obtain that
which she wanted most—the restitution of Gibraltar.
Great Britain had suffered defeat, but her position at the
end of the war was by no means a humiliating one. For
Britain had kept Gibraltar, that symbol of her power, and
her pride, founded upon her maritime supremacy. That
pride is well illustrated in an observation contained in a
memorial submitted to the Foreign Office early in 1783:
"We must still consider ourselves as the first maritime
power (tho' now with somewhat less insolence than usual
with us), as we are still in reality so superior to the rest of
the world."[1] Both British and Spanish statesmen recognized that Gibraltar remained the fundamental obstacle to
a true reconciliation between the two nations, and in the
post-war years they tried to solve the problem of the Rock.

Despite the outcome of the war and peace negotiations,
England was not opposed to the restitution of Gibraltar,
if thereby she could break the connection between Spain
and France. British statesmen had held the same viewpoint since the secret negotiations preliminary to the
Treaty of Aix-la-Chapelle in 1748. A tract published
shortly after the signature of the preliminaries in January 1783 and inspired by Lord Shelburne expressed the
British position in the following terms:

1. From a memorial entitled "Some Memoranda for Treating with
Spain," in F.O. 72:1.

If ever hereafter it should be found expedient to give up that fortress to the Spaniards, it will be of the highest importance to us to do it without the interference of France, and to render it the means of detaching Spain from the family compact, and of restoring that country to its natural alliance with England.[2]

It should be noted also that English opinion of the value of Gibraltar was at its lowest ebb after the peace of 1783, because of the substantial decline of Britain's Mediterranean trade and of the loss of Minorca, for which Gibraltar had served as a point of support.[3]

Spain attempted to re-open the subject of Gibraltar on various occasions between the conclusion of the peace and the end of 1786. For the first time, the Spanish presented their overtures on bases of expediency, instead of on threats or on any real or pretended right to restitution. The Spanish king still cherished the desire of recovering Gibraltar, but Floridablanca's enthusiasm toward the project was questionable. In any event, the aging of Charles III and the illness of his chief minister lessened the vigor of Spanish diplomacy after the war, and the Spanish court was really content to rest on its laurels.

Heredia, Spanish chargé at London, initiated the efforts to re-open the Gibraltar question in conferences with the British ministers during January 1783. In a conversation on January 25, Heredia disclosed to Lord Grantham that Spain had been willing (in October 1782) to give Spanish Santo Domingo directly to England in exchange for Gibraltar. Grantham expressed surprise and interest at this revelation, especially when he learned that France had blocked the proposal and had forthwith proceeded to take over the negotiation and prevent any such direct offers to England. According to Heredia, this disclosure seemed to increase Grantham's interest in closer relations

2. *Considerations on the Provisional Treaty with America and the Preliminary Articles with France and Spain* (London, 1783), pp. 120–121. Written by Andrew Kippis, under the direction of Lord Shelburne.

3. See below, chap. XI and Tables I and II, pp. 267–268.

with Spain and in the possibility of a future exchange of Gibraltar.[4]

When Bernardo del Campo went to London in March 1783 to assume the ministerial post, he carried instructions to offer East Florida, together with a money payment, in exchange for Gibraltar.[5] On his arrival, Campo found it inexpedient to open the subject of Gibraltar because of the political confusion arising out of the overthrow of Shelburne by Fox. "Under the existing circumstances," he wrote, ". . . I have not wished to submit any paper on the slight importance of Gibraltar [to England]; but I am comforted by the fact that the lords, the gentlemen, the merchants, and others with whom I talk unanimously confess it."[6]

Although the Spanish minister had decided to postpone any mention of Gibraltar, a favorable opportunity presented in a conference with Fox (foreign secretary in the new Fox-North coalition) changed his mind. Campo suggested that an article be placed in the final treaty which would provide for a subsequent negotiation on the basis of a mutually favorable exchange. Fox refused to consider the inclusion in the treaty of peace of any article on Gibraltar, but he did not appear averse to its cession. Indeed, he stated: "If we should come to another war and Spain remained neutral to the end of it that would be perhaps a good opportunity to give up Gibraltar." Campo retorted that the cession of Gibraltar would be the best guarantee against any future wars between the two nations.[7] Floridablanca approved this overture, and told Campo to continue to press the subject when opportunity

4. Heredia to Aranda, Jan. 29, 1783, Spain, Archivo General de Simancas, Estado, Legajo 2617, no. 40 (Cunningham transcripts—L.C.).

5. Floridablanca to Campo, March 17, 1783, Simancas, Est., Leg. 2617, no. 40 (L.C.). Campo's instructions also authorized him to repeat the old offer of Orán for Gibraltar, and perhaps to offer other inducements, including a free port at the Straits or in the Mediterranean.

6. Campo to Floridablanca, March 31, 1783, Simancas, Est., Leg. 2617, no. 40 (L.C.).

7. Campo to Floridablanca, April 20, 1783, Simancas, Est., Leg. 2617, no. 40 (L.C.).

offered. He authorized Campo to offer Tobago (which France had offered to Spain in return for a portion of Spanish Santo Domingo) in addition to East Florida as an exchange.[8]

The Spanish did not attempt to press the suggestion that an article on Gibraltar be included in the treaty of peace. Campo did not even submit a formal memorial on the subject to the British ministry. In order to prepare the ground for a future negotiation, however, he established contacts with those who favored the cession. He cultivated both Commodore George Johnstone and Richard Cumberland, two of the principals in the secret negotiation with Spain during the war. Johnstone of his own accord suggested that Puerto Rico and one of the Floridas be offered for Gibraltar. Campo pretended to be scandalized at the extravagance of this proposal, but he did not completely discourage it. More important was an expression from Admiral Rodney, whom Campo met while paying a visit to Cumberland's home. Rodney, Campo reported, "paid a thousand compliments to our nation . . ., and added that he was of the opinion, and always would be, that [England] ought to give us Gibraltar, seeking equivalents which would be agreeable to both nations."[9]

After the signature of the definitive treaty of peace on September 3, 1783, Spain returned to her old policy of making the possession of Gibraltar as irksome as possible to the English. The Spanish refused to reëstablish communication between Gibraltar and the mainland on the pre-war footing; and all British ships that touched at Gibraltar and subsequently put into Spanish ports were placed under quarantine for forty days, however perishable their cargoes. Robert Liston, the new British minister at Madrid, protested vigorously to Floridablanca, but without avail. The Spanish were determined to render the

8. Floridablanca to Campo, April 26 and May 15, 1783, Simancas, Est., Leg. 2617, no. 40 (L.C.).

9. Campo to Floridablanca, June 8, 1783, Simancas, Est., Leg. 2617, no. 40 (L.C.).

possession of Gibraltar inconvenient to Great Britain, in order to foment opinion among English merchants in favor of the return of the fortress to Spain.[10]

In addition to the Spanish attempt to isolate Gibraltar, the old dispute over the territorial jurisdiction of the fortress again came to the fore after the conclusion of the four-year siege. General Elliot attempted to settle disputes over the demolition of the Spanish siege works and over the occupation of the "neutral" ground before the British fortifications with the local Spanish commander, but was unsuccessful; and the matter became the subject of diplomatic controversy for some years. The British contended that the jurisdiction of the garrison should be returned to the *status quo ante bellum*. Floridablanca insisted that the British lines be restricted to the extent specified by the convention entered into after the siege of 1727, for he claimed that the British had gradually advanced their posts during the succeeding decades. Unfortunately, no copy of that convention could be found either in Madrid or in London; and it should be recalled that, although such an agreement had been made, the two nations had not at the time been able to agree on its interpretation, and the jurisdiction of the fortress had never actually been settled.[11] Efforts to effect a settlement during 1784 met with no greater success. General Elliot continued to post guards at several disputed points and to insist that the Spanish withdraw to their permanent fortifications, which apparently they did. The dispute over territorial jurisdiction was again renewed during 1787, and the matter hung in issue for many years thereafter.[12]

These disputes over the Spanish "quarantine" of Gi-

10. Robert Liston to Charles James Fox, Oct. 9, Oct. 13, and Nov. 17, 1783, F.O. 72:1. Liston to Viscount Mountstuart, Jan. 2, 1784, Add. MSS. 36,806, fol. 58.

11. See above, chap. V.

12. Exchanges between Robert Liston and the Marquis of Carmarthen, Jan. 15, 1784—Jan. 10, 1785, F.O. 72:2, 3, 4. Instructions prepared for the Earl of Chesterfield on his appointment as ambassador to Spain, March 17, 1784, F.O. 72:2. Memorial of Bernardo del Campo, April 30, 1784, F.O. 72:2.

braltar and over the land boundary were chiefly of importance as impediments to the settlement of the more vital
issue—the restitution of the fortress. The miscarriage of
the contemporaneous overtures toward restitution no doubt
can be laid in part to the ill feeling created by these lesser
questions.

The Spanish minister Campo continued to prepare the
ground for an eventual consideration of the exchange of
Gibraltar by suggesting at every opportune moment the
slight value of the Rock to England, and the willingness
of Spain to grant a satisfactory equivalent for it. He reported (December 1783) that there was a growing feeling
in all ranks of society—especially among the nobility—in
favor of the cession. Many of the larger London merchants
held the same opinion. Campo urged that when the time
came to discuss the exchange, it would help a great deal if
Spain would grant substantial commercial concessions to
English merchants in order to secure their support.

In a conversation at the beginning of December, Secretary Fox told Campo that he thought the exchange of
Gibraltar for an adequate equivalent practicable, and
that the project was not contrary to his own ideas. Inter-
estingly enough, Campo thought that Fox was the most
tractable toward the exchange of Gibraltar among the
English ministers, present or prospective. Fox showed no
great interest in either Orán or East Florida as an equivalent for Gibraltar. Campo noted that the English had lost
their interest in Mediterranean trade and that they were
concentrating on improving their position in India and
the West Indies. Fox did suggest that Gibraltar might be
given up if Spain would agree to a mutual guarantee of
possessions; such a guarantee would of course have gone
far to nullify the Family Compact.[13]

The political turmoil in England during the early part
of 1784 prevented Campo from renewing the discussion
of Gibraltar for some months. Fox was overthrown by the

13. Campo to Floridablanca, Dec. 13, 1783, Simancas, Est., Leg. 2617,
no. 40 (L.C.).

king's machinations, and succeeded by William Pitt, with the Marquis of Carmarthen as foreign secretary. In the meantime, Floridablanca began to show his own disinclination toward pressing the exchange of Gibraltar. "It seems to me better not to make it," wrote the Spanish minister, "for [if we do not have Gibraltar] we will live with greater care, and the nation with more uneasiness, and [consequently with greater] preparation."[14] In other words, Gibraltar in English hands served as a stimulus to overcome the inherent lethargy of Spain. Floridablanca also stated that the territorial guarantee suggested by Fox as an equivalent would not be granted save as a last resort.[15] In consequence of this newly expressed attitude of Floridablanca, Campo made no effort to press the consideration of the exchange upon the new British ministry.[16]

During the summer of 1784 the French admiral, Count d'Estaing, conceived the idea of exchanging certain of France's East Indian possessions (among others, the islands of France and Bourbon—or Mauritius and Reunion, as they are known today) for Gibraltar, Spain in return to give France part of Spanish Santo Domingo. D'Estaing discussed his plan with Aranda at Paris and formally presented it to Floridablanca in a private letter on September 14, 1784. The Frenchman founded his belief that England would hearken to the project on the fact

14. Floridablanca to Campo, Jan. 2, 1784, A.N., Est., Leg. 4256 (L.C.).

15. Floridablanca to Campo, March 23, 1784, Simancas, Est., Leg. 2617, no. 40 (L.C.).

16. Campo to Floridablanca, July 23, 1784, Simancas, Est., Leg. 2617, no. 40 (L.C.). Campo reported a private conversation with Lord Shelburne, in which the latter had agreed that Gibraltar was worth sacrificing if by that act England could break the ties between Spain and France. Shelburne admitted that the value of Gibraltar to England had considerably decreased since the loss of Minorca. Campo noted that Shelburne and others with whom he conversed on the subject expressed no particular concern about the cession of Gibraltar; they were primarily interested in securing an adequate equivalent for it. Campo also stated that he had tried on a number of occasions to sound Pitt on the Gibraltar question, but without success. He hesitated to push the matter too openly because of Floridablanca's "repeated instructions not to be too forward or to work with precipitation on anything relating to Gibraltar."

that all reports from London showed that English colonial ambitions were now centered in the Far East.[17]

As soon as he heard from Aranda about d'Estaing's project, Floridablanca submitted it to Gálvez, the Spanish colonial minister, for consideration. Gálvez approved the cession of part of Santo Domingo, or all of it if necessary; and he stated further that if the East Indian possessions were not enough to satisfy England, the Spanish king might also be persuaded to give Orán (which Gálvez termed as great a burden for Spain as Gibraltar was for England) or a sum of money.[18]

The d'Estaing proposal fell on barren ground. The French ministry was more than cool toward the project. The French were determined, if Gibraltar should ever be restored to Spain, that it be accomplished through French offices, so that Spanish dependence would be continued. Floridablanca himself discouraged the proposal in a private letter to d'Estaing. "It is believed here that that place [Gibraltar] is not as important as has been thought," he wrote, "and that we will be more vigilant over the entrance of the Mediterranean without it. This viewpoint is held by some who know the indolence of our nation; and others consider that we will be able to acquire it for very little on the first occasion that England has need of us."[19]

The English took the initiative in November 1784 in suggesting that an exchange for Gibraltar might be considered. At a private luncheon with Carmarthen and Fraser, an assistant of the Foreign Office, Campo found them anxious to bring up the subject in a guarded fashion. The Englishmen harped on the dependence of Spain upon France, and insinuated that Gibraltar could be

17. Aranda to Floridablanca, July 27, 1784; and d'Estaing to Floridablanca, Sept. 14, 1784, Simancas, Est., Leg. 2617, no. 40 (L.C.).

18. Gálvez to Floridablanca, Floridablanca to Campo, and Floridablanca to Aranda, all dated at San Ildefonso, Aug. 11, 1784, Simancas, Est., Leg. 2617, no. 40 (L.C.).

19. Floridablanca to d'Estaing, Oct. 21, 1784; and Campo to Floridablanca, Dec. 11, 1784, Simancas, Est., Leg. 2617, no. 40 (L.C.).

given up if that connection were broken. They asserted with great vehemence that it was perfectly evident that the French did not wish to see Gibraltar restored to Spain, "as they showed very plainly by the coolness with which they handled that point in the late negotiation for peace." Campo concluded that their observations were not casual but were intended to elicit a definite proposal from Spain. English readiness to discuss the question of Gibraltar at this time grew out of disturbances in northern Europe— above all, the conflict with France for the control of Holland. This was but the first of several overtures made to Spain on the subject of Gibraltar between the end of 1784 and the fall of 1786, designed to prevent Spain from giving active support to her ally. Campo and Floridablanca recognized its true purpose, and Campo showed no eagerness to follow up the lead presented by the British secretaries.[20]

Floridablanca himself introduced the question of Gibraltar in his conversations with Robert Liston at the beginning of 1785. The Spanish minister began by asserting that "he could not dissolve the Alliance subsisting between the Kings of Spain and France . . . yet he could confine it within such limits as to prevent its standing in the way of an advantageous connection between this country and England. . . . He said he must avow with frankness that his intention was not that Spain should be the servile dependent of any country; that She had too long languished in shameful subjection to France; that he meant She should be henceforth her own Mistress, the friend but not the slave of those whom nature had pointed out as her allies." Floridablanca went on to state that Gibraltar was the one great stumbling block to friendship with England; that Gibraltar was itself of very small value to Spain, but "there was a point of honor in our having it"; that if it were given up, Spain would grant to England a free port in the Straits, or on one of the Mediterranean islands, to

20. Campo to Floridablanca, Nov. 5 and Dec. 11, 1784; and Floridablanca to Campo, Nov. 25, 1784, Simancas, Est., Leg. 2617, no. 40 (L.C.).

be used as an entrepôt "upon the same footing as Sweden
has ceded Gothenburg to France"; and that the cession of
Gibraltar "might afford us a pretext for treating you with
favourable distinction" in a new commercial agreement. A
few days later the Spanish minister again introduced the
subject, this time in connection with the dispute over the
logwood settlements in Central America. He suggested
that Spain might make some concessions on that point if
England would agree to enter into a negotiation for the
cession of Gibraltar. Floridablanca reiterated that Gibraltar as an English possession would always be "a bone
of Contention, and would continue to prove (what it had
been stiled with great justice) the best ally of France."
The French, Floridablanca said, were so sensible of that
fact that they would by no means wish to see the place in
the hands of Spain. Several of the Spanish ministers, who
had pro-French feelings, held this same opinion.[21]

The British minister forwarded the report of this new
overture to England, together with a Spanish memorial
on the subject of the logwood settlements. Section three of
this memorial read:

But as this Negotiation cannot be undertaken with Success
without some Pretext, Equivalent, or Recompense in Favor
of Spain for her Concession of better terms than stipulated
for in the Treaty, an Equivalent shall be taken into Consideration, and in this Negotiation shall be included that of
finding Means for the Cession of Gibraltar, treating this
matter either jointly or separately.[22]

It should be noted that the equivalent proposed was *treating about* the cession of Gibraltar, not the cession itself;
the real equivalent for Gibraltar would have to be found
elsewhere. Carmarthen did not respond to this memorial
until three months later, and then he avoided giving any
answer to Spain on Gibraltar. In a private letter to Liston,
he remarked: "I think the less that subject is touched

21. Liston to Carmarthen, Jan. 7, 1785, F.O. 72:4.
22. F.O. 72:4.

upon the better."[23] It is perfectly obvious from the correspondence that the English ministry had no disposition to combine Gibraltar or any other subject with the settlement of the logwood dispute.

The difficulties over the logwood settlements created a good deal of bitterness in Anglo-Spanish relations throughout 1785. Floridablanca expressed his open distrust toward the professions of the English that they desired to settle the dispute. On the other hand, Liston reported at the end of the year that greater friction existed between France and Spain than at any time since 1778, when the French had made their treaty with the Americans. Liston emphasized the opportunity for a rapprochement with Spain, if only the outstanding controversies could be solved. In response, the Marquis of Carmarthen rather bluntly said: "Whatever may be the opinion of Count Floridablanca respecting a more intimate connection between the two Courts, he ought to be persuaded that the Family Compact must be annulled before England can ever treat with Spain in the light of a friendly or at least an independent power."[24]

Anglo-Spanish relations became almost critical during January and February of 1786. The French were doing their best not only to break up any negotiations between Great Britain and Spain, but also to secure the adherence of Spain to their new alliance with Holland, which in effect would have been a reaffirmation and strengthening of the Family Compact. Liston applied to London for definite assurances that the logwood dispute would be settled amicably as soon as possible. Unless such assurances were forthcoming, Spain seemed certain to adhere to the Franco-Dutch Alliance.

In response to Liston's appeal, Carmarthen promptly forwarded a detailed and amicable response to the Spanish memorials on the subject of the logwood settlements, and laid the basis for a satisfactory conclusion of that dis-

23. Carmarthen to Liston, March 3, 1785, F.O. 72:5.
24. Carmarthen to Liston, Jan. 31, 1786, F.O. 72:7.

pute later in the year. An accompanying private and confidential letter to Liston is worth quoting in some detail:

Unless Fl. Bl. is desirous of collecting a Hundred and one
more Grievances I cannot account for his strange Language,
and still more extraordinary conduct. Should his View have
been only to bully us into a quick Settlement *of the dirty
petty-fogging Dispute* [over the logwood settlements], I am
satisfied, provided he will keep clear of the lately contracted
[Franco-Dutch] Alliance. We are really serious in wishing
to cultivate not only the Friendship, but, if possible, the
Confidence of Spain, and could we but once see a Probability
of a permanent and efficient Connection with that Country,
I see scarce an Object which might not be rendered perfectly
satisfactory to Spain (not even excepting Gibraltar itself).
This Consideration however would require the most ample
and mature Deliberation, more perhaps on account of popular though very honorable Prejudices than from the real and
intrinsic Value of that Place. . . . You will observe I give
an Opening for Count Florida Blanca to explain the Wishes
of his Court, upon Points of any *possible Description*, as well
as upon those either of a political or commercial Nature.
Gibraltar may probably occur when you communicate this
Part of my Dispatch [the public dispatch of this same date]
to him; and should he mention it, you will take it *ad referendum*, still repeating your Assurances of this Court being
ready to listen to every Subject Spain may wish to communicate.[25]

On receipt of this communication, Liston submitted to
Floridablanca a detailed memorandum, the concluding
paragraph of which read:

There is no point, however delicate, or apparently liable to
difficulty, whether of a political, a commercial, or any other
possible description, on which the English ministry are not
willing to enter into the most ample discussion wherever

25. Carmarthen to Liston, March 16, 1786, F.O. 72:7.

either the interest or even the wishes of Spain can at all be concerned.[26]

It must be noted that this very open overture was an extreme measure to block Spanish adherence to the Franco-Dutch treaty. Although he did not say so explicitly, Carmarthen implied that friendly negotiations over Gibraltar and other points could take place only if the Family Compact were expressly annulled or at least tacitly given up.

In his conferences with Floridablanca, Liston found that the Spanish minister evinced no disposition to respond to this opening. In a private letter to Carmarthen of April 19, Liston significantly stated:

. . . there is one observation which from its importance cannot perhaps be made at too early a period.—It is, that if Your Lordship and the rest of His Majesty's Ministers are convinced that no connection with Spain deserves the attention of Great Britain which has not for its basis a *formal rupture* of the Family Compact, it is more adviseable to drop the project at once: for I cannot persuade myself that, so long as the present King of Spain and Count Florida Blanca hold the reins of this Government any such proposition will ever be listened to with favour, or even with patience.[27]

Since the only equivalent which the British had seriously considered for Gibraltar had been the rupture of the Family Compact, it is obvious that there was scant possibility of a negotiation about its cession at this time, and for some time to come.

In connection with an attempt to negotiate a new Anglo-Spanish commercial treaty, Campo was approached in March 1786 by a Mr. Woodford[28] on the subject of Gi-

26. F.O. 72:7.

27. Liston to Carmarthen, April 19, 1786, F.O. 72:7.

28. I have not been able positively to identify Woodford. He was a subordinate (of the Foreign Office?), engaged in the attempted negotiation of a commercial treaty with Spain. I assume that he was Ralph Woodford, later minister extraordinary to Denmark, who was granted a baronetcy in 1791 and died in 1810.

braltar. Woodford hinted that the commercial treaty, combined with a mutual guarantee of territory, might free the Spanish from their dependence on France and pave the way for the cession of Gibraltar. Campo considered that Woodford's proposals were also instigated by English fears that Spain would join the Franco-Dutch Alliance (the principal object of which, according to Campo, was to combat British superiority in the Far East) ; and the Spanish minister expressed his distrust of any British insinuations on Gibraltar under such circumstances. Floridablanca held the same opinion. "Your Excellency may tell them," he wrote, "that they are throwing out a proposal with no real intention of doing anything about it, and that we recognize it." During April Woodford again raised the proposal of an alliance with Spain as a means of solving the problem of Gibraltar. He stated openly that if Spain and England would join in an alliance of a similar character to that recently entered into between France and Holland, the cession of Gibraltar would surely follow. Campo made no response to his overtures, merely reporting them to Floridablanca.[29]

In spite of his distrust of English motives, Floridablanca transmitted to Campo the most definite proposal on the subject of Gibraltar made during the post-war years. As a part of the general commercial treaty then in process of negotiation, he offered, in return for the cession of Gibraltar: 1, to enter into a mutual territorial guarantee, similar to that in effect between Spain and Portugal; 2, to grant to England a free port in the Straits, with warehouses and other necessary facilities, to be open to both merchant and naval vessels; 3, to pay for the English armaments and materials at Gibraltar; 4, to grant certain commercial concessions, such as a 25 per cent rebate in customs on the importation of non-competitive British

29. Campo to Floridablanca, March 6 and April 20, 1786; and Floridablanca to Campo, April 6, 1786, Simancas, Est., Leg. 2617, no. 40 (L.C.). Also Campo to Floridablanca, April 20, 1786, Simancas, Est., Leg. 8143 (L.C.).

manufactures, including iron and steel and Irish linen, and free entry of codfish, for a limited time.[30] At about the same time, Floridablanca sent Campo a memorandum in which he satirized the usefulness of Gibraltar to England. This memorandum, together with other expressions of Floridablanca made in these years, seems to confirm the indifference with which the Spanish secretary personally viewed the recovery of Gibraltar.[31]

Woodford did not broach the subject of Gibraltar to Campo again until September. In a private conversation he then said that England would be glad to cede Gibraltar for a reasonable equivalent. Campo responded by suggesting that Spain would give England a free port and perhaps agree to a neutralization of the Mediterranean. Not satisfied with this, the Englishman pressed Campo to make a definite offer, and asserted that England was more than ever ready to give up the Rock in return for a reasonable equivalent. Campo felt certain that Woodford had been prompted to make this overture by the ministry, but he refused to open himself on the subject, since Woodford was not properly charged to discuss foreign relations.[32]

After Floridablanca received Campo's report of Woodford's latest overture, the Spanish secretary once more brought up the point of Gibraltar in his conferences with Liston on the subject of the commercial treaty. Liston stated that he had no instructions to discuss the subject, but that he did not doubt that the "friendly inclinations of his Government . . . might even lead them to listen to a negotiation on the subject of Gibraltar, with the prospect of a cordial union with Spain." The English minister asserted, however, that since such a negotiation could be founded only upon a rupture of the Family Compact, which Floridablanca had assured him on repeated occa-

30. Floridablanca to Campo, May 17, 1786, British Museum, Egerton MSS. 373, fols. 57–58.

31. "Relación de las utilidades que saca la Gran Bretaña de la posesión de la Plaza de Gibraltar," in Egerton MSS. 373, fols. 59–60.

32. Campo to Floridablanca, Sept. 5, 1786, Simancas, Est., Leg. 2617, no. 40 (L.C.).

sions was an impossibility, he had presumed that the subject had been dropped. The Spanish minister assured Liston that the cession would permit him to grant Britain valuable commercial privileges. "He ended," reported Liston, "by mentioning for the first time what he meant by the *middle term* which he thought might serve to counterbalance the family compact, or be an equivalent to its dissolution. It was, to make a treaty with England containing a reciprocal guaranty of the possessions of the two countries, of which he explained the operation so as to endeavour to prove that it rendered the Family Compact virtually null and void." Floridablanca told Liston that personally he cared little whether or not Spain secured Gibraltar; he felt that the cession of Gibraltar would lull the Spanish nation into a false sense of security, and diminish its interest in the maintenance of a strong naval and military power. But, Floridablanca said, the earnest desire of the Spanish king and people for the recovery of the fortress forced him to waive his personal views on the subject; and he was prepared to negotiate on the above basis, if the English would do so promptly. If they would not, he would abandon forever his efforts to obtain the fortress.[33]

The efforts of England to negotiate a new commercial agreement with Spain were overshadowed by the new Anglo-French commercial treaty of September 26, 1786. That treaty forecast a general improvement in relations between Great Britain and France, and consequently lessened the desirability of a closer union with Spain. The nightmare of French control in Holland began to clear by the end of the year; by the middle of 1787 Britain and her ally Prussia succeeded in ousting the French from The Hague and dissolving the Quadruple Alliance projected by France with Spain, Austria, and Holland. Floridablanca's proposal for a new treaty with England, that would in a measure neutralize the effectiveness of the Fam-

33. Liston to Carmarthen, Oct. 11, 1786, F.O. 72:8. Floridablanca to Campo, Oct. 5, 1786, Simancas, Est., Leg. 2617, no. 40 (L.C.).

ily Compact and at the same time secure Gibraltar, fell on
barren ground. The improvement of England's diplomatic position by the end of 1786 cooled the ardor of the
British ministry for a general settlement with Spain at the
price of Gibraltar.

Indeed, in the period after the treaty of peace, both
Britain and Spain had introduced the question of Gibraltar at strategic moments as an offset to the claims or diplomatic maneuvers of the other power. Spain had proposed
the cession of Gibraltar as a counter-measure to balance
the demands of England in the logwood dispute and in the
negotiations for a commercial treaty. On the other hand,
the British had expressed their willingness to consider the
cession only when Spain had been threatening to join the
Franco-Dutch Alliance. Both nations had approached the
subject in the most guarded fashion, and under pressure.
With that pressure withdrawn, no excuse remained to continue the negotiation. Neither nation desired to continue
it. The old specter of popular prejudice to the cession
haunted the Pitt ministry. Although English statesmen
had not yet opened their eyes to the prospect of British
power in the Mediterranean, they preferred not to run the
gauntlet of partisan opposition which the cession of Gibraltar would surely have aroused, unless that measure
were compensated by a substantial equivalent and the rupture of the Family Compact. Age and illness had robbed
the Spanish king and Floridablanca of that vigorous enthusiasm with which they had followed the quest of Gibraltar in earlier years. King Charles was not prepared to depart from the French alliance, which for so long had been
the mainstay of the Spanish diplomatic system. Thus,
while the statesmen of both nations had handled the question of Gibraltar with a moderation unmatched in previous negotiations, their efforts to arrange a settlement
were fruitless.

The conferences of Liston and Floridablanca in October
1786 brought to an end the efforts of England and Spain
to adjudicate the problem of Gibraltar in the post-war

years. Carmarthen made no response to Floridablanca's final overture. Not until the arrival, in June 1788, of William Eden as regular ambassador to the Spanish court did the Spanish secretary again mention the subject; and then he admitted the futility of attempting to renew the issue. Eden's record of this interview admirably summarizes the position of the two nations on the question of Gibraltar:

In speaking of the long interval still likely to elapse before the Russian Fleet could make its appearance in the Mediterranean, he [Floridablanca] entered into a wide field of speculation respecting the navigation of that Sea, He said that particular epochs had occurred in which it might have been both a practicable and a wise measure for such of the European Powers as have Ports and Possessions in the Mediterranean to have jointly stipulated that no other Power should be permitted to enter with armed vessels.—He said that for so good a purpose he would readily have concurred in giving to Great Britain for the ground of such limitation a free port upon the coast of Spain.—This line of conversation led us to the mention of Gibraltar.—He told me that about three years ago he had written much on that subject to M. del Campo. He considered it as a possession which, though overrated as to its solid importance and value, was a perpetual thorn in the side of Spain, and a great obstacle to the establishing any compleat cordiality:—he had turned it much and long in his mind:—he could see many ample equivalents in the eye of national wisdom, but there were prejudices in England on the subject which would supersede any just reasonings.—He made mention in different statements of the question sometimes of Porto Rico, sometimes of the Caraccas, sometimes of specific commercial advantages, with a general guarantee of all possessions; which last measure he has occasionally stated in argument with Mr. Liston as one mode of removing our objections to the Family Compact without any breach of faith towards France. —I endeavored, without giving offence, to make him feel the

difficulty of giving to any new possession, however valuable,
the same immoveable security, that we possess in the place in
question. He dismissed the subject by saying in a tone of regret, bordering on peevishness, that all such speculations
were a waste of time, that no British Ministry of the present
Century would have the courage to look the question fairly
in the face, and that he was determined to think no more
about it.[34]

34. Eden to Carmarthen, June 10, 1788, Add. MSS. 34,428, fols. 75–76.

XI

THE VALUE OF GIBRALTAR

HOW valuable was Gibraltar as a British possession in the eighteenth century? How greatly did this factor of value influence the diplomatic history of the Rock? Was Gibraltar of sufficient worth to compensate for the diplomatic complications that followed Britain's refusal to restore it to Spain? These questions can not be answered categorically. Contemporary opinion on the value of Gibraltar as a British possession varied widely. In 1783, for example, one observer (a civilian) commented: " 'Tis Gibraltar alone which gives us the importance we want there [in the Mediterranean]. Our *Flag* and our *passport* would sink with the loss of that place to a level with those of other nations;"[1] another (a naval officer) referred to the Rock contemptuously as "the Golden Image of English Idolatry."[2] With such differences of opinion to confound him, the student of today may well be forewarned against the expression of any positive judgment on the wisdom of England's retention of Gibraltar.

The English based their decision to keep Gibraltar and Minorca partly on their belief that these strongholds would serve as sureties for their Spanish and Mediterranean trade. They also hoped to develop the ports of Gibraltar and Mahón as trading centers to aid in an expansion of their commercial interests in the Mediterranean area. At least as far as Gibraltar was concerned, these expectations very largely failed of realization.

1. "Some Memoranda for treating with Spain," a memorial by an unidentified writer, undated but probably written early in 1783, F.O. 72:1, fols. 101–109.

2. Sir Roger Curtis to Evan Napean, Feb. 2, 1783, Shelburne MSS., vol. 87 (L.C.). Curtis at this time held the rank of commodore; he had taken an active part in the relief of Gibraltar and other naval operations in the Mediterranean area during the war.

Gibraltar itself had very little commercial value in the eighteenth century. It produced nothing that entered into the channels of trade. The only local trade of consequence in the first half of the century was in provisions and supplies for the garrison. The British made Gibraltar a free port, hoping that it would become an important entrepôt for trade with the adjacent Spanish and African coasts. A number of factors helped to frustrate this design: Spain did her best to discourage any local trade with Gibraltar—under the Treaty of Utrecht land communication was restricted to the emergency supply of the garrison, and trade by sea was interrupted after 1728 by the subterfuge of "quarantine."[3] The corrupt and arbitrary administration of the Rock led English merchants to avoid it, and most of the local trade was handled by Moors, Jews, and Genoese.[4] The situation of the Bay of Gibraltar in relation to the prevailing winds through the Straits often made it inexpedient or impossible for merchant vessels to stop there.[5] The roadstead was open and dangerous in bad weather. Docking facilities for private ships were inadequate; and the port had practically no means of repairing or servicing merchant vessels.[6]

The more friendly spirit in Anglo-Spanish relations after 1748 led to a relaxation of the restraints imposed by Spain on trade with Gibraltar. In addition to the provisioning and supply of the garrison and visiting ships, the Gibraltar merchants began to participate in other channels of trade. They imported wine from Spain and south-

3. See above, p. 126.
4. "Sur Gibraltar," by M. Durand, March 10, 1760, in M.A.E., Mem. et Doc., Angleterre, vol. 58, fols. 103–106.
5. *Ibid.*
6. "So little are they prepared at Gibraltar to relieve any occasional distress, that in the year 1774 one of my ships called the Mercury of about 150 Tons, after having delivered a Cargo of fish at Barcelona, lost her cable anchors, between that place and Gibraltar, where she put in to refit; but there was none to be had but those in the King's Stores, and the Vessell was therefore obliged to proceed to England without them." Francis Baring to Lord Shelburne, Dec. 28, 1782, Clements Library, Shelburne MSS., vol. 83.

ern France, and sent it to England and America. American vessels brought rice, sugar, rum, lumber, and other products and exchanged them at Gibraltar for wine and African goods. About five or six thousand mules were purchased annually in Africa and shipped from Gibraltar to America. Other African products that moved through Gibraltar were hides, brass, morocco leather, almonds, wax, and ivory. Between thirty and thirty-five small vessels were regularly employed in handling the African trade of the Gibraltar merchants.[7]

The possession of Gibraltar gave the British a base for smuggling goods into southern Spain. Thomas Gordon, the first protagonist of Gibraltar's worth in the ranks of the pamphleteers, emphasized that "it gives us the means of carrying on a private and advantageous Commerce with Spain, notwithstanding all the Prohibitions they can make or Precautions they can use."[8] Six decades later a memorialist advised the Foreign Office: "From thence the smuggling trade into Spain can at any time be let loose to different degrees."[9] The Spanish minister Floridablanca complained in 1786 that Gibraltar furnished an "asylum for many bad actors and smugglers."[10] Yet the British never exploited this advantage to any considerable degree; indeed, on occasion they coöperated with the local Spanish authorities in suppressing the smuggling of tobacco, the principal item of illicit trade.[11] Apparently the combination of English and Spanish restraints that stifled local commercial activity at Gibraltar affected equally both legitimate and illegitimate trade.

Contemporary critics stressed the value of Gibraltar as

7. This paragraph is based on a "Mémoire relatif à Gibraltar," by Count Roffignac, dated 1782, in M.A.E., Mem. et Doc., Espagne, vol. 208, fols. 171–172. Roffignac's account, the most detailed description of local trade at Gibraltar that the author has discovered, apparently applies to the situation as it existed on the eve of the War for American Independence.

8. *Considerations Offered . . . upon the Importance of Gibraltar to the British Empire* . . . (London, 1720), p. 18.

9. F.O. 72:1, fol. 106.   10. Egerton MSS. 373, fols. 59–60.

11. See above, p. 170 n.

a menace to insure the good behavior and proper respect of the piratical Barbary states toward British commerce. Partly for this reason, the governor of Gibraltar was charged with the conduct of Barbary relations. Although the value of British trade with the Barbary powers was relatively insignificant (less than £50,000 annually),[12] their good conduct toward English merchant vessels engaged in the Mediterranean trade was of course an important asset. In actual practice, the relative strength of British naval power and the payment of tribute, rather than the argument of Gibraltar, governed the attitude of the Barbary states toward British commerce. When Britain lost her naval control in the western Mediterranean, the "friendship" of the Barbary powers vanished.[13]

What of the larger channels of trade with Spain and the Mediterranean for which Gibraltar served as a surety and protection? Instead of keeping pace with the rapid expansion of British commerce, the value of trade with Spain and the Mediterranean area (except that with Italy) became diminishingly significant in Britain's commercial outlook; it declined from one-fifth to one-tenth of the total during the course of the eighteenth century. Even during the periods of most friendly relations, England's commerce with Spain failed to increase appreciably during the century.[14] Far from preserving and promoting trade with Spain, England's possession of Gibraltar helped to engender no less than five Anglo-Spanish wars

12. L. A. Harper, *The English Navigation Laws* (New York, 1939), p. 289.

13. "It may be urged that we shall lose our consequence with the States of Barbary by ceding it [Gibraltar] to Spain. In answer to that argument it is scarcely possible for the Emperor of Morocco to be more hostile than he is at this moment, and I should think Algier and Tunis not only from their remote situation but what they have felt from the arms of the British Navy, which was fresh in their memory a few years ago, when I visited them, will not change their policy upon it." Sir John Jervis to Shelburne, Sept. (?), 1782, Shelburne MSS., vol. 83. Jervis at this time was a captain in the Navy who had seen much service in the Mediterranean. Subsequently he became Earl of St. Vincent and admiral of the Fleet.

14. See Tables I and II at the end of this chapter.

between 1713 and 1789, wars that curtailed or eliminated Spanish trade for extended periods. One trade for which Gibraltar afforded a measure of protection in the first half of the century—that with Spanish America via Cádiz— virtually disappeared after the removal of the ban on direct trade between other Spanish ports and the Indies. The declining significance of Britain's trade with Spain and the Mediterranean helps to explain the growing indifference of informed British opinion toward the possession of the Rock and the maintenance of British power in the Mediterranean area.

Aside from the relative decline of Britain's Mediterranean and Spanish commerce, contemporaries doubted that Gibraltar had any great value as a guardian for trade through the Straits. "Should Gibraltar not remain in the possession of Great Britain," wrote a London merchant in 1782, "that trade will still go on, and in war time in the same manner [in neutral bottoms] it has for the last three or four years."[15] Another merchant advised Lord Shelburne that a lower rate of insurance for British commerce was the principal peace-time advantage attributable to the possession of Gibraltar.[16] The failure of England to maintain her naval power in the western Mediterranean during the years of Spanish participation in the War for American Independence forced the British to transfer their Mediterranean trade to neutral bottoms.[17] This development strengthened the growing conviction of many merchants that British commerce in time of war should be carried in neutral vessels.[18] In reality, not Gibraltar but

15. John Motteux to Shelburne, 1782, Shelburne MSS., vol. 83.
16. Samuel Garbett to Shelburne, Dec. 1782, Shelburne MSS., vol. 83.
17. See above, p. 163.
18. "I thought it very possible, that before a future war, the system of *neutral shipping* might secure a [*sic*] little Mediterranean [trade] we had left better than Gibraltar." Benjamin Vaughn to Shelburne, Dec. 4, 1782, Clements Library, Vaughn MSS., vol. I. "In time of War our Commerce with the Mediterranean and Levant ought to be in Neutral Bottoms, not only because freight and Insurance will be cheaper by Neutrals, but because our Sailors are then of great importance to the State." Garbett to Shelburne, Dec. 1782, Shelburne MSS., vol. 83.

British naval power in time of peace, and naval superiority over France and Spain in time of war, provided the only sure protection for the Mediterranean trade.

Contemporaries frequently criticized Gibraltar as an expensive luxury for which England received no commensurate return. The cost of maintaining the garrison mounted steadily as the century progressed; it was estimated at £60,000 in 1718, £120,000 in 1760, and upwards of £200,000 twenty-five years later. In wartime the expense was far greater; between December 25, 1780 and December 24, 1781, it amounted to £351,000.[19] These sums do not include the costs of naval supply and protection. The expense of Minorca must have been roughly equivalent to that of Gibraltar, and the cost of maintaining a Mediterranean fleet (without which those possessions would have had slight value) an additional burden. The value of Britain's Spanish and Mediterranean trade (about £3,500,000 annually) hardly justified such expenditures. Yet one cannot calculate solely on that basis. A French critic, in a confidential mémoire to the French Foreign Office in 1760, concluded that Britain's outlay for her Mediterranean possessions and fleet was probably justified. In his opinion, Britain's commercial and strategic interests in the Mediterranean area required the maintenance of her power there; without Gibraltar and Minorca it would probably have cost her even more to maintain her position; Minorca, though of greater value than Gibraltar, could not have been held without the latter's support; and Britain's power in the Mediterranean was of value not only in itself but also because it gave her "a part of the influence which she has in the general affairs of Europe."[20]

The British used Gibraltar as a local base for their naval operations in the vicinity of the Straits and in the western Mediterranean. The deficiencies of Gibraltar as a

19. John Sinclair, *The Propriety of Retaining Gibraltar Impartially Considered* (London, 1783), pp. 20–21.
20. Durand mémoire, M.A.E., Mem. et Doc., Angleterre, vol. 58.

naval base have already been mentioned. Until the end of the period under discussion in this study, Gibraltar had but scant facilities for servicing a fleet. In 1725, the dock facilities were so inadequate that only fifth- and sixth-rate ships could be repaired;[21] and very little seems to have been done during succeeding decades to improve this situation. Sir John Jervis wrote Lord Shelburne in 1782 that "the Mole being very small will not admit of more than one Line of Battle Ships at a time to careen, therefore it cannot be considered as a place of equipment."[22] The cannon range of the Spanish fortifications erected in 1730–1732 covered nearly four-fifths of the safe anchorage area, making the harbor virtually useless in time of war. Gibraltar's sole advantage as a naval base, in comparison with any site within an easy radius of the Straits, was its relative invulnerability.

From the standpoint of naval strategy, the most important utility of Gibraltar was its service as a base for supporting a British fleet in the Straits sufficiently strong to keep the Atlantic and Mediterranean fleets of Spain and France divided in time of war. "Gibraltar has been described as that happy spot, which in the possession of Great Britain, divides France from France, and Spain from Spain, and consequently as a place which ought not on any account to be relinquished."[23] Furthermore, Britain's naval control of the Straits protected her Mediterranean trade in wartime. Divorced from British naval control, Gibraltar by itself was helpless to achieve these objectives. "Spain is unquestionably as entirely in the command of the Straits of Gibraltar," wrote Captain Jervis in the fall of 1782, "and as capable of annoying and intercepting the Trade of Great Britain bound up the Mediterranean, as if she was in possession of Gibraltar."[24]

Gibraltar's eighteenth-century garrison of between

21. *Gibraltar a Bulwark of Great Britain . . . . By a Gentleman of the Navy* (London, 1725).
22. Shelburne MSS., vol. 83.
23. John Sinclair to Shelburne, July 17, 1782, Shelburne MSS., vol. 83.
24. Shelburne MSS., vol. 83.

three and four thousand men constituted one of the largest permanent establishments of the British army. An early argument against the retention of the Rock involved this very point: As Gibraltar and Minorca would require large permanent garrisons, and as a standing army was against the English tradition, those possessions should be given up.[25] Far from taking advantage of Gibraltar as a pretext for maintaining a large standing force, the British limited the garrison to the bare minimum necessary to man the defenses.

The inordinate desire of Spain to recover Gibraltar led her to concentrate at all times a considerable portion of her military force in the vicinity of the Rock. In time of war Gibraltar acted as a magnet to draw Spanish forces that might otherwise have been used to attack more vulnerable English outposts in America. On the other hand, the defense of Gibraltar required an English diversion of military and naval strength that might have been put to better use elsewhere in the wars of the eighteenth century. Floridablanca finally came to the conclusion (perhaps a somewhat jaundiced one) that Britain's possession of Gibraltar was really useful from the Spanish viewpoint: Not only did it divert British forces that might have been sent against the Indies, but also it acted as a stimulus to the inherent lethargy of Spain, by prompting her to maintain a more vigorous military and naval establishment.[26]

Gibraltar had another value of real significance from the military standpoint. It served as an observation post, from which Britain could easily keep watch on movements of Spanish and French naval vessels and Spanish military preparations on land. In view of the close coöperation of the Bourbon powers under the Family Compact through

25. *Concordia Discors: or an Argument to Prove, that the Possession of Dunkirk, Port Mahon, Gibraltar, and Other Places by the English, may be of Worse Consequence* . . . (London, 1712).

26. See above, p. 243. Floridablanca's attitude toward Gibraltar is also revealed in a satirical memorandum to Del Campo, 1786, Egerton MSS. 373, fols. 59–60; and in the *Instrucción reservada,* written in 1787 and edited by Andrés Muriel (Paris, 1838), pp. 243–248, 372–382.

much of the eighteenth century, the vantage point of Gibraltar provided the English with a rather accurate gauge of Franco-Spanish symptoms of hostility. On the eve of the American Revolution, in the late 1760's and early 1770's, Spanish diplomacy exhibited every symptom of desiring to precipitate an immediate clash with England; yet the British knew, because of information gathered by spies sent out from Gibraltar into southern Spain, that Spain's military preparations lagged far behind her belligerent attitude. Further, military activity in the immediate vicinity of Gibraltar provided a useful index of the true intentions of Spain throughout the century.

Many critics in the eighteenth century believed that Gibraltar was of far less value to England than Minorca. One need only recall the attempt of Pitt in 1757 to recover Minorca by offering Gibraltar to Spain. One contemporary referred to Minorca as "a place which has all the advantages that Gibraltar has, tho' in a much higher degree, and none of the disadvantages."[27] From the standpoint of commercial value, Minorca undoubtedly eclipsed Gibraltar. On the other hand, Gibraltar possessed one attribute that Minorca lacked: It proved invulnerable to the Spanish assaults of the eighteenth century, whereas Minorca easily succumbed on two occasions. It is difficult to show, however, that this advantage of Gibraltar exercised any degree of influence in the one negotiation where a choice of keeping one or the other presented itself. In 1782, the British king and ministry attempted to exchange Gibraltar for Puerto Rico and the return of Minorca.

Gibraltar as a British possession had one utility of a nebulous but nevertheless important character—its psychological value. "It will give us Reputation and Figure in those Seas," wrote Thomas Gordon in 1720, "which are always rewarded with Power and Riches."[28] For reasons

27. [Doctor Lind], *Three Letters Relating to the Navy, Gibraltar, and Port Mahon* (London, 1757). (Written in 1748.)
28. *Considerations Offered . . . upon the Importance of Gibraltar,* p. 20.

not easy to explain, after 1720 Gibraltar captured the imagination of the English people and maintained its position as their favorite and unreasoning "prejudice."[29] "It is not probable that the Bulk of the Kingdom will think anything an Equivalent for Gibraltar," wrote a correspondent of Lord Shelburne in 1782.[30] Faced with such popular enthusiasm for Gibraltar, British statesmen, whatever their private opinion of its value, on most occasions evinced the greatest reluctance to embrace any scheme for parting with the Rock. Aside from its intrinsic worth, therefore, the possession of Gibraltar undoubtedly bolstered the national morale and patriotic sentiments of the English people. This was especially true after the heroic and widely publicized defense of the Rock by the gallant General Elliot in the great siege of 1779–1783. The failure of that siege established more firmly than ever the tradition of Gibraltar's invulnerability. Gibraltar, in short, became a symbol of British power and invincibility.

To answer the first question raised at the beginning of this chapter, Great Britain undoubtedly derived a measure of benefit in the eighteenth century from her possession of Gibraltar. Because the Rock failed to live up to original expectations that it would be a valuable point of support for British commerce and because of its grave deficiencies as a naval base, the great majority of qualified contemporary critics condemned it as of little value. They tended to ignore or underestimate the significant but less obvious advantages that Gibraltar gave to Britain. The Rock was a valuable military outpost, not as a base for offensive operations against Spain, but as an observation post to watch Spanish military preparations and as a magnet to divert Spain's military efforts in time of war. Perhaps Gibraltar's greatest value was psychological; it acted as a fillip to British pride and patriotism. Without

---

29. *National Prejudice, Opposed to the National Interest, Candidly Considered in the Detention or Yielding up Gibraltar and Cape Briton* . . . (London, 1748), pp. 29–30.
30. Garbett to Shelburne, Dec. 1782, Shelburne MSS., vol. 83.

taking into account the wider range of injury to Britain's diplomatic and economic position caused by her refusal to restore the Rock, I believe that the benefits which Britain derived from Gibraltar more than offset its shortcomings as a naval base and commercial outpost and justified the heavy expense of its upkeep.

To what extent did the value of Gibraltar determine the fate of the fortress in British diplomacy? Certainly the bulk of "informed" opinion—the expressions of British statesmen, naval officers, and merchants—held that Gibraltar had but a moderate or negligible value, and that it would be well worth sacrificing in return for Spanish friendship and an advantageous equivalent. On the other hand, the force of British "public" opinion—the voice of the man in the street—was in the opposite direction. For the average Briton the Rock of Gibraltar held a special appeal that had little to do with any rational arguments for or against its utility. Despite the absence of the forms of democracy, public opinion exerted a powerful control over the course of British policy in the eighteenth century. The conflict between informed and general public opinion as to the merit of the Rock influenced the course of the Gibraltar question in British diplomacy in a rather obvious manner. British statesmen proposed restitution or exchange on a number of occasions; the hostility of public opinion toward such a step helped to check and frustrate the consummation of every one of these efforts.

A more pertinent question remains to be answered: Was Gibraltar sufficiently valuable to warrant Britain's keeping it at the expense of Spanish hostility and other diplomatic complications? The answer to that question must be no, if by its restoration England could have cultivated Spanish friendship, improved her commercial position, and preserved her naval power (by securing some alternative base) in the western Mediterranean. It is by no means certain that the return of Gibraltar at any time in the eighteenth century would have acted as a panacea to heal Anglo-Spanish relations. Even if Britain had tried to pacify Spain by restoring Gibraltar, it is unlikely that Spanish resentment of British trade encroachments—legal and illegal—in the Spanish Indies would have disappeared. No matter how badly they wanted Gibraltar, the Spanish could never bring themselves to offer in exchange an alternative base in the vicinity of the Straits acceptable to the British. Nevertheless, if we consider the

TABLE I[31]

The Value of England's Mediterranean and Spanish Trade
(Expressed in Percentages) in Relation to the Value
of All English Trade, and Trade with
America and East India

		1698–1701	1722–1725	1751–1754	1770–1773	1789–1792
(a)	Total English Trade	100.00	100.00	100.00	100.00	100.00
(b)	With Italy	3.46	4.00	4.12	5.64	4.63
(c)	With Venice	.73	.51	.24	.59	.24
(d)	With Turkey	4.13	3.84	1.59	.75	1.09
(e)	Total Mediterranean	8.32	8.35	5.95	6.98	5.96
(f)	With Spain	8.55	6.68	7.28	5.18	3.67
(g)	With Straits	3.24	4.07	3.74	.47	.51
(h)	Total Spain, Straits, and Mediterranean	20.11	19.10	16.97	12.63	10.14
(i)	With East Indies	7.26	6.92	9.19	10.96	14.39
(j)	With Jamaica	2.72	3.67	5.66	6.77	7.92
(k)	With American Continental Colonies (U.S.)	5.73	6.17	10.57	14.36	11.41

31. Tables I and II have been compiled by the author from George Chalmers' copy of Charles Whitworth's *State of the Trade of Great Britain in Its Imports and Exports Progressively from the Year 1697* (London, 1776). This copy is in the Manuscripts Division of the Library of Congress. Chalmers corrected and extended Whitworth's figures in manuscript. The figures on which these two tables are based include the value of trade in both dutiable and free goods, but exclude currency and bullion shipments. L. A. Harper, in *The English Navigation Laws*, pp. 286–291, presents similar statistics and conclusions with regard to the decline of the Mediterranean and Spanish trade of Great Britain in the eighteenth century.

question solely from the contemporary viewpoint of affairs, I believe that Great Britain would have profited from the restoration of Gibraltar to Spain in 1721, in 1748, or in 1782. This belief is founded upon the speculative (and therefore unhistorical) opinion that such an act would have materially improved Britain's strategic and economic situation and eliminated a constant lurking danger to her international position.

TABLE II

The Relative Increase or Decrease in the Value of England's Trade with Spain, the Mediterranean, America, and the East Indies, 1698–1701 vs. 1789–1792. (Expressed in Index Numbers: 1698–1701 Equals 100.)

	Exports	*Imports*	*Total*
(a) Total English Trade	323	314	319
(b) With Italy	813	290	426
(c) With Venice	57	138	105
(d) With Turkey	81	85	83
(e) Total Mediterranean	297	188	228
(f) With Spain	123	151	136
(g) With Straits	45	–	50
(h) Total Spain, Straits, and Mediterranean	148	174	160
(i) With East Indies	1056	491	629
(j) With Jamaica	847	970	929
(k) With American Continental Colonies (U.S.)	880	326	638

XII

SUMMARY

GIBRALTAR will be as great a Rock in the negotiation as it is in the sea." This observation, repeated
on several occasions by British ministers, strikes
the keynote to the failure to resolve one of the more perplexing questions in the diplomacy of the eighteenth century. After an initial stage of indifference and neglect,
the English people acquired an attachment for Gibraltar
that defied the calculated opinion of English statesmen
that the Rock had at best a very moderate utility as a
British possession. Ministers might wish to effect a true
reconciliation with Spain or to disrupt the Family Compact by restoring Gibraltar; but popular antagonism to
such a step overawed their better judgment. The "terrible
aversion with the generality of mankind" to the restitution that frightened James Craggs in 1720; the "violent
and almost superstitious zeal among all parties in this kingdom against any scheme for the restoration of Gibraltar,"
as Townshend expressed it in 1728; these and similar
evidences of the unreasoning prejudice of public opinion
stayed the hands of British ministers and kept Gibraltar
a British possession. As the Spanish minister Floridablanca "peevishly" remarked in 1788, "no British Ministry of the present century would have the courage to
look the question fairly in the face."

Gibraltar, like so many other portions of the modern
British Empire, was acquired almost accidentally. After
its capture in 1704 the English did not at once decide to
keep it. As the War of the Spanish Succession progressed,
however, they resolved to make it a permanent possession
of the English Crown in spite of treaties with Holland
promising the Dutch an equal share in any acquisitions
from Spain. Using methods not above reproach, they

"persuaded" the Dutch to relinquish their claim to the Mediterranean strongholds of Gibraltar and Minorca by presenting their ally with a *fait accompli* after secret Anglo-French peace negotiations in 1711. At the same time, the English stirred the hopes of King Philip of Spain for the recovery of Gibraltar by hinting, in the initial stages of the negotiation, that it might be returned for a sum of money. Indeed, although Louis XIV and his nephew had no choice but to give up the Mediterranean strongholds that England was determined to keep, the French and Spanish monarchs were determined to retrieve Gibraltar and Minorca at the first opportune moment. That opportunity would come, they hoped, with the anticipated internal disturbance in England over the succession at the death of Queen Anne. The British themselves were responsible for a more immediate threat to their tenure of Gibraltar. Great Britain treated her new offspring as a foundling, ignoring the pleas of successive commanders for adequate supplies and repairs. So shameful was her neglect that Lord Portmore gravely warned the ministry in 1714 that "it is a great question if the town of Gibraltar will be long in her Majesty's possession."

The death of the Grand Monarch in 1715 provided the first favorable turn in the fortunes of Gibraltar as an English possession. The insecurity of the Duke of Orleans as Regent of France led him to negotiate an alliance with Britain which postponed for two decades the partial realization of a Bourbon union between France and Spain as envisioned by Louis XIV. This alliance also estopped French support for the Pretender, and helped prevent the revolution in England upon which Louis XIV had counted as the main chance of regaining the concessions awarded to the British in the Treaties of Utrecht.

Soon after the negotiation of the Anglo-French Alliance, the Whig ministry of George I, under the leadership of James Stanhope, took a step that threw the question of Gibraltar into the arena of European diplomacy. England and France sponsored a project designed to reconcile the emperor and King Philip of Spain and pacify southern Europe. This project, known as the Quadruple Alliance, proposed a compromise settlement of the Austro-Spanish wrangle over Italian possessions that neither monarch desired to accept. Stanhope, believing Gibraltar to be virtually worthless as an English possession, authorized the French regent to offer it to Spain as a *douceur* to overcome Spanish objections to the Quadruple Alliance. The Spanish spurned this offer in 1718, and embarked on a brief and disastrous war that forced them to come to terms two years later. Without the knowledge or approval of the British ministry, the Regent of France renewed the offer of Gibraltar as an enticement to persuade the Spanish to capitulate. Although admitting that England was no longer legally bound to restore Gibraltar as a *quid pro quo* for Spanish adhesion to the Quadruple Alliance, the French regent believed, and was led by Stanhope to anticipate, that Britain still intended to restore Gibraltar as one step in the settlement of the troubled affairs of southern Europe.

When the English Parliament convened in January 1720 rumors were afloat that the ministry proposed to give up Gibraltar. Almost overnight, Stanhope encountered a tide of protest that made him tread warily in forwarding the restitution of the Rock. This wave of parliamentary and popular hostility to the cession of Gibraltar had a variety of origins. Stanhope at this time faced a growing opposition in Parliament, not only from the Tories but also from the dissenting Whigs led by Robert Walpole; in December 1719 his proposal to limit the peerage was defeated, and the following month the South Sea Company's project for refunding the national debt met strong opposition when introduced into Parliament. The South Sea Company, with ministerial backing, triumphed over the rival offer of the Bank of England, but not without swelling the ranks of the opposition. The opponents of Stanhope were fortified by the airing of the Gibraltar question before the public in a pamphlet by Thomas Gordon, who championed the retention of the Rock with a hodgepodge of arguments which were to be echoed for many decades.[1] Stanhope's proposal to cede Gibraltar offered an ideal target for his opponents, and he felt obliged to promise that he would do nothing without parliamentary approval.

Stanhope's inability to push through an immediate restitution of Gibraltar almost caused a break in the Anglo-French Alliance. The Duke of Orleans felt that England's failure to fulfill the promise he had given to King Philip would compromise his honor; knowing that both Stanhope and King George favored parting with Gibraltar, he could not understand their hesitation. Parliamentary clamor? The regent would be delighted to furnish any amount of money necessary to purchase enough votes in Parliament to secure approval of the cession. Stanhope of course refused such assistance; but in order to soothe the regent's injured feelings, he himself went to France to patch up this misunderstanding which threatened his whole program for the pacification of Europe. At Paris Stanhope managed to convince the duke that he sincerely intended to push through the Gibraltar project as soon as parliamentary opposition subsided. Under the auspices of a projected international congress, he would arrange the exchange of Gibraltar for further trade advantages in the Spanish Indies.

In the summer of 1720 the King of Spain unwisely tried to force Stanhope's hand by arbitrarily suspending England's trade with the Indies and notifying the English that he would not rescind this action until they gave him a definite promise that Gibraltar would be restored. Stanhope, annoyed by this irresponsible action, and anxious above all that the subject of British trading privileges in the Spanish dominions should not be a topic of discussion at an international gathering, at once decided to settle all

1. Thomas Gordon, *Considerations Offered . . . upon the Importance of Gibraltar to the British Empire* (London, 1720).

outstanding problems with Spain by a private negotiation
in advance of the impending congress. For this purpose
he drafted a treaty project which included the exchange
of Gibraltar, and planned to go to Madrid himself to conduct the negotiation.

A domestic crisis intervened to thwart this plan. The
bursting of the South Sea Bubble forced Stanhope to
postpone his trip to Madrid and devote all his attention to
an internal upheaval that threatened to overthrow his
ministry. The financial debacle that followed the orgy of
speculation in the summer of 1720 left the English public
in an ugly mood. To have proposed the exchange of Gibraltar at this moment would have been suicidal. In this
instance, a situation totally extraneous to any consideration of the Gibraltar question on its own merit blocked a
solution of the problem. Yet Stanhope, having secured the
support of Walpole and many of the opposition Whigs,
still intended to carry out his proposal as soon as this new
tumult quieted. Through the French, he pledged his solemn word in January 1721 that Gibraltar would be restored to Spain within the following year.

The French in the meantime opened secret negotiations
with Spain to adjust their own private differences before
the projected congress. With Stanhope's renewed pledge
on Gibraltar in hand, they expected to lay the ground-
work for a tripartite treaty to settle all questions in dispute between Spain on the one hand and Britain and
France on the other. The sudden death of Stanhope (and
his colleague Craggs) in February 1721 interfered with
this project. The French had already promised their good
offices to support the Spanish claim to Gibraltar, but because they were uncertain of the attitude Stanhope's successors would assume, they abandoned the idea of bringing
the British into the negotiation. Instead, they left their
ally ignorant of their engagement on Gibraltar in the
secret Franco-Spanish treaty of March 1721.

As the French had anticipated, the new British secretaries failed to share Stanhope's enthusiasm for parting

with Gibraltar. The incorrigible Philip almost immediately antagonized them by issuing a new ultimatum renewing his threat to suspend all English trade until a definite promise on Gibraltar was forthcoming. Yet the English could not completely ignore Stanhope's pledges. They agreed to send a letter, phrased in obscure terms, promising that the king would present the question of Gibraltar to Parliament at the earliest opportune moment. This letter, while not included in the text of the particular treaty signed by England and Spain in June 1721 renewing all previous trade agreements, was nevertheless made a contingent and integral part of the negotiation through a separate agreement, signed by the British minister at Madrid and the Spanish secretary. This agreement stipulated that if such a letter were not delivered, the signature of the particular Anglo-Spanish treaty would be considered null and void. That the famous letter of George I on Gibraltar was a binding obligation can not be doubted. That the English ministry acted with insincerity and with no intention of ever fulfilling this obligation if it could be avoided seems equally apparent. The stage was set for decades of Anglo-Spanish wrangling and bitterness over the citadel of the Straits.

In my opinion, four basic factors foiled the sincere attempt of James Stanhope to restore Gibraltar to Spain as a step in the pacification of Europe under the hegemony of English diplomacy. First, popular interest in Gibraltar, artificially stimulated by the partisan tactics of the day, suddenly manifested itself in the spring of 1720. Second, a series of fortuitous occurrences, almost wholly unrelated to any judgment of the proposal on its merit, blocked Stanhope at critical moments in the negotiation. Third, King Philip of Spain, by his obstinate and arbitrary efforts to coerce the English, injured his own cause by arousing the antagonism of many leaders who otherwise might have backed Stanhope's project. Lastly, the problem of Gibraltar became one of the first crucial tests of ministerial responsibility to Parliament. Heretofore, the conduct of foreign affairs had been considered a part of the royal prerogative. The king, through his ministers, proposed to cede a possession of the Crown which had never been officially annexed to the "realm" of England. Apparently George I and his ministers believed that they had a perfect right to do so without consulting Parliament. In this instance Parliament challenged the action of King George and his great minister, and forced Stanhope to admit that he could not carry out his proposal without the consent of Parliament.

It is a commonplace that Robert Walpole in his long ministry from 1721 to 1742 had as his primary goals in foreign policy the preservation of peace and the promotion of English trade. The problem of Gibraltar which he inherited from Stanhope promised to interfere with both of those objectives. Spanish friendship hinged upon the fulfillment of the royal pledge "to make use of the first favorable opportunity to regulate this article [the restitution of Gibraltar] with the Consent of My Parliament." In return for this promise, Spain had renewed England's trade treaties, with the implication that they might again be suspended if England failed to carry out her part of the bargain. To maintain Spanish peace and commerce, and at the same time refuse to execute King George's promise, called for statesmanship of the first magnitude. Until 1730, Walpole allowed his secretaries of state—Carteret, Townshend, and Newcastle—the principal voice in the conduct of foreign affairs, and these gentlemen did their best to avoid reopening the Gibraltar question.

The pompous and empty proceedings of the Congress of Cambrai, where England and France assumed the rôle of joint mediators in an effort to iron out the differences between King Philip and the emperor, served to postpone the subject for nearly four years. As long as he was dependent on England's diplomatic support, Philip could not afford to press the question of Gibraltar.

The abrupt Austro-Spanish "reconciliation" in the Treaties of Vienna of 1725 ended this period of suspense.

The Spanish king resumed his efforts to coerce Britain into the restitution of Gibraltar, first by renewing his threat to suspend Britain's Indies trade, then by openly preparing for war. Under Townshend's leadership, the British met the menace of the general European war forecast by the Vienna alliance by organizing a rival block of powers under the Alliance of Hanover. With Europe divided into hostile camps roughly equal in strength, the emperor abandoned any intention he may have had to precipitate a war. But he could not prevail upon King Philip and his termagant queen to do likewise. Angered by the English refusal to negotiate on the subject of Gibraltar on any terms whatsoever, the Spanish monarchs tried to touch off general hostilities by laying siege to the Rock. Almost before the first gun had been fired, the Austrians, French, and British began to draft preliminary articles of peace, which they forced the Spanish to accept. Left in the lurch by his ally, Philip had to turn once more to a quest for Gibraltar through diplomatic channels.

The complicated and nugatory negotiations that culminated in the Congress of Soissons served only to reveal more clearly than ever how unwilling were the British to accept a settlement that left any loophole for a continuance of Spanish pretensions to Gibraltar. They now adopted the position that King George's letter had never had the character of a binding agreement, and that Spain's hostile measures had erased any moral obligation they were bound in honor to fulfill. England's uncompromising attitude widened the breach with Spain; but without Austrian support the Spanish did not dare to renew hostilities. Instead of resorting to open violence, they took steps to harass and curtail British trade with the Indies by a variety of artifices, and to cut off all contact between Gibraltar and the Spanish mainland in order to make the Rock as useless as possible to Great Britain. Such tactics angered the British commercial classes, and brought the two powers to the verge of war in the spring and summer of 1729.

Out of this hostile atmosphere there emerged a new and favorable Anglo-Spanish treaty which pushed the question of Gibraltar out of sight for the time being. The Treaty of Seville of November 1729 did not spring from any moderation of the belligerent sentiment existing in both England and Spain. Elizabeth Farnese, who dominated her husband and the course of Spanish policy, at last perceived how shamefully the Austrians had deluded her. Once convinced of their duplicity, she lost no time in seeking a reconciliation with England and France, in order to obtain their support for the furtherance of her Italian ambitions. This about-face forced her to thrust aside the grievances of Gibraltar and trade. To be sure, Philip and his ministers did their best to insert in the treaty draft some wording that would imply English recognition of the Spanish pretension to Gibraltar. The English, for their part, tried to induce the Spanish monarch to make a specific renunciation of his claims to the Rock. Both had to be satisfied with a compromise; the point of Gibraltar was passed over in silence. Nevertheless, the Treaty of Seville buried the royal promise of 1721 beyond recall.

France, under the astute direction of Cardinal Fleury, did not neglect the opportunity of seeking a reconciliation with Spain by dangling before King Philip a promise of continued good offices on behalf of his claim to Gibraltar. Fleury secretly transmitted this offer before the signature of the Treaty of Seville, and the knowledge that France would pledge her continued support to the Spanish quest for Gibraltar undoubtedly helped to induce Philip to agree to the Seville treaty. The French did not stop there. They aimed to draw Spain into the French diplomatic orbit by negotiating a Bourbon family alliance. England's decision to realign herself with Austria gave impetus to France's efforts, and the first Family Compact slowly took shape. In its negotiation, Gibraltar was a most important bait to lure Spain into the arms of France. In the Escurial treaty of 1733, the French promised not only continued good offices but also to use force "if it shall be necessary" to secure the return of Gibraltar to Spain. The French never made any effort to execute this pledge. In the heyday of the Anglo-French Alliance under the Duke of Orleans, the French sincerely desired to see Gibraltar restored to Spain. Once that brief hiatus in the norm of Anglo-French enmity had passed, and Spain had become a diplomatic satellite of France, the French manifestly preferred to have England keep Gibraltar and allow the Rock to remain an insurmountable obstacle to Anglo-Spanish friendship.

In the half-century between the Treaty of Seville and the entrance of Spain into the War for American Independence, the question of Gibraltar came to the surface on only a few occasions. It ceased to be an active subject in Anglo-Spanish diplomacy. No treaty, however, could dissipate the yearning of the Spanish people for the recovery of the Rock. The refusal of England to part with it left a rankling bitterness in Anglo-Spanish relations that continued through most of the century. There were, of course, other causes of Anglo-Spanish hostility, but none so deep-rooted and long-lived as Gibraltar.

After a long interval of peace (barring the minor conflicts of 1719 and 1727) England and Spain finally became involved in war over American issues—trade and colonial conflicts—in 1739. The issue of Gibraltar had no direct connection with this conflict, though one of the incentives of England in declaring war was a belief that France and Spain had concluded a new offensive treaty providing for an attack on the Rock. This new treaty—a reaffirmation of the Family Compact of 1733—was not actually signed until 1743, when France entered the general European war that revolved around the Austrian succession. Again, France promised her good offices and the use of force against Gibraltar; but she did not lift a finger to fulfill this engagement either during the war or in the peace negotiation.

Spain herself sought the restoration of Gibraltar in

secret peace negotiations with England during 1747 and
1748. The English ministry seriously considered granting
this request. The English anticipated that they might be
confronted with the choice either of giving up Gibraltar
or of relinquishing Cape Breton, which they had captured
from the French in 1745. Several ministers, among them
Lord Chesterfield and the Duke of Bedford, believed that
the voluntary cession of Gibraltar would be the best means
of detaching Spain from her Bourbon alliance. Actually,
the choice between Cape Breton and Gibraltar never had
to be made; the French insisted on the former's return and
made no effort to secure the latter for Spain. In secret
conversations with the Spanish emissary Richard Wall,
the ministry probably went so far as to say to the Spanish
that in return for a separate peace, Great Britain would
be willing to consider the restitution of Gibraltar at a subsequent date. Before any action could be taken on this
overture, a general treaty of peace was signed at Aix-la-
Chapelle. The extended secret Anglo-Spanish negotiations
of 1747–1748 had as their chief by-product a new formula for the restitution of Gibraltar: the British then and
at intervals in the succeeding decades agreed that it would
be sound strategy to cede the Rock if by that step they
could permanently dissolve the Family Compact.

The French conquest of Minorca in 1756 set the stage
for one of the best-known incidents in the history of Gibraltar—the offer of William Pitt to restore the Rock. Almost immediately after the stunning news of Minorca's
loss reached England, Henry Fox conceived the idea of
enlisting Spain in the new war with France and promising
Gibraltar in return for aid in the recovery of Minorca.
Moved by the military plight of England, Pitt sent his
famous letter of August 23, 1757, proposing that Spain
enter the war on England's side and offering Gibraltar as
compensation. The Spanish brusquely rejected Pitt's proposal, for they earnestly desired to remain neutral. No
project, however alluring, could have altered this determination. Thus the only real significance of Pitt's offer

lay in its revelation of Britain's attitude toward Gibraltar. With Spain as an ally, the British were perfectly willing to surrender that stronghold in order to secure the return of Minorca, which they deemed the more valuable of their Mediterranean outposts.

The accession of Charles III to the Spanish throne in 1759 marked the end of a brief era of comparative harmony in Anglo-Spanish relations. Unlike his predecessor, Ferdinand VI, King Charles shared his father's dislike for England. In sharp contrast to both his father and half-brother, the new king was an intelligent and capable monarch, under whose wise direction Spain emerged into a brief renaissance of her former power and glory. The first turn in the new and more vigorous foreign policy of Spain, however, had almost disastrous consequences. After some hesitation, Charles entered into a new Family Compact with France, at a moment when French fortunes in the war were as desperate as those of England had been in 1757. When the English learned of this renewal of the Bourbon alliance, they promptly forced Spain into the war and pounced upon Havana. The Spanish emerged from the conflict with feelings of bitterness and revenge akin to those of the French.

The revival of Anglo-Spanish hostility, the recovery of Spain, and the desire for revenge against England prepared the way for a new and supreme assault on Gibraltar—both military and diplomatic—during the War for American Independence. This new quest—a climax in Spain's century-long effort to recover the Rock—had four phases. Initially, after France allied herself with the new American nation in February 1778, the Spanish sought, under the guise of mediation, to force England to cede Gibraltar as the price for Spain's continued neutrality in the war. Then, following the secret Convention of Aranjuez with France in April 1779, specifying that France would never make peace until Gibraltar had been won for Spain, the Spanish entered the lists against England and launched a four-year siege of the fortress. Again, during

the war, the Spanish carried on secret parleys with England through which they hoped to obtain the cession of Gibraltar in return for their withdrawal from the conflict.
Finally, in the peace negotiation of 1782, the Spanish
stood their ground so firmly that they actually persuaded
the British Cabinet to approve the cession of Gibraltar,
only to lose this one golden opportunity for the recovery
of the Rock through the artifice of the French minister
Vergennes.

Gibraltar was very clearly the primary goal in Spain's
tender of good offices before her entry into the War for
American Independence. Yet this phase of Spanish action
had little significance other than to illuminate their determination to capitalize on Britain's predicament. Although
England and France cautiously accepted the Spanish offer of mediation, they did so with evident insincerity and
presented irreconcilable terms. Indeed, Spain's own attitude smacked of insincerity. Cannon were being hauled
toward Gibraltar before the Spanish representatives at
London and Paris presented the formal offer of mediation.
From the Spanish viewpoint, this protracted negotiation
(April 1778–April 1779) served a dual purpose: It
frightened the French into granting far more favorable
terms in the Convention of Aranjuez than otherwise might
have been obtained; and it gave Spain more than a year
to prepare for active military participation in the war.

The great siege of Gibraltar (1779–1783) had no direct bearing on the diplomatic story. Indirectly, however,
England's brilliant defense of the Rock prepared the
Spanish to offer a more generous compensation for it in
the peace negotiation. Likewise, Spain's success in capturing naval control of the Straits, thereby isolating Gibraltar and interrupting Britain's Mediterranean trade,
helped to reconcile the British to the idea of parting with
the Rock. This feeling was strengthened by the fall of Minorca in 1781; despite this second manifestation of its vulnerability, George III and many of his subjects expressed
their preference for Minorca over Gibraltar if one or the

other had to be ceded to Spain. The outcome of the siege and accompanying naval operations served to modify both the British and Spanish diplomatic positions and bring them within reconcilable range in the peace negotiations of 1782.

The origins of the secret Anglo-Spanish negotiations associated with the mission of Richard Cumberland to Madrid in 1780 are obscure; at any rate, Floridablanca thought he discerned some disposition on the part of England to sacrifice Gibraltar if Spain would withdraw from the war. His suspicion was not unfounded; several members of the British Cabinet advocated the exchange of Gibraltar for a substantial equivalent and Spain's severance of all connection with the conflict—a move that would almost inevitably have disrupted the Bourbon alliance. The Spanish, however, had no intention of deserting their ally; they would promise only to interpose their good offices between the British and Americans on the one hand, and the British and French on the other, in order to arrange a compromise peace reasonably satisfactory to all parties concerned (except, possibly, the Americans). But the British absolutely refused to permit any intermediary to intervene in their American quarrel; and they certainly would not have ceded Gibraltar voluntarily unless assured of the termination of the Bourbon alliance. Given these circumstances, and barring a catastrophic turn in the military fortunes of England, the Hussey-Cumberland negotiation had no hope of success.

Many historians have dealt with the peace negotiation of 1782, both competently and in detail; yet it still offers a fertile field for investigation. One of the commonly expressed misapprehensions is that Britain tenaciously refused to cede Gibraltar to Spain; whereas in fact the British Cabinet approved the cession and offered it on terms that the Spanish were willing to accept. The wily and astute French minister Vergennes saw to it that this offer never reached the Spanish court; instead, he hastily concluded a peace without Gibraltar in violation of France's pledge in the Convention of Aranjuez. That he succeeded in doing so, and in persuading the Spanish court to accept his handiwork, is a tribute to his diplomatic genius. In my opinion, Henri Doniol in his monumental treatise[2] concealed this duplicity of Vergennes beneath his paeans of praise for the high and noble plane of French diplomacy during the War for American Independence. Actually, Doniol scarcely does Vergennes justice. It was certainly a greater triumph to be the active agent in blocking the reacquisition of Gibraltar by Spain—a step wholly consistent with French policy for the previous half-century— than to be represented as unable to obtain the cession of the Rock because of English intransigence and because the Americans by making a separate preliminary peace forced France to accept less satisfactory terms on behalf of Spain. True enough, Vergennes explained his action to the Spanish and to posterity on those grounds. In view of the evidence presented in the body of this study, I cannot accept Doniol's conclusion that Vergennes allowed himself to be outmaneuvered by the British and Americans.

During the brief interval of peace between 1783 and the French Revolution, the English and Spanish carried on desultory negotiations on the subject of Gibraltar. These fruitless and temperate efforts to solve the old problem were a definite anticlimax to the determined and single-minded quest by Spain during the preceding war and peace negotiation. English opinion of Gibraltar was at its lowest ebb, and the chief novelty in the post-war diplomacy was that the English themselves initiated discussion of the subject on several occasions. Floridablanca hesitated to press the question; to his minister at London he confessed his private opinion that it was better for Spain to have England keep Gibraltar. In any event, the Spanish minister was unwilling to act upon the only basis on

2. Henri Doniol, *Histoire de la participation de la France à l'établissement des Etats-Unis d'Amerique,* 5 vols. and supplement (Paris, 1886–1899).

which the English would agree to its restoration, that is, the severance of all Spanish ties with France.

The French Revolution ushered in a new chapter in the diplomatic history of Gibraltar. The downfall of the French monarchy dissolved the Family Compact, and the common menace of revolutionary France forged an alliance between Britain and Spain. Great Britain's titanic struggle with Napoleon revived her interest in Mediterranean power as a means of checking France and maintaining the balance of power on the Continent. Six decades later, the opening of the Suez Canal so magnified the importance of Gibraltar, by making it a vital stronghold on the "life-line" to the East, that the notion of restoring it to Spain took on the character of an absurdity. But the history of the Rock in British diplomacy since 1789 must await a future telling.

BIBLIOGRAPHICAL NOTE

BIBLIOGRAPHIES AND GUIDES

Wilbur Cortez Abbott's *Introduction to the Documents Relating to the International Status of Gibraltar, 1704–1934* (New York, 1934) contains an excellent, but not exhaustive, list of the printed works on the history of the Rock, and some references to manuscript material. A useful bibliography of Spanish works on the subject, both printed and manuscript, is to be found in *Las llaves del estrecho: estudio sobre la reconquista de Gibraltar* (Madrid, 1882), by José Navarette. Francis G. Davenport compiled a valuable guide to the manuscript material in the British Museum entitled "Materials for English Diplomatic History, 1509–1783," published in the *Eighteenth Report* of the Royal Commission on Historical Manuscripts (London, 1917), appendix II, pp. 357–402. For the period of the War for American Independence the *Guide to the Diplomatic History of the United States, 1776–1921* (Washington, 1935), by Samuel F. Bemis and Grace G. Griffin, is indispensable. The excellent work of Clyde L. Grose, *A Select Bibliography of British History, 1660–1760* (Chicago, 1940), appeared after most of the research on this study had been completed. The best modern bibliography of Spanish history is that of B. Sánchez Alonso, *Fuentes de la historia española* . . . (Madrid, 1919). The author is indebted to many other bibliographies and guides to manuscript material, and to the published guides to the English and French archives and the British Museum.

MANUSCRIPTS

This work has been based principally upon material obtained from the manuscript collections of six depositories: the Public Record Office and British Museum in London; the archives of the French Foreign Office in Paris; the Library of Congress in Washington; the William L. Clements Library of the University of Michigan at Ann Arbor; and the New York Public Library.

286   GIBRALTAR IN BRITISH DIPLOMACY

The Public Record Office

The State Papers Foreign provide the greatest fount of information for the diplomatic history of Gibraltar in the eighteenth century. In this collection, the most valuable series is S.P.F. 94, correspondence with the British ministers in Spain. The correspondence with representatives at Paris, in S.P.F. 78, is of particular importance in the early decades of the century, especially after 1716 during the period of the close Anglo-French alliance. I have made use of scattered volumes in other series, notably S.P.F. 100 (Foreign Ministers); S.P.F. 104 (Foreign Entry Books); S.P.F. 105, for the secret negotiations leading to the Treaties of Utrecht; and S.P.F. 103, for the background and negotiation of the Treaty of Seville.

With the establishment of the Foreign Office in 1782, diplomatic correspondence was arranged in new series under that name. The French series, F.O. 27, is important for the peace negotiations of 1782; the Spanish correspondence, F.O. 72, contains some information on the secret overtures to effect the restitution of Gibraltar after the peace of 1783.

The Colonial Office records are not very revealing on the diplomatic history of Gibraltar. I have examined carefully the first sixteen volumes of C.O. 91, a series which contains the correspondence between the governor and the ministers in London, together with much miscellaneous material. These volumes vividly illustrate the misgovernment and inefficiency in the administration of Gibraltar during the first half of the eighteenth century. Colonial Office 95:3, an "Historical Abstract of Matters Concerning Gibraltar, 1704–1726," has some useful material to supplement the diplomatic correspondence in the State Papers Foreign.

The British Museum

The Department of Manuscripts of the British Museum has a wealth of material on eighteenth-century English diplomacy, because of the custom followed by many English statesmen of personally retaining much or most of their official correspondence after their term of office. A notable example may be cited: Lord Carteret, secretary of state for the Southern Department in 1721, kept all of the correspondence, both originals and copies, relating to the background and transmission of the famous letter of George I, promising to present the question of the restitution of Gibraltar to Parliament. A few years later his successor, the

Duke of Newcastle, had to seek special permission to borrow the official correspondence from Carteret's country estate for a few weeks. Afterward it was returned to Carteret, and never thereafter was it in the possession of British diplomats in the eighteenth century. No wonder the circumstances surrounding the writing of that letter became clouded in the minds of later British ministers!

The Newcastle Papers, an extraordinary source of information on English history and diplomacy during the duke's long tenure of office, are the most important collection among the Additional Manuscripts for the purposes of this work. I have made particular use of these volumes for the years 1726–1734 (Add. MSS. 32,746–32,784) and for other intervals when the subject of Gibraltar was active. Among the other collections of Additional Manuscripts, I found the following to be especially valuable: the Strafford (Raby) Papers, relating to the secret negotiations of 1711, Add. MSS. 22,205–22,206; the Carteret Papers, official correspondence for the years 1721–1723, Add. MSS. 22,515–22,521; the Townshend Papers, of value for the years 1725–1726, Add. MSS. 38,502–38,504; the Hardwicke Papers, especially Add. MSS. 35,883–35,884; and the Grantham Papers, correspondence with Lord Grantham while he was ambassador to Spain, 1771–1779, Add. MSS. 24,165, 24,174–24,176. A number of other volumes of Additional, Stowe, Egerton, and King's Manuscripts furnished useful information, as cited in footnote references.

Archives du Ministère des Affaires Etrangères

My work in the archives of the French Foreign Office has been limited to the examination of correspondence covering certain periods during which France was intimately involved in the diplomacy of Gibraltar. For the year 1711, when the French king persuaded his grandson to relinquish Gibraltar to England, I have used volumes 232–236 of the Correspondance Politique, Angleterre, and 206–207 of the Correspondance Politique, Espagne; for the offer of Gibraltar to Spain in 1718, vols. 314–315, Angleterre and 267–272, Espagne; for the difficulties of the regent over England's refusal to give up Gibraltar, and the secret Franco-Spanish Treaty of March 1721, vols. 327–331 and supplementary vol. 6, Angleterre, and 300–302, Espagne; for the attitude of France toward the Treaty of Seville and her secret negotiations with Spain, vols. 363–368, Angleterre and 364–366, Espagne; for the negotiation of the first Family Compact of 1733, vols. 403–408, Espagne; for France's probing of Pitt's offer of Gibraltar in 1757, vol. 522, Espagne; and for the peace negotiations of 1782, vol. 539, Angleterre and vols. 609–610, Espagne, which contain material that supplements the transcripts and photocopies in the Library of Congress (see below). In the Mémoires et Documents collection, vol. 58 in the English series and vols. 142 and 208 in the Spanish contained some useful information.

The Library of Congress

The Manuscripts Division of the Library of Congress possesses a large number of transcripts and photographic reproductions of European diplomatic correspondence for the period of the American Revolution and subsequent years. This material has been arranged according to the original archival designations and provenance. I have made particular use of the English, French, and Spanish correspondence in the following volumes, all relating to the peace negotiations of 1782, except as noted: English, F.O. 27:2–3, both transcripts and photocopies; French, transcripts of Cor. Pol., Espagne, vols. 608–609, and Cor. Pol., Angleterre, vols. 538–539, and photocopies of Cor. Pol., Angleterre, vol. 538; Spanish, Archivo Histórico Nacional, Estado, Legajos 4199 and 4199bis (Spanish mediation in 1778–1779), 4203, 4215, and 4256, all photocopies; and the Cunningham typescripts of correspondence in the Archivo General de Simancas, Estado, Legajos 2617 and 8143, on Anglo-Spanish relations after the peace of 1782. In addition to these volumes of diplomatic correspondence, I am indebted to the Manuscripts Division for the use of transcripts and photocopies of the Shelburne Papers, vols. 34, 71, and 72, the originals of which are in the Clements Library at Ann Arbor; and for access to a copy of Charles Whitworth's *State of the Trade of Great Britain in Its Imports and Exports Progressively from the Year 1697* (London, 1776) which was owned by George Chalmers, and in which Chalmers corrected and extended Whitworth's figures in manuscript.

The William L. Clements Library

The Clements Library has a large collection of the political and diplomatic correspondence of Lord Shelburne, originally part of the vast collection of Lansdowne Manuscripts, the balance of which are in the British Museum. The collection at Ann Arbor relates principally to the peace negotiation of 1782, but contains in addition a good deal of miscellaneous material; I have made particular use of volumes 9–12, 35, 38, 83, 87, and 168. Besides the Shelburne Papers, the Clements Library has a number of other collections, both originals and copies, which have been of some assistance. Among these I may mention: the Sackville (Germain) Manuscripts, which furnished some new material on the Hussey-Cumberland negotiation of 1779–1781; the Benjamin Vaughn Manuscripts (photocopies of typescripts), especially vol. 1, correspondence relative to the peace negotiations of 1782; three photocopy volumes of Holland House correspondence, 1782–1784, the papers of Charles James Fox; and the Fortescue typescripts of the correspondence of King George III, vols. I and II (1783–1788), which provide a continuation of the correspondence edited by Fortescue cited below.

The New York Public Library

The Hardwicke Papers in the manuscript collection of the New York Public Library are mostly duplicates of similar material in the British Museum. This collection contains, however, a number of volumes of original correspondence once the property of Sir Luke Schaub. Volumes 54–56 and 59–60 of these Schaub Papers furnished some useful information on the negotiations of 1720–1721.

PRINTED SOURCES

THREE general source collections, covering the whole period under review in this study, have been used extensively. The publications of the Royal Commission on Historical Manuscripts of Great Britain have been especially helpful, not only for the material calendared therein but also as a guide to manuscript and other published collections. The appendices of the eighteen *Reports* (London, 1870–1917) and the many separate series under individual titles published since 1899 have furnished scattered information that, collectively, has been of great value, particularly for the period before 1730. The Royal Historical Society has published four volumes of *British Diplomatic Instructions, France, 1689–1789*, Camden 3rd Series, vols. XXXV, XXXVIII, XLIII, and XLIX (London, 1922–1934), that are worthy of special mention; they have been edited with illuminating introductions by L. G. W. Legg, one of the foremost authorities on British diplomacy in the eighteenth century. The French Commission de Archives Diplomatiques has undertaken the publication of a somewhat similar series, the *Recueil des instructions données aux ambassadeurs et ministres de France* (Paris, 1844 ff.); vols. XII and XIIbis, *Espagne, 1701–1793,* are the only ones of value to the story of Gibraltar.

For the secret Anglo-French peace negotiations of 1711–1712, I have made particular use of the *Letters and Correspondence, Public and Private, of the Right Honourable Henry St. John, Lord Visc. Bolingbroke; During the Time He was Secretary of State to Queen Anne,* 4 vols., edited by Gilbert Parke (London, 1798), vols. I and II; Bolingbroke's own account of his part in the negotiation published in his *Works,* 5 vols. (Dublin, 1793), vol. II, pp. 401–489; the *Mémoires de Torcy pour servir à l'histoire des négociations . . .,* 3 vols. (London, 1757); and "Torcy's Account of Matthew Prior's Negotiations at Fontainebleau in July 1711," a long memorandum from the French archives edited by L. G. W. Legg and published in the *English Historical Review,* XXIX (July 1914), 525–532. There are few printed sources for the period of intense activity of the Gibraltar question from 1718 to 1733; aside from the general collections cited above, a few of the documents have been printed by Coxe in volume II of his *Memoirs of Sir Robert Walpole,* by Mahon in his *History of England,* and by other secondary authorities. The second volume of the *Annals and Correspondence of the Viscount and the First and Second Earls of Stair,* 2 vols., edited by John Murray Graham (Edinburgh, 1875), contains some correspondence of the British ambassador at Paris, relating to the negotiations of 1718–1721, not to be found in the public archives. The publication of *The Private Correspondence of Sir Benjamin Keene* (London, 1933) was cut short by the untimely demise of its learned editor, Sir Richard Lodge; this volume consists principally of Keene's private exchanges with Castres, British minister at Lisbon, after the peace of Aix-la-Chapelle, and contains practically nothing on Gibraltar. For the peace negotiations of 1782, two source collections proved of some value: the last volume of *The Correspondence of King George the Third, 1760–1783,* 6 vols., edited by Sir John Fortescue (London, 1928); and, of less importance, vols. V and VI of *The Revolutionary Diplomatic Correspondence of the United States,* 6 vols., edited by Francis Wharton (Philadelphia, 1889). In the works of Doniol, Danvila y Collado, Yela Utrilla, and

Bemis (*Hussey-Cumberland Mission*), cited below, there is a considerable amount of French and Spanish diplomatic correspondence pertaining to the War for American Independence of which I have made some use. Passages in *Gobierno del rey Carlos III, ó instrucción reservada para dirección de la junta de estado que creó este monarca,* edited by D. Andrés Muriel (Paris, 1838), reveal Floridablanca's attitude toward Gibraltar after the peace of 1783. For texts of treaties, I have relied on *A Collection of Treaties Between Great Britain and Other Powers,* 2 vols., edited by George Chalmers (London, 1790), and *Tratados, convenios y declaraciones de paz y de comercio. . . . Desde el año de 1700 hasta el día* (Madrid, 1843), edited with valuable introductory notes by D. Alejandro del Cantillo. The published records of parliamentary debates on the Gibraltar question are fragmentary and in some instances non-existent; for example, there is no published record of the heated debate which took place in January and February 1720. Occasionally, however, the *Journals of the House of Commons* (London, 1742 ff.), the *Journals of the House of Lords* (London, 1767 ff.), *The Parliamentary History of England . . . to the Year 1803,* 36 vols., edited by William Cobbett (London, 1806–1820), and *A Collection of Parliamentary Debates in England from the Year MDCLX to the Present Time,* 24 vols. (London, 1740–1749), have been helpful.

PAMPHLETS AND TRACTS ON GIBRALTAR

THE voluminous and contentious pamphlet literature of the eighteenth century furnishes an important guide to public feeling and the political cross-currents of the day, but is rather barren of factual information. The pamphlet literature on Gibraltar is nevertheless of some value, not only as an index to public opinion on the Gibraltar question, but also because it marshals the arguments for and against the value of the Rock and the desirability of restoring it to Spain better than any other source of information. *A Narrative of Sir George Rooke's Late Voyage to the Mediterranean . . .* (London, 1704), an anonymous work often attributed (erroneously) to Rooke himself, gives a eulogistic account of the admiral's part in the capture of Gibraltar. *The Report of the Commissioners Sent into Spain, . . . Relating to Gibraltar . . .* (London, 1728) is an exposé of the wretched administration of the Rock in its early years as an English possession. *Concordia Discors: or an Argument to Prove, that the Possession of Dunkirk, Port Mahon, Gibraltar, and Other Places, may be of Worse Consequence to these Nations, Than if They Continued in the Hands of the French, or Spanish* (London, 1712) argues that, since the English tradition is against a standing army, and the possession of these places would require the maintenance of large permanent garrisons, they ought not to be kept. The most famous of the pamphlets in defense of Gibraltar, *Considerations Offered upon the Approaching Peace, and upon the Importance of Gibraltar to the British Empire* . . . (London, 1720), written by Thomas Gordon and inspired by the rumor that Stanhope proposed to cede the fortress, set the standard—indeed, it furnished the precise language in several instances—for the protagonists of the Rock during the remainder of the century. Later in the same year (Nov. 5, 1720) Gordon wrote a more abusive and menacing attack on Stanhope's proposal, "Reasons to Prove that We are in no Danger of Losing Gibraltar," published in *Cato's Letters* . . . (London, 1733), I, 1–5. *A Letter to the Lords Commissioners for Trade and Plantations, Concerning the Advantage of Gibraltar to the Trade of Great Britain. By a Turkey Merchant* (London, 1720) echoes Gordon's arguments. *Gibraltar, a Bulwark of Great Britain, with Proposals for Erecting a Civil Government There*. . . . *By a Gentleman of the Navy* (London, 1725) emphasizes its potentialities as a naval base, and stresses the value of Gibraltar as a sanction to secure the good behavior of the Barbary states. Daniel Defoe's *The Evident Approach of War* . . ., *With Plan and Description of Gibraltar* (London, 1727) urges that Gibraltar be kept, but is of no value to the diplomatic story. The title of *Some Short Reflections on the Situation of Gibraltar and Its Importance to the Trade and Maritime Force of This Kingdom* . . . (London, 1731) indicates the position of its anonymous author. The *Danverian History of the Affairs of Europe for the Memorable Year 1731. With the Present State of Gibraltar* (London, 1732) stresses the value of the Rock and has a good description of the new Spanish works constructed in front of the fortress; this work, usually ascribed to Nicholas Amhurst (Caleb D'Anvers), is in reality an attack on the inaccuracy of Amhurst's reports of European news. *National Prejudice, Opposed to the National Interest, Candidly Considered in the Detention or Yielding Up of Gibraltar and Cape Briton by the Ensuing Treaty of Peace* . . . (London, 1748) presents a strong argument in favor of returning Gibraltar to Spain, in order to secure Spanish friendship and trade for Great Britain. The anonymous *Reasons for Giving Up Gibraltar . . . with an Appendix Containing Extracts of the Addresses to the Throne from the City of London Regarding the Importance of Gibraltar* (London, 1748) urges, sarcastically, that Gibraltar be surrendered to Spain because its administration was so bad that its example might corrupt the whole British colonial system; actually, this is a plea for the reform of the government of Gibraltar and for its retention by Great Britain. A letter written by a Doctor Lind in 1748, published in *Three Letters Relating to the Navy, Gibraltar, and Port Mahon* (London, 1757), stresses the many disadvantages of the Rock, and advocates its exchange for a worthwhile equivalent (the writer suggests one of the Canary Islands). Dissertation XXXV, advocating the retention of Gibraltar, in the second volume of *Britain's Commercial Interest . . .*, 2 vols. (London, 1757), by Malachy Postlethwayt, is practically a reprint of Gordon's *Considerations*. Finally, after the preliminary peace of 1783, John Sinclair published *The Propriety of Retaining Gibraltar Impartially Considered* (London, 1783), a strong argument for the restitution of Gibraltar to Spain, as the surest means of effecting an Anglo-Spanish reconciliation and disrupting the Family Compact.

SECONDARY AUTHORITIES

General Works

Many of the general histories of England and continental Europe have been used for reference and guidance in the writing of this study. Only the most useful need be listed here. Of the English histories, I have resorted most frequently to vols. IX and X in the Hunt and Poole *Political History of England: The History of England from the Accession of Anne to the Death of George II (1702–1760)* (London, 1909), by I. S. Leadam, and *The History of England from the Accession of George III to the Close of Pitt's First Administration (1760–1801)* (London, 1909), by William Hunt; their bibliographies have been particularly helpful. The same may be said for vols. V and VI of *The Cambridge Modern History* (New York, 1908–1909). Of the older general histories, the *History of England, 1713–1783*, 7 vols. (London, 1836–1854) and *History of England, . . . 1701–1713* (London,

1870) by Philip H. Stanhope (Lord Mahon), and the *History of England in the Eighteenth Century*, 8 vols. (London, 1878–1890), by W. E. H. Lecky have been the most helpful; Stanhope devotes far more attention than Lecky to diplomacy, and the intimate relation of the Stanhope family with the early history of Gibraltar and Minorca as English possessions has led Stanhope to emphasize their history. The best general surveys of Spanish and French history are the *Historia de España y su influencia en la historia universal*, 9 vols. (Barcelona, 1919–1936), by Antonio Ballesteros y Beretta, and the coöperative *Histoire de France depuis les origines jusqu'à la revolution*, 9 vols. (Paris, 1900–1911), edited by Ernest Lavisse. The first volume of the *Manuel historique de politique étrangère*, 4 vols. (Paris, 1896–1926), by Emile Bourgeois, gives the best broad survey of European diplomacy in the eighteenth century. There is no general history of British diplomacy before 1783; the Introduction by Sir A. W. Ward in vol. I of *The Cambridge History of British Foreign Policy* (New York, 1922) presents a brief summary of the subject. For general reference, I have used frequently such publications as the *Dictionary of National Biography*, the *Gentleman's Magazine* (London, 1731 ff.), the *Annual Register* (London, 1758 ff.), and the lists and guides to correspondence of *British Diplomatic Representatives, 1689–1789*, edited by D. B. Horn, published by the Royal Historical Society, Camden 3rd Series, vol. XLVI (London, 1932).

Works on Particular Subjects and Periods

The *Memoirs of the Kings of Spain of the House of Bourbon . . . 1700 to 1788*, 5 vols. (2d edition, London, 1815), by William Coxe, is still the best general survey of Anglo-Spanish relations during the eighteenth century, though naturally Coxe has been corrected in detail by more recent historians. Coxe's several histories were the fruit of patient research in the private papers of British statesmen, and he left a mass of transcripts which have been preserved in the British Museum. Two Spanish histories of Anglo-Spanish relations have appeared: Jerónimo Becker y González, *España e Inglaterra. Sus relaciones políticas desde las paces de Utrecht* (Madrid, 1906), and Mariano Marfil García, *Relaciones entre España y la Gran Bretaña desde las paces de Utrecht hasta nuestros días* (Madrid, 1907); neither makes any important contribution to the story of Gibraltar. The biography of *Elisabeth Farnese, 'the Termagant of Spain'* (London, 1892), by Edward Armstrong, is practically a history of Anglo-Spanish relations during the reign of the Italian wife of Philip V, based primarily on the diplomatic correspondence of Benjamin Keene and his predecessors.

The learned and brilliant work of Alfred Baudrillart, *Philippe V et la cour de France* . . ., 5 vols. (Paris, 1890–1901), is in a class by itself. This masterly exposition of Franco-Spanish relations, 1700–1746, founded upon exhaustive research in the French and Spanish archives, contains a more illuminating and accurate treatment of the Gibraltar question than any other secondary authority.

For an introduction to the establishment of British sea power and influence in the Mediterranean area, two naval historians have contributed the outstanding works: Julian S. Corbett, *England in the Mediterranean* . . . *1603–1713*, 2 vols. (London, 1904), and Alfred T. Mahan, *The Influence of Sea Power on History, 1660–1783* (Boston, 1889). Of less consequence is Walter F. Lord, *England and France in the Mediterranean, 1660–1830* (London, 1901).

The initial period of Gibraltar's history as an English possession is covered most adequately by George Macaulay Trevelyan's *England under Queen Anne,* 3 vols. (London, 1930–1934). The only general work in English which describes the background and negotiation of the Treaties of Utrecht is that of James W. Gerard, *The Peace of Utrecht* (New York, 1885). A more scholarly treatise, by Ottocar Weber, *Der Friede von Utrecht* (Gotha, 1891), throws some light on the attitude of the Dutch toward England's acquisition of Gibraltar. The origins of the secret negotiations of 1711 are described by G. M. Trevelyan in "The 'Jersey' Period of the Negotiations Leading to the Peace of Utrecht," published in the *English Historical Review,* XLIX (Jan. 1934), 100–105. *Matthew Prior: a Study of his Public Career and Correspondence* (Cambridge, 1921), by L. G. W. Legg, describes Prior's important rôle in the secret Anglo-French peace negotiations.

Turning to the active and complicated period in the diplomatic history of Gibraltar that followed the offer of Stanhope to restore the fortress in 1718, one finds a wealth of useful secondary material. The work of Baudrillart already cited is the most notable, but there are a number of others worthy of special men-

296   GIBRALTAR IN BRITISH DIPLOMACY

tion. I am particularly indebted to three works of Basil Williams:
the first, "The Foreign Policy of England under Walpole," published as a series of articles in the *English Historical Review*, XV
(1900), 251–276, 479–494, 665–698, and XVI (1901), 67–83,
308–327, 439–451, a lucid review of England's foreign relations
in the three decades after Utrecht; the second, his excellent biography, *Stanhope, a Study in Eighteenth Century War and Diplomacy* (Oxford, 1932); and, most recently, his volume entitled
The Whig Supremacy (Oxford, 1939), a general history of England during the reigns of the first two Georges. The scholarly
Englische Geschichte im Achtzehnten Jahrhundert, 4 vols. to
date (Leipzig and Berlin, 1896–1937), by Wolfgang Michael, is
a practically definitive work on the period from the accession of
George I to the fall of Walpole; the first two volumes of an English translation (London, 1936–1939) have already appeared. In
vol. II, pp. 256–282, Michael has contributed a clear and accurate review of the origins of the Gibraltar question. The much
older work of William Coxe, the *Memoirs of the Life and Administration of Sir Robert Walpole*, 3 vols. (London, 1798), also
devotes special attention to Gibraltar and publishes a good deal
of relevant correspondence. For particular segments and aspects
of this period, I have made use of: James F. Chance, *George I
and the Northern War* (London, 1909), a study of the involve-
ment of England in the Hanoverian interests of her new German
king, and an excellent introduction to English diplomacy under
George I; Sir Richard Lodge, "The Anglo-French Alliance,
1716–1731," in *Studies in Anglo-French Diplomacy during the
Eighteenth, Nineteenth, and Twentieth Centuries*, edited by
A. Coville and H. Temperley (Cambridge, 1935); P.-E. Lémontey, *Histoire de la Régence*, 2 vols. (Paris, 1832), which contains valuable references to the secret negotiations of 1717–1718;
Emile Bourgeois, *La diplomatie secrète au XVIIIe siècle. Ses
débuts*, 3 vols. (Paris, 1909), a detailed account of the formation
of the Quadruple Alliance and secret Franco-Spanish negotiations, 1716–1723; Louis Wiesener, *Le Régent, l'Abbé Dubois et
les Anglais*, 3 vols. (Paris, 1891–1893), a lengthy study of Anglo-
French relations, 1715–1723, based almost solely on English
sources; an article by P. Bliard, "La question de Gibraltar au
temps du Regent, d'aprés les correspondances officielles, 1720–
1721," in the *Revue des questions historiques*, LVII (1895), 192–
209; Jean Dureng, *Le Duc de Bourbon et l'Angleterre (1723–*

1726) (Toulouse, 1912), a sequel to Wiesener's work; Gabriel Syveton, *Un cour et un aventurier au XVIIIe siècle: le Baron de Ripperda* (Paris, 1896); J. F. Chance, *The Alliance of Hanover* (London, 1923), an exhaustive treatise on the diplomatic crisis of 1725 and 1726; Arthur M. Wilson, *French Foreign Policy during the Administration of Cardinal Fleury, 1726–1743* (Cambridge, Mass., 1936), an excellent study, but with scant reference to secret French diplomacy relating to Gibraltar; Sir Richard Lodge, "The Treaty of Seville," in *Transactions* of the Royal Historical Society, 4th Series, XVI (London, 1933), 1–43, a clear review of the troubled background of that famous treaty; A. Goslinga, *Slingelandt's Efforts towards European Peace* (The Hague, 1915), especially thorough on the Congress of Soissons; and Paul Vaucher, *Robert Walpole et la politique de Fleury (1731–1742)* (Paris, 1924), a scholarly monograph based on research in the British and French archives.

There are very few special works that throw any light on the problem of Gibraltar during the middle decades of the century. The volume by Sir Richard Lodge, *Studies in Eighteenth-Century Diplomacy* (London, 1930), is an important exception; Lodge concentrates his attention on the secret Anglo-Spanish peace negotiations during 1747 and 1748, in which Gibraltar was an active ingredient. Mention should also be made of Lodge's address entitled "Sir Benjamin Keene, K.B.: A Study in Anglo-Spanish Relations," published in *Transactions* of the Royal Historical Society, 4th Series, XV (1932), 1–43, a brief appreciation of one of the most human and able British diplomats of the century, who, by his tact, cultivated Spanish friendship after 1748 and kept the question of Gibraltar submerged. In the third volume of *The Life and Correspondence of Philip Yorke, Earl of Hardwicke*, 3 vols. (Cambridge, 1913), by Philip Chesney Yorke, there is a brief record of the Pitt proposal to surrender Gibraltar to Spain in 1757, with extracts from the Newcastle-Hardwicke correspondence.

After slumbering for nearly four decades, Gibraltar again became a pressing question in Anglo-Spanish diplomacy during the era of the American Revolution. The best guide to the diplomacy of this period is *The Diplomacy of the American Revolution* (New York, 1935), by Samuel Flagg Bemis, a brief but definitive treatise, based on an exhaustive study of the published material and manuscript collections in the principal European archives. For French diplomacy, the monumental *Histoire de la participation de la France à l'établissement des Etats-Unis d'Amerique,* 5 vols. and supplement (Paris, 1886–1899), by Henri Doniol, is the master work; I believe that Doniol must be used with some caution, for he wrote with the intention of eulogizing the vigorous and successful diplomacy of Vergennes in an effort to inspire a similar policy in the vacillating French government of the late nineteenth century. Louis Blart, *Les rapports de la France et de l'Espagne après le pacte de famille, jusqu'à la fin de ministère du duc de Choiseul* (Paris, 1915), is a useful dissertation, based exclusively on French sources, on the revival of the Family Compact. The work of Manuel Danvila y Collado, *Reinado de Carlos III,* 6 vols. (Madrid, 1893–1896), the best history of the reign of Charles III, pays a great deal of attention to Anglo-Spanish relations; the text contains many quotations and abstracts from Spanish archives not published elsewhere. The *Historia diplomática de América,* 2 vols. (Pamplona, 1920–1924), of Valentín Urtasún covers only the background and diplomacy of the War for American Independence; curiously, the author made no use of Spanish archives. The leading work on Spanish participation in the War for American Independence, J. F. Yela Utrilla, *España ante la independencia de los Estados Unidos,* 2 vols. (Lérida, 1925), is most valuable (to this study) for the period before 1779. S. F. Bemis has written a monograph on *The Hussey-Cumberland Mission and American Independence* (Princeton, 1931) which portrays the secret effort of Spain to secure the fortress by diplomacy during the progress of the war. In addition to the works already mentioned, the brief biography of the Spanish minister at Paris, *Die Politik des Grafen Aranda* (Berlin, 1929), by Richard Konetzke, contains some valuable information on the part played by its principal in the peace negotiations of 1782. I have been unable to discover any secondary authorities who treat the post-war negotiations to effect the restitution of Gibraltar with more than passing mention.

Histories of Gibraltar

The histories of Gibraltar all provide much the same pattern of information, with emphasis (for the eighteenth century) on the English capture and three Spanish sieges. For its diplomatic history they are of very slight value; their authors have not made use of either the British diplomatic correspondence or the Colonial Office records. Omitting a number of tracts and longer works dealing exclusively with the military history of the Rock, I am listing here the English and Spanish works I have examined.

Of the English works, the first to appear was *The History of the Herculean Straits, Now Called the Straits of Gibraltar,* 2 vols. (London, 1771), by Thomas James; the second volume is devoted to the history of Gibraltar, and has some excellent maps and pictures of the Rock. A decade later, *The Ancient and Modern History of Gibraltar* (London, 1781), by James S. Dodd, appeared; Dodd based this volume on a Spanish manuscript describing the siege of 1727, and added thereto accompanying material notable for its gross inaccuracies. Of the many printed accounts of the great siege of 1779–1783, the best known is that of John Drinkwater [Bethune], *A History of the Late Siege of Gibraltar with a Description and Account of that Garrison from the Earlier Periods* (London, 1783). Another work principally concerned with this siege, John Heriot, *An Historical Sketch of Gibraltar* (London, 1792), is worthy of mention only for its beautiful binding; certainly it is the handsomest work on Gibraltar that ever appeared! Vol. VII of the *History of the British Possessions in the Mediterranean* (London, 1837), by Robert M. Martin, deals with Gibraltar. James Bell, *The History of Gibraltar, from the Earliest Period of its Occupation by the Saracens* (London, 1845), is an abridgment of the Spanish history of López de Ayala, cited below, with some additional material. Frederic Sayer, *The History of Gibraltar and its Political Relation to Events in Europe* (London, 1865), makes an effort to trace the diplomatic story; his account is based solely on English published works such as those of Coxe and Pitt's correspondence. The next three works to appear, none of which added anything of value to this study, were: John H. Mann, *A History of Gibraltar and its Sieges, with Photographic Illustrations* (London, 1869); Frederick G. Stephens, *A History of Gibraltar and its Sieges* (London, 1870); and George J. Gibbard, *A Popular History of Gibraltar* (Gibraltar, 1887), really a guide book, with a very brief account of the history of the fortress. Two recent volumes complete the list: E. R. Kenyon, *Gibraltar under Moor, Spaniard, and Briton* (London, 1938), primarily a description of the military defenses of Gibraltar at various periods in its history; and G. T. Garrett, *Gibraltar and the Mediterranean* (London, 1939), which contains a brief survey of the eighteenth century, based almost exclusively on secondary works.

The best known of the Spanish histories of Gibraltar, and the most important work on its history before the English occupation, is the *Historia de Gibraltar* (Madrid, 1782), by Ignacio López de Ayala. In the mid-nineteenth century, the renewal of Spanish agitation for the restoration of Gibraltar explains the appearance of a number of histories and tracts on the Rock, in both Spain and England. I have been unable to locate a copy of the first of these Spanish works to appear, the *Historia de Gibraltar* (Seville, 1852), by Angel María Monti. The *Historia de Gibraltar y de su campo* (Cádiz, 1860) of Francisco María Montero is based entirely on secondary works, and makes no original contribution to the diplomatic history of the Rock. The work of Francisco María Tubino, *Gibraltar ante la historia, la diplomacia, y la política* (Seville, 1865), is fairly accurate, in contrast to many of the Spanish accounts. That much cannot be said for *La cuestión de Gibraltar, apuntes históricos, críticos y políticos* (Madrid, 1869), by Liborio Acosta de la Torre. The small volume of José Navarette, *Las llaves del estrecho; estudio sobre la reconquista de Gibraltar* (Madrid, 1882), is useful only for its bibliography of Spanish works. With the advent of the first World War, Spanish hopes for the recovery of Gibraltar again revived; several argumentative and inaccurate tracts appeared, typical among them being *La cuestión de Gibraltar: apuntes históricos* (Madrid, 1915), by Jorge de Aragón. It is a pleasure to record, as a final entry, a significant exception to my general opinion that the Spanish accounts of Gibraltar of the past century are inaccurate and almost worthless; the brief study with the lengthy title by Julian Juderias y Loyot, *Gibraltar, apuntes para la historia de la pérdida de este plaza, de los sitios que le pusieron los españoles y de las negociaciones entre España e Inglaterra referentes á su restitución, 1704–1796* (Madrid, 1915), is, within its limitations (based almost solely on secondary accounts), both accurate and objective.

INDEX

Act of Settlement, 28

Adams, John, American envoy, on grand assault of Gibraltar, 208–209

Aix-la-Chapelle, Treaty of (1748), 157, 279

Alberoni, Giulio, Cardinal, Spanish minister, policy, 30; rejects Gibraltar offer, 34–35; downfall, 38–39

Algiers, British relations with, 259 n See also Barbary states

Almodóvar, Pedro, Marquis of, Spanish envoy, in Spanish mediation, 183–187

Amelot, Jean-Jacques, French minister, in negotiation of second Family Compact, 140, 142

American colonies. See United States

American Revolution, France and, 179–180; Spain and, 179–181, 264; summary of Gibraltar in, 280–283

Anglo-French Alliance (1716), origin, 29, 270; keynote of Stanhope's foreign policy, 33, 64; threatened by Gibraltar dispute, 46–48, 272; DuBois' support of, 61; British determination to adhere to, 81; weakness, 107; dissolution, 114, 117

Anne, Queen of Great Britain, 270; and Dutch claim to Gibraltar, 14–17; announces peace terms, 18

Antilles. See West Indies

Aranda, Pedro, Count of, Spanish envoy, anti-British policy, 177; advocates war, 178, 181; Spanish peace envoy, 200–202, 204–205; submits Spanish terms, 210; seeks new instructions, 211; policy in peace negotiation, 211, 223, 233–236; Vergennes and, 215, 222–225; modifies Spanish demands, 218; confers with Rayneval, 218–219; accepts English peace terms, 229–230; reaction to his conduct, 232; confers with d'Estaing, 243–244

Aranjuez, Convention of (1779), signature and terms, 188–189, 280–281; conflict with Franco-American Alliance, 189; proposed renewal of Gibraltar article, 235 n; violation of French pledge, 282–283

Asiento, promised to England, 12; interrupted, 53; annulment threatened, 60; extension proposed, 79 See also Trade, Spanish Indies; South Sea Company

Asturias, Prince of, 232

Aubeterre, Joseph-Henri, Marquis of, French envoy, 168

Austria, alliance with Britain, 29; and Congress of Cambrai, 73; proposed mediation in Gibraltar dispute, 76–77; Spanish subsidy, 80; attempts to restrain Spain, 87–88; and Congress of Soissons, 101–102; opposes execution of Treaty of Seville, 115–116; mediation (1781), 197–198 See also Charles VI; Vienna, Austro-Spanish Treaties of

Austrian Succession, War of, origins, 138; Gibraltar in, 143–144; peace negotiations, 144–158

Bahamas, in peace negotiations of 1782, 205 n, 210, 217–218, 221, 227

Banda Oriental (Uruguay), Spanish-Portuguese conflict over, 177–178

Barbary states, Gibraltar as a factor in British relations with, 6,

East Florida, Spanish interpretation of boundary, 219; offered for Gibraltar, 239–240, 242
See also Florida; West Florida
East Indies, British trade with, 267–268
Eden, William, British envoy, interview with Floridablanca, 254–255
Elliot, General George Augustus, 209, 241
England. *See* Great Britain
Escarano, Spanish chargé, 178; in Spanish mediation, 182–183
Escurial, Treaty of (1733), and Gibraltar, 119–120, 277–278
See also Family Compact
Estaing, Charles, Count d', secret mission, 213–215; proposes basis for exchange, 243–244

Falkland Islands, dispute over, 175
Family Compact, Gibraltar as factor in formation and maintenance of, 2, 57–58, 84, 119–122, 138–143, 214, 234 n, 237–238, 246–247, 249, 251–254, 269, 277; origins, 57, 64, 112–113; first (Escurial, 1733), 118–121; influence on Anglo-Spanish relations, 137; Patiño and, 138; second (Fontainebleau, 1743), 139–143, 278; under Ferdinand VI, 144, 159; abrogation of, as basis for Gibraltar's cession, 153–155, 169, 237–238, 279, 282; proposed renewal, 168–169; third (Paris, 1761), 171–172, 280; under Charles III, 174; revival, 177; fourth (Aranjuez, 1779), 188–189, 280; proposed Anglo-Spanish territorial guarantee to neutralize, 242, 252; Floridablanca and, 245; dissolved by French Revolution, 284
See also France; Spain
Far East, increased British interest in, 244
Farnese, Elizabeth, Queen of Spain, control over Spanish policy, 30;

urges cession of Gibraltar, 77–78; and Austro-Spanish Alliance, 79; characterization of, 81; policy, 92, 98, 101–102, 144; turns against Austria, 105, 277; supports Great Britain, 115; anti-French policy, 118; dislike of Fleury, 137
Ferdinand VI, King of Spain, policy, 144, 159, 169, 280; and Gibraltar, 164
Fisheries. *See* Newfoundland fisheries
Fitzherbert, Alleyne, British envoy, replaces Grenville, 202; on Spanish terms, 203 n; instructions to, 207, 211, 227; receives Spanish terms, 210, 212; Vergennes and, 215; rejects Gibraltar article, 235
Fitzmaurice, William. *See* Shelburne, Earl of
Fleury, André Hercule de, Cardinal, French minister, supports Great Britain, 89, 95–96; Spanish policy, 91 n; British suspicions of, 101, 107; promises secret declaration on Gibraltar, 112, 277; policy, 115; false assurances to Britain, 121; opposes war, 140, 142–143; death, 143
Florida, proposed exchange for Gibraltar, 60, 213, 216, 240; conflict over, 174; in peace negotiations of 1782, 199, 207, 210–211, 217–221, 224–227, 231–232
Floridablanca, José Moniño, Count of, Spanish minister, on "quarantine" of Gibraltar, 126 n; policy, 180–181, 232–233, 245, 254–255, 269; and Franco-American Alliance, 181; and Spanish mediation, 182–187; dismisses Grantham, 189; and Hussey-Cumberland negotiation, 190–191, 193–197; instructions to Aranda, 200, 204, 211–212, 223–224, 229; wishes to be rid of Orán, 211 n; threatens re-opening direct negotiations with Britain, 224; professed secret opposition to Gibraltar's recovery, 238, 243–244, 251–252,